We're

Not

Dead

Yet

By

Lynda Davis

2020

1

Dedication

To my hunka hunka burnin' love

ISBN: 9798636299882

Introduction

Baby boomers are accustomed to being the centre of attention, the driving force of the economy. We put an end to the war in Vietnam; we wrote and performed the best popular music ever; we made blue jeans a staple of the everyday fashion lexicon. Microsoft, Apple, Amazon . . . all created by boomers.

If you were born between 1946 and 1964, you are probably preparing for retirement, or perhaps you have retired already. You may or may not have lost a spouse, partner, best friend or sibling. Most likely, you've lost one or both parents. You're as grown up as you'll ever be and you've learned so much along the way. You have made your share of mistakes and have the wisdom to prove it.

One consequence of aging is we become invisible. The older we become, the less people notice us or take us seriously. Other than close relatives, who cares about what we are up to, what we think, what we support or participate in?

According to Oprah Magazine, baby boomers are the healthiest, wealthiest and most engaged generation in history. We control 70% of disposal income in the country today and spend 250% more than the general population. The bottom line is, we have money and we're spending it. So, why do businesses, the government, and marketing strategists ignore us?

This book is a series of essays that speak for, to, and about baby boomers. We wish to go on record as still being a viable demographic. We're still protesting; we're still relevant; we still count. We're not dead yet!

Lynda Davis

Table of Contents

Chapter 1   Boomer Fashion and Beauty

Chapter 2   Lifestyle

Chapter 3   Aging

Chapter 4   Remember When?

Chapter 5   Mind, Body, Soul

Chapter 6   Food

Chapter 7   Current Events

Chapter 8   In the Year 2020

Chapter 9   Business

Chapter 10   Final Thoughts

Chapter 1

Boomer Fashion and Beauty

Girls just gotta have shoes

It was love at first sight. As soon as my eyes landed on that incredible pair of Jimmy Choo python pumps in Vogue, I found myself longing not only for the shoes but for my twenty-year-old feet to put in them. Even though it has been years, or more like decades since I've been able to strut my stuff in killer heels, the old longing and feeling of empowerment bestowed on us by stilettos never leaves us.

The objects of my affection.

I could so easily picture my former self wearing those python beauties around the office in my power suit or slipping them on with skinny jeans (the jeans, not me) for a stylish stroll through the mall on a Saturday. Just looking at those babies made my heart beat faster. My imagination conjured up fantasies I haven't had in years. There was a giant smile on my face just thinking about the possibilities those beauties could bestow on my life. Boomer women totally understand how Cinderella was completely transformed as soon as she put on those magic glass slippers. It's no fairy tale.

In the late sixties and early seventies, I lived and worked in downtown Toronto. Too broke and too cheap to invest in subway tokens, I hoofed it everywhere in heels, usually on the run. From Bloor Street to Front Street I made my way around

If only we could buy new feet.

the downtown core to and from work, to meet friends, to shop and out at night, always on foot. And those young, size seven feet were always shod in the latest fashion. I've twisted ankles falling off my platforms, caught spike heels in sidewalk grates and suffered burns and blisters on the balls of my feet from the heat of summer sidewalks burning through thin leather soles. Not once did I think my feet would outlive their best-before date.

Baby boomer women now have a different set of criteria when shopping for shoes. Toe cleavage and strappy high heels have given way to arch supports and low heels with rubber soles, and not the kind the Beatles sang about in 1965. Back in the day, our shoe purchases were treated like decadent works of art, affirmation of our sexiness and stylishness. I'd actually place newly purchased shoes on the dining room table to admire them when I brought them home. Or I'd position them on my night table, so they'd be the first things I'd see when I woke up in the morning. Talk about getting a high. Gorgeous shoes were like little magic carpets that carried us into a fantasy land where we were invincible. And, unlike dress or pant sizes, shoe size was immaterial. In fabulous shoes, our feet looked great no matter what size they were.

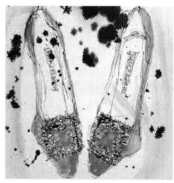

After clomping around in rubber sandals for the past several weeks, I recently squeezed my feet into a pair of stylish suede boots that don't see much action these days. My back hurt from bending down to put the socks and then the boots on and my feet felt like they were going to explode by the time I got home from shopping. Mes pieds are just not used to such harsh discipline and they object strenuously to any form of confinement. I soooo miss the feet I had when I was twenty years old.

I wonder if those python Jimmy Choos come with industrial strength arch supports and cushy rubber soles? If I win the lottery, perhaps I'll buy them and prop them up on my mantle, just to admire them like the works of art they are. I could reflect on the days when I used to listen to the original *Rubber Soul* while wearing my Mary Quant mini skirts and platforms, back when I could still wear fantasmic shoes. As the Everly Brothers sang so eloquently and in perfect harmony, *"All I have to do is dream. Dream. dream, dream",* the siren song of Jimmy Choo and those fabulous shoes.

Who cares if it's swimsuit season . . . again?

Many years ago I read about a magazine editor who quit her job at a high-profile international women's magazine because she just couldn't face overseeing another annual swimsuit edition. I know how she must have felt because I can't face another swimsuit season either. All the current magazines are full of tips on how to match a bathing suit to our individual figure types, how to look our best and feel confident. Pages and pages in the spring and summer fashion mags have been dedicated to the latest swimsuit styles. The tropical patterns and colours are yummy and some of

Seriously?

those scraps of fabric cost hundreds of dollars. The Photoshopped models look gorgeous. The reality is grim.

I'll admit some styles are infinitely more flattering than others, but let's face it, we're never *ever* going to resemble anything close to those pubescent nymphets modelling the various styles featured in the magazine spreads. In fact, most boomers are even reluctant to go out in public in *shorts* much less a bathing suit.

Those with cottages or winter homes in Florida can't avoid wearing a swimsuit occasionally but they're usually hidden under diaphanous lightweight coverups when we're not actually under water.   It is virtually impossible for swimsuit designs to overcome what makes so many boomer broads self-conscious about beach wear. No amount of

I'll have what she's wearing!

9

underpinning, tummy panels, supportive straps or bum tuckers will compensate for what nature has bestowed upon us after many decades of living our lives.

By the time we've tried on dozens of unflattering designs in cramped fitting rooms with scary fluorescent lighting, cried a river, paid our dues at Weight Watchers, spray tanned our cellulite and waxed our lady parts to an unsightly, red rash, we're fed up with the entire exercise.

Sure, they tell us to feel good about ourselves regardless of our body shape. That's easy to say when you're in your twenties or thirties. I sympathize with that fed-up magazine editor. This summer you will find me sitting in the shade and privacy of my back-yard gazebo, wearing elastic-waist shorts and a tee shirt, reading the latest New York Times' best seller on my iPad mini. The beach is no longer my thing and even if it were, give me a birkini any day.

Help! I've OD'd on black and white

At what point does safe, so-called classic dressing become just plain boring? We've always been told that basic black and white is a never-fail look for any occasion. It's safe, easy to assemble and accessorize and we can be assured of never feeling self-conscious. I've religiously adhered to that principle for far too long and my closet now looks like a nun lives here. It's time I kicked the "habit". I'm embarrassed to tell you how many pairs of black pants I own, not to mention black and white blouses, tee shirts and sweaters. How many times have we shown up for lunch with girlfriends when most, if not all of us are wearing some combination of black or white pants and top?

Assembling a travel wardrobe is one instance however when I think black and white is recommended. Who cares if you wear the same outfit several times? You can easily rinse out pieces in hotel sinks if they need freshening up and an assortment of colourful scarves brings a basic look to life. It makes packing easier and lighter while relieving us of wondering what to wear. Easy peasy.

Summer should be about colour. It took some mental convincing to force myself to buy a pair of pants at Chico's in a colour called *Malibu Punch* which is a kind of coral pink. Seeing them on a baby boomer fashion blog that I follow (susanafter60) persuaded me that they could work and I'm glad I bought them. And, naturally, I have a million white tops to wear with them. Now, I'm waiting for a sunflower yellow linen blazer to go on sale and when it does I'll have another piece to brighten up my wardrobe and my spirits. It will look amazing with all those black and white pants I own as well as both dark and light skinny jeans.

Few women wore white jeans and a black tee shirt better than Jackie Kennedy. However, lacking her innate beauty and grace, I need a bit more help. While I still lean heavily on that classic black and white look, I am making a serious effort to brighten up my wardrobe. When summer sales are on, I intend to change my habit and go for pink, blue, yellow and red.

Even though I know I already have far too many white tops, just the other day I scoped out a cute little sleeveless blouse I saw in the window at Massimo Dutti in the mall. Fortunately, they did not have my size, or I'd have another one to add to my collection. I'm ashamed to admit that I think I actually have some white tops in my closet that I've never even worn. Needs and wants are quite different. I cannot resist the siren's call.

The September issue of Vogue blows

Every year I look forward to writing a bitchy critique of the famous September issue of Vogue magazine. At upwards of 800 pages, it arrives with a heavy thud in my mailbox (a couple of years ago the postman actually rang my doorbell and personally handed it to me) and usually gives me a couple of hours of entertainment.

Most of what Vogue offers up is utter nonsense and completely irrelevant to the average woman. Despite this, somehow, I usually manage to find one or two tiny sparks of inspiration in its superficial pages. This year? There's nothing to write about. No inspiration. Nadda. Zero. Rien. Ziltch. Not a single thing. Vogue is barren of anything relevant or worthwhile to this old boomer.

Is it just me or are fashion magazines seriously out of touch with their readers? I'm becoming increasingly fed up with fashion media, despite their few and infrequent pathetic attempts at recognizing older readers, a.k.a. baby boomers. As the saying goes, *"I don't know why I botha'."* Who's out of touch? Me? Or them?

What exactly is 'disposable' fashion?

Are you sitting down? Burberry recently incinerated $37 million worth of their luxury brand merchandise that did not sell. Rather than dilute the cachet of their brand by offering it at discounted prices to the great unwashed masses (like you and me), they torched it. It must be lovely to have a business with such generous markups and profit margins that you can afford to just set fire to $37 million.

That act of destruction reminded me of how casually we treat our possessions regardless of the cost. Not only are fashions from Zara, The Gap and other mass retailers treated as disposable fashion, so are premium brands. Our "affluenza" and consumerism have reached ridiculous proportions.

We need to be more thoughtful about what we buy and conscientious about managing our belongings. This comes on the heels of a sobering documentary *Clothing Waste – Fashion's Dirty Secret* which aired on CBC's *Marketplace*. It's available for streaming.

It highlighted the negative effects of disposable clothing on the environment and the facts presented left me feeling ashamed and totally committed to changing my wanton ways. I used to feel vindicated when I dropped off old clothing at a charity bin until I saw on *Marketplace* what in fact happens to my donations. Giant bales of excess used clothing sit in warehouses until they're shipped to places like Africa or India. They're then sold in street markets as used clothing which seems all fine and dandy until we're shown the piles of clothing being burned behind the

stalls, clothing that doesn't sell. Brand names like Tommy Hilfinger, H&M, Old Navy and others, all go up in smoke. Even third world countries *don't want or don't know what to do with* our cast-offs.

We didn't start off this way

When boomers were growing up we didn't have the vast,

Clothing goes from here . . .

disposable wardrobes that are common today. In addition to a few everyday school clothes, we had a good Sunday outfit which did double duty for going to birthday parties or Christmas concerts. One winter coat, one pair of boots, one pair of everyday school shoes and one pair of good shoes was the norm and they lasted until we outgrew them.

Our parents' wardrobes were equally modest. Some of us perhaps remember our fathers having shoes resoled to extend their life. I grew up in a house built in the 1880s with no closets. My spartan wardrobe was either folded in a couple of dresser drawers or hung on hooks on the back of my bedroom door and I did just fine with fewer items.

How far we've fallen. How many boomer gals have commandeered the entire master bedroom closet for racks of clothes (many of which we don't wear, or they don't fit) and relegated our partners' clothes to the spare bedroom closet? It's an insidious process, a slippery slope and regular culling unfortunately tends to invite more buying.

To here.

When I first started working in 1965, I was thrilled to finally have my own money to spend on mini dresses, shoes and even fabric to sew my own version of Twiggy-inspired fashion. How could we not fall in love with what fashion was offering in the sixties? It was a total transformation from boring and practical to colourful and fun. Over the years, boomer gals have spent small fortunes on dressing for success, weekend wear and special event dresses. To this day I'm still filled with self-loathing when I think that I spent the equivalent of nearly a week's wages on that burgundy ultra-suede suit that I wore for one season in the seventies. Then, there are all the matching shoes, purses, coats, jackets, accessories. Well, you get the picture. Who among us wouldn't love to have some of that wasted money now earning interest in our RRSP.

I know my triggers. From now on I'm going to be more discriminating about what I purchase and avoid the following potential hazards:

- Shopping trips just acquaint me with more things I do not need so I will minimize the number of times I visit the mall. Ditto for internet shopping.
- Fashion magazines are bait for suckers like me. Seeing something I like starts me longing for it. See Item 1 above.
- When I see things on women's television shows that include fashion and home decorating segments, I'm motivated to shop. I would be further ahead reading my books or going for a walk instead of watching those programs.
- Comparing myself with the beautiful people is counterproductive. How often do we think if we just had that blouse, that bracelet, that designer handbag or pair of sunglasses, our lives would be complete?
- Advertising for the latest skincare or makeup product guaranteed to solve all our

And finally, here.

problems is so tempting and generally a complete waste of money. I must work on tuning out the marketing 'noise' and stick with whatever basics work for me, preferably organic.
- The wellness industry including thousands of websites such as GOOP are constantly setting us up to think we need improving with supplements, diets, cleanses and other new age gimmicks. Tune out.

This is not a definitive list but it is a good start. These steps are actionable immediately and would make a difference not only in my self-esteem and the environment but more importantly, my bank account. We can still feel great about ourselves without being sucked into the vortex of disposable fashion, useless health and beauty products and general consumerism. Regular culling of our closets serves to remind us that we already have too much, and we should be more discriminating about what we buy. I definitely buy into that. Starting now.

Raising eyebrows . . . literally, one microblade at a time

I did it! Several months ago, I mentioned that I was considering getting my eyebrows microbladed and if I did, I'd let you know how it went. Well, the deed has been done and I'm absolutely thrilled with the results.

Like most baby boomer women, I plucked my eyebrows into extinction during the seventies when thin, arched brows were the fashion. Stupid. Stupid. Stupid. They never grew back. If only the hair removal on my other body parts (chin, legs, bikini area etc.) had been as effective I'd have been spared years of maintenance.

The procedure requires three appointments:

1. **Consultation:** Before undergoing microblading, I had a mandatory free consultation with the technician to ensure I was a safe candidate, i.e. not pregnant, no auto-immune issues, not a diabetic, etc. During the consultation, the technician measured the optimal shape of my new brows and with a conventional eyebrow pencil drew in what they would look like. This took about 15 minutes.

2. **Procedure:** A few days later I went in for the main procedure. Over a period of slightly more than two hours, the technician:

   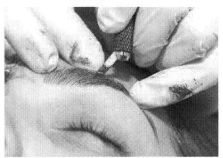

   - Measures and maps the final brow design using plastic templates and guides. She carefully angled and marked the outline, the borders, extremities and overall shape. Then, she applied a numbing cream which

   It was surprisingly painless as the technician used a topical numbing cream beforehand.

   she left on for about 25 minutes to activate before starting the procedure. And, I signed pages of legal waivers.

- Together we selected the pigment colour. I was reminded that the colour would initially look much darker than the final outcome. I selected *milk chocolate,* not too ashy and with a bit of warmth. I'm naturally fair with blue eyes so I didn't want anything too harsh. I also insisted she not make the arch too sharp and I didn't want the inner corners squared like I've seen some brows done. I wanted them to look completely natural but better than what Mother Nature endowed me with.

- For the actual microblading procedure, the technician uses a blade to etch and deposit pigment into the brow area. It was painless, which really surprised me. She first plucked a few stray natural hairs and that was the only part that was slightly uncomfortable. I do have a high pain threshold so others might might experience a bit of discomfort, but I found it painless. Microblading is not exactly the

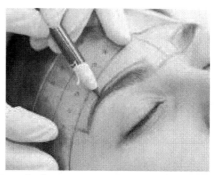

Detailed mapping and measuring ensures the correct, most flattering shape.

same as tattooing. Pigment cream is deposited into tiny hair-shaped cuts in the brow area which results in a far more natural look than tattoo ink. There are many variations in colour and shape you can choose from depending on whether you want a natural or more dramatic look.

The technician was incredibly precise and patient as she carried out the procedure. About 90 minutes later she showed me the first glimpse of my completed brows and I was thrilled. My followup instructions involved applying a special white ointment to the brows with a Q-Tip several times a day to preserve and protect the new

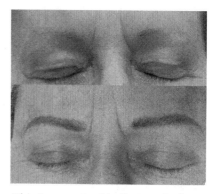

This is my actual before and after.

brows. I was advised not to get them wet for a couple of weeks. They will appear flaky and crusty at first, but I am not to pick or brush the brows. Just let them heal. I experienced no swelling, just a tiny itch after a day or two which is natural, and I didn't scratch.

3. **Followup and touch-up:** I was scheduled to go back six weeks after the procedure for a final touch-up and assessment. It is still a fairly new technique so I expect I may need touch-ups once a year or so which is an easy path to perfect eyebrows. And it is so lovely to wake up in the morning with eyebrows.

If you decide to go ahead with the procedure be very careful to only use an experienced licensed technician. You don't want to risk infection or poor artistry. She'll be happy to show you pictures of her previous work to help make your decision.

My queendom for the perfect eyeliner

Things change as we get older. I won't go into detail as you know what I'm talking about, but one issue that I haven't been able to resolve is finding the perfect eyeliner. Back in the olden days (the sixties and seventies), I could execute a perfect swipe of eyeliner faster than . . . well, the blink of an eye. My eyelids were taut, receptive and beautifully enhanced by whatever I applied, in whatever colour. And I applied plenty.

As we age, less is better. We no longer apply foundation with a spatula, mascara with a broom, or blusher with a mop. A delicate touch is now the order of the day. But boomer gals still like makeup and we have a sizeable inventory to back this up. Every so often I purge my supplies while trying not to calculate the money invested/wasted on products that

Can you believe, nothing in my vast inventory of eyeliners works.

didn't work for one reason or another. Sometimes when I go through my 'retired' makeup and skin care products, I discover I own multiples of the same thing.

Eyeliner is my current challenge. My eyelids are now a bit crepey which means I can't get the exact result with eyeliner that I used to. Liquid eyeliners are just too difficult to control and the result is a bit too harsh, even after smudging. Pencils scratch, pull and refuse to stay put. I've had the most success with wetting a brush and using cake eyeliner or eyeshadow to apply a line that can be softened with the finger or a sponge wand. But even careful application doesn't give me nearly the result I used to get when my eyelids were . . . well, you know, young.

While I keep searching for the definitive, perfect eyeliner solution, I decided to go through my existing inventory and was shocked at what I already own. Any thoughts of purchasing something new were immediately wiped out by the humiliating sight of an entire tray of assorted eyeliner products. You name it, I've tried it. What I've invested in eyeliners alone would probably pay off the national debt of a third world country. And that doesn't include skincare products, hair products and makeup. I'm not proud of it. Just stating the facts.

I recently had my eyebrows microbladed which will hopefully take care of the brow pencil issues. And don't even suggest getting my eyeliner tattooed on. There are just too many downsides to that procedure for me to even consider it as an option. In the meantime, I need to figure out what I'm going to do with a queen's ransom in eyeliner pencils that I don't use.

What's up in men's underwear?

Have you taken a close look at men's underwear lately, other than what turns up in your weekly laundry? I had occasion to peruse the men's lingerie section of a major department store the other day and I can't tell you how much fun it was. The names the marketing people come up with to describe men's skivvies are just too hilarious. They surely deserve a Nobel Prize for creative fiction. The brand names are all riffs on size, power and even *calibre*! Check these out:

- Magnum
- Big Eagle
- Champion
- Colt
- Performance
- Prodige
- Hero
- UrbanTouch (seriously??)

What I didn't see was:

- Crop-duster
- Skidmark
- Babyface
- Rust belt

I don't think I've ever seen women's underwear with similarly ambitious names. Our frillies are usually just called "Thong, Bikini, Hi-rise leg" or a similar fairly obvious description. Maybe there's an opportunity here for creative marketers to jump on the bandwagon with new names for women's underwear:

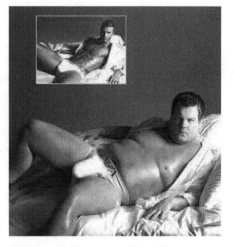

- Steel magnolia
- Stud buster
- You wish
- Secret treasure
- In your dreams

There could be a considerable discrepancy between what is advertised and what is actually in the package.

Men's underwear names are ego-enhancing and denote power, which I am quite sure is not always reflective of the contents or the wearer. But then, most women know men's egos need constant stroking! Baby boomer women were raised to be good listeners. As soon as we

19

started dating, we were coached to ask our dates about themselves, and they were only too happy to oblige . . . for hours and hours and hours. We have already proven *our* staying power.

I know it's always risky to generalize but when I read about dates-gone-bad in the agony columns in local newspapers, the challenges never change. Even enlightened millennials are forced to suffer through painful first dates with guys who are so self-absorbed it never occurs to them that *we* might have something of value to say as well. *"All he did was talk about himself; his work, his car; his sports"* is a common complaint from women in the dating market. And they wonder why they're ghosted.

Some things never change, including what's up in men's underwear. Until attitudes change and women start insisting upon proof in advertising, we'll just have to double check for inferior goods and not fall for false claims. If they aren't willing and happy to meet us on equal ground and recognize that we're also worthy of such labels as Heroine, Boss Lady or Conqueror, then just leave 'em on the shelf for some other less discriminating poor soul. Thank heavens we were born women and don't have to suffer the stress of constantly stroking our ego, through our underwear.

When fashion's in, I'm out. When I'm in, fashion's out

You would think by now I would have a fairly good handle on what works best for me, fashion-wise. For the most part I do, at least with the basics. My tastes lean more toward classic with splashes out in accessories, hence the big red glasses, and blue ones, and pink ones, and tortoise shell ones with yellow arms. I'm generally not a slavish follower of trends, usually dragging my comfortable-height heels until I'm absolutely sure the trend is going to become a classic. I thought that was the case with skinny jeans. Now they're being usurped by flares (again!), boot-cut and even culottes (give me strength!). I realize it's all part of forcing us to keep spending our hard-earned money through planned obsolescence, but I always seem to be on the wrong end of the fashion cycle.

I never did give up on high-waisted jeans (thank you *Not Your Daughters Jeans*) because boomer muffin top was never compatible with those ridiculous 7-inch rises that excluded most of the female population. Most boomer gals still have decent legs which we're able to showcase in well-fitted jeans with high waists and loose tops worn over. Great boots or booties amp up the look even more so we can achieve 'sexy'. But when they start moving the hemlines up to mid-calf, well, that's only going to make those of under six feet tall (which is 99 percent of the population) look just plain dumpy.

A couple of seasons ago, jeans with frayed hems started making the scene. As usual, my cynical reaction was, "What a cheap, unimaginative trick by designers to get us to buy new jeans. I'll take a pass". I liked the pictures of bloggers I follow wearing the new look, but figured I'd ride it out. I fancy myself to be smart like that.

Now that the style is on its way *out*, I'm frantically sussing out frayed hem jeans at a price point I can justify. That means no Eileen Fisher or Rag & Bone. It would be quite simple for me to cut the hem off an old pair of NYD Jeans and fray the bottom, zip up a line of staystitching on my old Singer and call

Loving fashion is not limited only those born within the last twenty years.

it a day. It would require an investment of an hour of my time and zero money. But somehow, spending hours monitoring on-line sales and comparing prices, styles and spandex content makes it seem so much more satisfying. You know what I mean!

So, when you see everyone on the street except me sporting wide leg culotte jeans this season, stand by. Next year, I'll be packing up those home-made frayed-leg jeans for something even more ridiculous and expensive in search of fashion nirvana. I took the same approach toward boot-cut jeans, painter pants, acid-wash jeans and even skinny jeans when they first arrived on the scene.

I'm always just a little bit out of fashion with visions of myself achieving total coolness lurking in my imagination, but forever just slightly out of reach. At this point in life I guess I'll never get over that feeling of a dog chasing a car. Even if I caught it, I wouldn't know what to do. This boomer body just doesn't lend itself to

21

trends. So, I'll always be on the tail-end of fashion trying to be cooler than I really am. I may never be in sync with the fashion cycle, but it's still fun chasing cars.

Do you "get" fashion magazines like *Vogue* or *InStyle*?

The magazine industry has forsaken us. It's not as if I look to *Vogue* for the latest in how to camouflage boomer waistlines (or lack thereof) or the best high fashion shoes with serious arch supports, but I do look to magazines for basic inspiration and find them sorely lacking.

I clearly remember my very first magazine subscription. It was Chatelaine, the ubiquitous Canadian magazine for the so-called modern woman. The wonderful feminist and women's advocate Doris Anderson was the editor. The year was 1968 and I was living in my very first apartment by myself, on Vaughan Road in Toronto, after spending the previous three years living with a series of agreeable and not-so-agreeable roommates. I was so proud of that place because it was all mine. It was a bachelor apartment in a prewar three-storey walk-up with no elevator, no communal laundry room and no counter in the tiny kitchen. It did have two old white enamel sinks on the kitchen wall and a genuine old clawfoot bathtub (no shower, naturally) in the tiny bathroom. It also had an unlimited supply of mice which I gave up trapping after I'd disposed of nineteen of the cute little creatures.

Subscribing to a lady's magazine was an affirmation that I was an independent grownup, a career gal who could be trusted to be at the address I gave them and pay the annual subscription fee. Over the years, my love of magazines developed into a bit of a problem. I became a magazine junkie. At its peak, not that long ago, I subscribed to eighteen magazines a month. I'd be truly annoyed if a day went by and there wasn't a new magazine in my mailbox. I loved everything about them, their editorial content, their glossy pictures, the quality of the paper, the fold-over perfume samples, even the advertisements. I couldn't wait to make a pot of tea, sit down with my marker pen whenever a new one arrived and go through it slowly, page by page. It was my dream to be a magazine editor in my next life.

Things have changed. Just like my favourite women's shows on Sirius XM radio, the good ones started disappearing. *MORE* magazine, one of my favourites was cancelled about three years ago. *Easy Living* from the UK was cancelled but I managed to replace it with *RED,* which is similar, and I get it online cheaper and faster than waiting for it to arrive at Chapters/Indigo. Then, some of the decorating magazines that I got from the U.S. like *Veranda* and *House Beautiful* just became too weird or too arty so I let them go. But, out of patriotic loyalty, I kept up my subscriptions to Canadian decorating mags like *Canadian House and Home* and *Style at Home*. But their too-frequent features on mid-century modern and reviving seventies avocado green and macramé are starting to concern me.

My love affair with fashion magazines however is in serious jeopardy. I much prefer *ELLE Canada* over the American edition, but their targeting of the 18-35 demographic continues to annoy and frustrate me. *LouLou* is gone. *Maclean's* has cut back from once a week to once a month and after more than fifty years of subscribing to Canada's stalwart *Chatelaine* I'm actually considering not renewing my subscription. They've cut back to bi-monthly and it's a pretty lean publication geared more to young mothers who probably don't have the time or inclination to even read *Chatelaine*. What's a boomer gal to do?

Vogue is the source of most of my delicious criticism, however. I love to poke fun at *Vogue* and I've concluded that the only reason I still subscribe is because *Vogue* has become my most prized source of derision and blogging material. And the September issue alone costs as much on the newsstand as my entire year's subscription.

What would I have to bitch about if I didn't get my monthly *Vogue*? Its level of irrelevancy is astounding. Where fashion magazines should be inspirational and somewhat aspirational, *Vogue* is an exercise in complete idiocy. I still like the

In what universe is there even one thing in these images that we can relate to or draw inspiration from?

folded perfume samples but only the old classic French scents. As an old classic myself, most of the new fragrances all have a common chemical kind of smell that makes it impossible to distinguish one from another. Maybe my nose has lost its sensitivity, but I don't think I'm that old.

How do the fashion mags retain their credibility and more importantly their readers with the ridiculous nonsense they put out each month? It's no surprise that magazine publishing is in peril. Boomer gals love fashion, after all, we are the ones who launched miniskirts, platform shoes and pant suits in the workplace in the sixties. But once we pass the age of thirty-five, we're suddenly invisible. I still wonder how the under-thirty-five demographic can relate to $5,000.00 handbags and scraps of rags photographed on anorexic teenage models leaping over garbage cans. I also subscribe to *InStyle* but I find their emphasis on skinny, young celebrities in evening gowns off-putting. Hard to relate. Rod Stewart sang our tune perfectly so long ago when his Dad said, *"We looked ridiculous"*. That's what most fashion mags are offering up today.

Back in the sixties and seventies when we were all whipping up our little A-line dresses and flared pants on our Singer sewing machines, we considered Vogue patterns the epitome of style and taste. Butterick, Simplicity and McCalls patterns were good for everyday fashions but for a special event a Vogue pattern tipped the balance for chic. We got our fashion inspiration from Vogue magazine and our lifestyle guidance from *Cosmo's* Helen Gurley Brown. In the sixties, those of us with sewing machines could replicate Vogue high fashion on our own.

Where does a boomer gal go for fashion inspiration today? We used to rely on quality magazines like *Vogue* to provide us with reliable fashion direction. **Most of my own fashion inspiration these days comes from like-minded bloggers and observing street fashion** when I'm out and about. I frequently approach women on the street or in the food court and ask where they got a particular item they're wearing, or who cut their hair.

Fashion magazines offer nothing relevant to baby boomer women. We're forced to find our own inspiration outside the publishing industry. I'll never understand why the Anna Wintours and Grace Coddingtons of the fashion world are so revered. Perhaps there was a time when their declarations had merit but exactly who are they serving today? Certainly not real women. Definitely not me and my boomer gal pals. I'm tempted to dust off my old Singer and see if I can't create something on my own that is wearable, flattering and inspired.

There are a few retailers now who are addressing our demographic. *Chico's* came to Canada for a brief period, but now have left, so I'm still waiting for others who are sensitive to our taste in fashion. *Chico's* has an affiliate lingerie business *SOMA* that has wonderful, appropriate lounge wear, lingerie and bathing suits for women our age, but so far they're only in the U.S. *J. Jill* is another one which hasn't arrived here yet but has great fashions at affordable prices. They both have wonderful on-line stores but the cost of importing and shipping combined with dollar exchange is often prohibitive. I have also had great luck buying *Eileen Fisher* pieces on sale at various on-line sites, but it requires patience and an American delivery address. I've scored some EF pieces at up to seventy percent off which puts her fashion items more within reach of our budgets.

I Marie-Kondo'd my bra drawer and feel so uplifted

Rachel Hollis, author of *Girl, Wash Your Face* was right: *Bras are the devil's work.* Over my lifetime, I've probably invested the equivalent cost of a luxury German imported car in a futile search for a comfortable bra. I am convinced they don't exist.

Yesterday as I was getting dressed to go out, I tried on no less than three different bras before I found one comfortable enough to wear to the mall. And when I got there I bee-lined it for the *Jockey For Her* section in the lingerie department in search of something wearable. I opted for one of those sports-like all-over stretch jobs with no clasps, trim or skinny bits to dig in. Much as I hate wearing a bra, a certain amount of decorum is required when going out in public, so we're forced to buckle up.

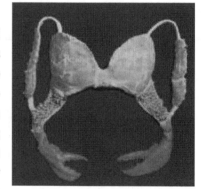

We all know that feeling.

When I got home the first thing I did, as usual, was rip my bra off. Then, I pulled everything out of my bra drawer, gave each one a quick test drive to determine whether it would live or die, then tossed the rejects into a big pile on my bed. I was merciless. The losers were too tight around the ribcage, didn't have enough banding around the ribcage, rolled at the ribcage, slipped off my shoulders or simply didn't properly accommodate the girls without spilling over or accentuating back fat. Am I too demanding? I don't think so. There was a time many generations ago when I was so proud to wear a bra. When my mother took me to buy my first 28AA training bra I felt so grown up. There was also a time when we were young that I loved buying all the lacey little contraptions that passed for a bra. But when we reached a certain age, comfort and performance became priorities, while still achieving a level of sexiness and femininity.

I have been measured many times at different stores and each one comes up with a different size combo. I accept that our size is not static and changes as we age and gain or lose weight, but maybe we need a computer-generated modelling system to get it right once and for all. If they can do it for jeans, why not bras? Could someone please task a grandchild to create an app for calculating the

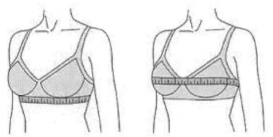

In theory this system should work but in the real-world sizes vary widely according to manufacturer.

correct bra size by manufacturer and style? The old ribcage measurement combined with breast size just doesn't compute in the real world. Hence, the huge pile of discarded bras on my bed. Only six (6) survived the purge, including the new Jockey-For-Her number. That should be enough by anyone's standards, but I have a feeling I'll soon be on the prowl again. *Fourteen (14)* regular bras and *eighteen (18)* sports bras are destined for the dumpster (Yes! That's a shameful total of *thirty-two (32)*), except textiles should not be thrown in the trash, so what do we do with them? That's a lotta landfill. I'll parcel them up for charity, if they'll take them, as most have hardly been worn. Hopefully, they will be useful to someone else. The Canadian Diabetes Association recycles clothing and I understand H&M stores have drop boxes for recycling clothing.

Then, I attacked another drawer full of camisoles and tank tops worn over bras under certain blouses and sweaters. The work never ends. It's a shocking and embarrassing thing to admit but how could any one person possibly need or wear 33 camis? We all have too much of everything and the recent culling of my bras

Yep! A total of thirty-two bras went for recycling
as well as thirty-three tank tops and camisoles.

and camisoles is a prime example of our excesses—well, mine for sure. Now I have a couple of empty drawers in my bedroom and I won't have to forage through dozens of rejects to find something to wear. Theoretically.

No longer burdened by a surplus of ill-fitting, uncomfortable bras, I feel strangely uplifted. Kondo was right, sort of. It wasn't about keeping only those that sparked joy (I can't imagine *any* bra sparking joy) but more accurately *getting rid of things* sparked the real joy. I recently took a pile of clothing to the consignment shop and a couple of bags of discards to the charity box.

Imagine how I would feel if I dared go down to the basement and tackled that quagmire. Naaah! I think I'll just sit back and enjoy the fruits of my lingerie liquidation before I get into something under foot that might be over my head. I'm feelin' fine. Let's just keep it that way. Have you had a good purge lately?

I think sports bras are the best all-round solution.

My Queendom for a decent nightgown

Am I the only person on the planet who still wears nightgowns rather than pyjamas? It's been more than two years since I've been able to rotate some of my old nighties out and replace them with new ones. The reason for this is not because I blew the budget on purses and shoes or that I haven't really tried. I've been scouring the department stores, lingerie boutiques, the internet and everywhere short of dumpsters looking for some new replacement nightgowns.

Everything, everywhere is *pyjamas, pyjamas, pyjamas*. Shorties. Thermals. Dorm-wear. Brothel-wear. Skimpy. Safe. Granny or gorgeous. Every kind of pyjama style, fabric and price point is available but no suitable nightgowns for old boomer broads like me. I'm not particularly demanding but I do have a few specific requirements:

- Not too short. They need to keep my bum warm under the covers and should keep my knees covered when wearing them around the house. (Who knew boomer gals would grow unsightly muffin top on our *knees*!)

- Not too long. I'm not keen on maxi length because I'm only 5'3" tall and full length usually means I'm tripping over it. Mid-calf midi (not maxi) length would be perfect. Handkerchief or asymmetrical hems are a nice touch too.

- No spaghetti straps. They just fall off our shoulders, requiring constant adjustments. Nice tank-style shoulder straps between one and two inches in width would do nicely. Despite the persistence of our hot flashes, we do not like our shoulders getting cold during the winter.

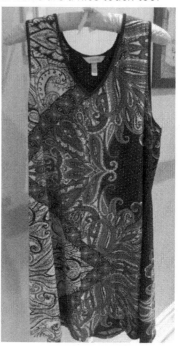

- No ruching or elastic under the bustline. Again, this calls for constant attention, untwisting and relocating things.

- Breathable fabrics. Those hot flashes still blast us every so often and our bodies need to breathe. Cotton jersey knit or bamboo are lovely and the better-quality fabrics feel divine.

- Feminine, sexy prints are preferred. Dark, *solid* colours fade in the wash and light colours are too transparent to be worn decently around the house. Animal prints are always fun. Painterly patterns can be lovely

If this nightgown were a bit longer, it would be perfect.

too. Orchids, calla lilies and other florals are cheerful. But no teddy bears, strawberries or bunnies puleez. We are not children. We are women who want to be appropriately feminine and a bit sexy, whether we sleep alone or not.

- Soft fabrics are essential. Preferably something that moves gently when we walk and feels delicious next to our skin. No scratchy, stiff or rough embellishments.

I really don't think I'm asking for too much. A midi-length tank-style, A-line nightgown in a soft printed fabric would make me the happiest old boomer broad in the world. I used to be able to score what I was looking for at *Soma* in the United States but even they have abandoned me the last couple of years. Donna Karen sometimes comes out with something acceptable. Natori is a bit pricey and haven't yet created one that I one hundred percent love.

I'm getting desperate. My inventory is seriously depleted and there seems to be no signs of hope to grasp on to. The other day I was so desperate I went into Victoria's Secret (a store I dislike) and asked if they had any nightgowns. The young nymphette working there looked at me for a few seconds like I was crazy before she shook her head *no.* The empress has no nightclothes and it's not a pretty sight. Am I a freak or does anyone else share my frustration?

Did you ever get rid of something and later regret it?

Back in the 1970s when I was finally making decent money, living the life of a modern career gal who wanted to put her best fashion foot forward, I invested in a winter coat that cost an embarrassing amount of money. It was by Canadian designer Pat McDonagh. Made of black and grey wool tweed shot through with cobalt blue, it came almost to my ankles, had giant banded sleeves and shoulder pads, and a large, soft pleat down the flared back. *I. Absolutely. Loved. That. Coat.* I wore it with a cobalt blue scarf, tall boots and felt like a

If I reduced the shoulder pads, this fabulous Pat McDonagh coat would be just as stylish today as it was when I bought it forty years ago. Mine was a darker mixed colour of tweed.

million dollars whenever I put it on. Why oh why did I ever get rid of it? Did I consign it or just stuff it into the bag for Goodwill? I was so casual about its disposal I can't even remember where it went. I regret it soooo much and wish I still had that coat.

My friend Perry had the rare privilege of living in swinging London in the sixties. Boomers will remember London as the epicenter of the fashion universe and one of the hippest stores at that time was *Biba.* Vogue's Anna Wintour worked in the fitting rooms at Biba back then. According to Perry, *"Biba was near where I used to live in London and was a mecca for all the dollybirds. I bought one of her Victorian-style lamps in velvet with a long fringe around the edge of the shade in a colour called Oxblood. It was my proudest possession. I sold it recently in a garage sale for $10.00."* Original Biba items now command hefty prices on eBay and perhaps if Perry had been a bit more discriminating about how she sold it, she could have supplemented her old age wine budget significantly.

The other night I was watching a television rerun of *Carnal Knowledge* from 1971 starring Jack Nicholson. There's a quick scene toward the end of the movie where he's flipping through a slide show of his previous lovers for his old college friend played by Art Garfunkle. In a quick couple of seconds, he skips over a black and white shot of a lean, dark-haired girl lounging in a Bentwood rocker.

That shot instantly transported me back nearly fifty years to when I first started to work for EllisDon. I was sharing an apartment with my friend Joan from my 1965-67 Willard Hall days. We lived downtown on Alexander Street in Toronto behind Maple Leaf Gardens. We were both broke, in transition, and the decor in our apartment reflected our pecuniary status. We had a rollaway cot in the living room that served as a couch. Beside it was a side table we'd fashioned from two stacks of old copies of the Yellow Pages. The nicest piece of furniture we had was a "chrome suite", an arborite kitchen table with four avocado green vinyl chairs.

The Bentwood rocker I purchased in 1971 was my idea of the ultimate in decorating chic.

In celebration of my new high-paying job ($115.00 per week; it was 1971), I went to Cargo Canada (an earlier incarnation of Pier I Imports) on Yorkville Avenue, before it became gentrified. There, I purchased a Bentwood rocker that elevated our decor to stratospheric levels. I had to splurge on a cab to get it home and buy a Philips screwdriver to put it together. I loved that chair and was so proud of it even though it had the peculiar habit of traveling across the floor whenever I rocked in it. A couple of years ago, after kicking around in my basement for too many years, I reluctantly sold it at a yard sale. As soon as I saw that chair on *Carnal Knowledge* I missed it and desperately wanted it back. Sigh!

And, what about all the lovely gold jewelry we've sold over the years for next to nothing? The retailer would weigh it, give us a pittance for its karat value and if there happened to be any precious stones like diamonds in the pieces . . . well . . . we'd get nothing extra for them. No wonder retailers love buying our old jewelry. Our taste in jewelry changes and often we inherit pieces that aren't to our taste so we're happy to unload it for whatever we can get. What can you do?

It's not just big-ticket items we regret disposing of. In the 1980s I had a CoverGirl eye shadow in a colour called "Brick" that I tossed after a few months of use, and I've never been able to find one I like as much. Or that Elizabeth Arden lipstick from the seventies in the most perfect shade ever invented called *Pink Coral.* It's funny how we remember such incidentals. We've all mourned lipsticks that the cosmetics companies quit producing and spend hours scouring the internet for end-of-line deals on discontinued cosmetics.

My friend Terry has kept something I hope she never gets rid of. Every so often she brings out a tiny, lime-green leather miniskirt that she used to wear in the sixties. It's probably a foot wide and a foot long and originally had a matching jacket. *"My father was always horrified when I walked out the door in that outfit, with long brown leather boots"* she said. That always brings on howls of laughter

Vintage cars are guaranteed to evoke fond memories.

when we see it and we start comparing stories of some of the outfits we wore back when. I think she should mount it in a shadow box and display it on the wall. It's a priceless example of when boomer fashion and boomers were actually cool.

If we asked the men in our lives what item they wish they still owned it would likely be an old car. Maybe that's why boomers love going to vintage car shows. We look at those shiny old Mustangs, Chevys and Ford Fairlaines that evoke memories of all the fun we had steaming up the windows in them with Phil Spector's wall-to-wall sound blasting on the car radio. I've kept my black and white Beatles bubble gum cards from 1963 and still have a few of my well-used old 45s and LPs but have nothing to play them on. Can't bring myself to part with them though. My husband still has the marked decks of playing cards he used to cheat with when he attended Ryerson University in the early sixties. He loves to bring them out and baffle the grandkids with their secret powers.

I've kept both of my wedding dresses. I sewed the first one myself and can't believe that I was once that skinny. It still has a little swipe of makeup on the neckline from having difficulty squeezing out of it when the zipper stuck. I had to get into my 'going-away outfit' (remember them?) after the reception that day in 1974. Wedding dresses back then were much more modest than they are today. We would have never considered displaying cleavage or bare shoulders in a wedding dress. Times were different. I also still have the wedding album from my first wedding in 1974 even though I never look at it and rarely keep photos of anything today. In fact, I don't even *take* many photos these days because I can't be bothered keeping track of them, and I'm horribly selfie averse.

There are probably other things I wish I'd kept but the larger problem has now become keeping too much. We don't miss those big old stereos, the huge televisions we spent way too much money on when big screens first hit the market, our wardrobes of sweat-inducing crimplene or that orange shag rug that had to be raked after it was vacuumed. We all have garages, basements, closets and even storage units full of crap we know we should get rid of. But it's hard to part with the story of our lives as represented by various possessions. Thanks to our hoarding habits, decluttering has now become a highly profitable multi-million-dollar industry. There are quite a few old boyfriends I am thankful I kicked to the curb and too many fashion mistakes I happily kissed goodbye. If I could have one thing back, though, I think it would be that Pat McDonagh winter coat. It would still work, and I still miss it.

Is Home Ec the answer to sustainable fashion?

We're finally realizing that we can't keep buying and indiscriminately disposing of clothing without giving consideration to what becomes of the millions of pieces of unwanted items in landfill. As I was reading an article in the morning paper about how a designer is taking 'vintage' clothing and reworking the pieces into something new and fashionable, a lightbulb went off in my head. Why aren't more people doing this, particularly the Gen Xs, Ys and Zs?

The answer is simple. The younger generations don't know how to sew. Not only can they probably not perform simple tasks like sew on a button or hem a pair of pants, most have likely never even *seen* much less operated a sewing machine. Maybe it's time to bring back *"Home Ec"* in schools. It would have to be given a cool twenty-first-century new gender-neutral name like *"Fun With Fashion"* or *"Practical Personal Growth"* in order to get buy-in from the selfie-obsessed Instagram set. Much as we hated those classes in the sixties, we definitely benefited from what we learned, even though I've never actually made

Disposable fashion has created an environmental disaster

an honest-to-goodness cheese soufflé (our first grade nine cooking project) in real life.

Our first sewing project in grade nine was an apron, a great starting point. We learned how to cut from a pattern, hand baste and gather material at the waist, and sew in a (reasonably) straight line. During our first year of Home Ec, we

It was fun modeling our home-made couture in the school gym.

worked on manual treadle sewing machines (I'm really old). As we advanced, and the school advanced to electric machines, we learned how to do collars, buttonholes, plackets, sleeves, zippers, pockets, and other refinements to make a shirtwaist dress that incorporated the complete spectrum of our dressmaking skills. Then, we put on a fashion show in the school gym for our mothers to come and see us model our creations. Great fun.

I was so inspired by my new skills, I even did some voluntary sewing during the summer holidays in high school. My creative cousins made their own Barbie doll clothes on my Aunt Betty's treadle machine. "Pop-tops" were all the rage in the sixties and were a snap to make. I whipped up a couple and with the left-over fabric bits, I fashioned a purse from the same material. Using an empty Kleenex box (the cardboard was much sturdier in those days), I covered it with fabric to match my pop-top, added a shoelace handle and proudly strutted my new fashion look uptown. You can imagine how I turned heads and generated smiles on Front Street from people obviously impressed with my tasteful, couture fashion statement.

I made my first wedding dress and saved a fortune. No bridezilla meltdowns involved. The dress was simple. I combined the draped sleeves from one pattern with the dress part of another pattern and added assorted lace appliqués I'd purchased at

Sixties fashion had simple lines and was easy to replicate on our home sewing machines. So is twenty-first-century fashion

Fabric Land until I ran out of lace. My sister-in-law at the time was an expert seamstress and she inspired me to try things I might not have attempted on my own.

As I reflect on our motivation back then, it was a combination of being creative and being broke. We weren't making much money in those days and economy was a great motivator. In the sixties and seventies, my boomer gal pals and I were always whipping up something on our little Singer sewing machines. The girls I worked with at the telephone company would turn up in stylish new outfits they had made over the weekend and we would compare fabrics and patterns. We could produce a little skirt from a yard of material in the evening and wear it to work the next day, at a fraction of the price we would have paid for ready-made.

It seems young women today have a lot more disposable income than we did, not to mention limitless credit cards. There's no incentive to be creative and save

money at the same time. We've become far too affluent and we're overloading landfill with our cast-offs that will never biodegrade. We have closets full of clothing and probably wear only fifteen or twenty percent of what we own. French women are known for owning fewer, better quality pieces and wearing them to death. There's a lot of merit in that approach.

I still have the heavy, cast-iron beige Singer sewing machine that I purchased in 1968 but it mostly gathers dust. I'm thankful that I still have it, however, for the times when I need to make a quick alteration or repair a seam. It's been decades since I've bought a pattern and fabric to make a dress or top. That doesn't mean that I don't think about it, though. When I look at the simplicity of

Get the current raw hem look at no cost. Anyone with a pair of scissors can do it.

Eileen Fisher clothing and the pricey cost, I still find myself fantasizing about taking some old linen curtain material and turning it into a wearable shift dress or tunic top. And I bet I would even have enough material left over to create a matching

37

purse. Reworking vintage clothing just makes sense. You do not have to make a business of it but if you could, that would be even better. Simply cutting the hems off old jeans to get the new "raw hem" look costs nothing, and I've done it.

Adding embellishments to tired garments, trading clothes with friends and recycling old leisurewear into sleepwear also costs nothing. What about cutting old dresses down to tunics. Removing sleeves, tapering oversize sleeves, layering tired old pieces over or under more current ones has possibilities. I'm sure there are a million ways we could reduce the amount of disposable clothing that goes into landfill by reworking or reimagining pieces we already own. Tory Burch has made a fortune copying and manufacturing sixties fashion.

Imagine once again teaching young people in high school to sew their own clothing or restyle vintage clothing into something current and *hip* (is that even a word they would use or is the word *hip* vintage too?) like the designer I read about in the paper. The fashion industry is a major contributor to environmental pollution, and we perpetuate it by continually hitting the malls and buying more disposable fashion. We're all guilty.

I've recently made a conscious decision to limit my trips to the mall in order to reduce impulse purchases although I must confess my online habit still needs work. I'm convinced the economy and Amazon depend solely on me.

At the very least, we should start looking more at vintage and consignment shops for new purchases. In the meantime, I have no plans to get rid of my sewing machine. Who knows? Maybe I'll pull a Scarlett O'Hara and turn those old linen curtains in the guest room into something spectacular that will turn heads and generate smiles at our Saturday night oldies dances. Do you have any ideas to share about helping to reduce, reuse, and recycle clothing?

They've just added another questionable chore to our beauty regimen . . . scalp exfoliation!

This should come as a surprise to no one, but the beauty industry has miraculously come up with another new product they insist needs our immediate attention. Get your credit cards out girls. In order to constantly create demand for useless and questionable beauty treatments, clever product lines are continually being introduced as *new and improved, now with blowfish and fairy wing DNA,* or, *cleaner, more natural, distilled from puppies' tears,* or whatever marketing magic they can conjure up to suck us in.

Give me strength. And we gleefully buy the newest version of an over-hyped new-age treatment product. This time it's scalp exfoliators. I guess that means they've tapped out all the possibilities for the various oils they've been foisting on us for the last couple of years. As if we're not already busy and broke enough keeping ourselves stocked up on all the latest shampoos and conditioners, volumizers, mousse sprays, and colour enhancers, now we're required to *exfoliate our scalps.* One such product recommended in the May issue of *ELLE CANADA* actually had a price tag of *$115.00!!*

If regular washing and conditioning with forty-two mutually dependent products they've sucked us into buying are not already enough, now we're expected to scrape all their carefully marketed earlier products off our filthy scalps with expensive and newly formulated exfoliation products. It's double jeopardy. We need the 'before' products to generate a need for the 'after' products. Scalp exfoliators are popping up everywhere and if we don't immediately buy-in, well, I hate to think of the consequences.

I don't know about you, but just keeping my feet exfoliated has pretty much become a full-time job as I've aged. And now that we can't get to salons for professional grinding and sandblasting, we're having to do it ourselves. And, as boomers, it's not easy reaching down there to attend to our lower digits. Regular body exfoliation is accomplished a couple of times a week in the shower with special facecloths that I buy at Walmart. They have terry cloth on one side

Maybe when I've finished exfoliating my feet.

and loofah on the other which does quadruple duty on my face, legs, arms, and body. Foolishly, I thought that was enough and I was done.

It's getting harder and harder to stay beautiful. As Norah Ephron once said in *I Feel Bad About My Neck,* maintenance issues can easily occupy as much as eight hours a day—a fulltime job. What with our cleansing, toning, moisturizing, masking, conditioning, exfoliating, hair removal, and deep treatments, we hardly have enough time left over to take care of the basics like washing our pits and brushing our teeth.

It's not easy being a woman. My husband's beauty regime, on the other hand, includes a mere *three items*—a bar of soap, a deodorant, and a tube of toothpaste. Any old brand will do. *My* products require an entire linen closet of baskets and organizers divided according to the type of products for hair, body, face and medicinal, and subdivided further according to makeup (further subdivided into blushers, lipsticks, foundations, etc.), shampoos, conditioners, nail products, . . . and the list goes on.

And now they want me to exfoliate my scalp. This concerns me. First of all, thanks to the ravages of menopause I'm going bald. Every strand of hair is precious and as worthy of protection as any rare insect in the Amazon rain forest. Would an exfoliator not break and remove fragile individual hairs? That would be disastrous for me. Can I sue if *all* my hair falls out as a result of exfoliating my scalp? Maybe there's an income opportunity here. Or maybe I'll just stick to a good brushing with a natural boar bristle hairbrush followed by scrubbing with my fingers and Neutrogena shampoo.

The quest for beauty is a never-ending journey. I'm content to settle for *good enough* under the circumstances. I never was and never will be anywhere close to the photoshopped images we see in fashion magazines. *No one is.* Not even the models in the photos. During our home lockdown, most of us have eschewed makeup, jewelry, street shoes, expensive hair appointments, and the accompanying fashion angst if we're not perfectly turned out. We're clean; we're comfortable, and we're surviving, despite the lack of mani-pedis, regular facials, and other so-called essential beauty rituals.

I look forward to the time when I can once again get dressed up to go out for dinner or enjoy a day of retail therapy followed by lunch with my boomer gal pals. But in the meantime, you'll have to ignore my unexfoliated scalp, my less-than-perfect pedicure, and my DIY hair. By the time we're set free once again, I may have forgotten the one hundred and twenty-eight steps required to make myself presentable each morning and you might see me facing the world *au natural*. Now that's a truly scary thought. And I like it. Have you exfoliated your scalp lately?

Chapter 2

My days as a trophy wife could be over

My descent into ordinariness started with my manicure, or lack of it. Lockdown has made me extremely lazy. It's an insidious process. Not having to get dressed for public appearances several times a week has created an entire generation of women who are awakening to the joys of freedom from regular and expensive mani-pedi treatments; freedom from constricting waistbands, makeup, and freedom from bras, particularly underwires. Ouch! We no longer worry about wearing lipstick and blusher because 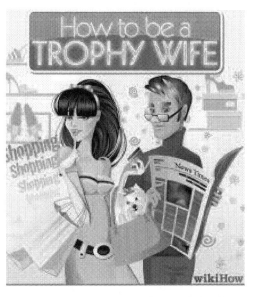 we're wearing masks everywhere for our infrequent excursions beyond the front porch. Who cares?

Men have always enjoyed the liberation of comfortable shoes and soft socks, going braless, not having to wear makeup, and not feeling embarrassed or self-conscious in any way about their Dad-bods. Women live under an entirely different and demanding set of standards. We've always accepted that it's our lot in life that our feet will be crippled by uncomfortable shoes in the latest fashion (designed by men), with half our salary (which is 76% of men's) going to stylish clothing and beauty treatments, and we have to keep toned and fit at expensive health clubs or suffer starvation and soul-destroying diet programs to remain in shape.

It's a new world

No more! We're throwing off our shackles. For most of the past five months, I've worn no nail polish. My nails get trimmed, filed, and buffed to a natural bareness and shortness by moi. I can bake without having to worry about destroying my manicure when I scrub baking pans or pick bits of cookie dough out from under longer nails. (No—this trophy wife does not make sourdough.) With a bit of stretching, which is cheaper than a gym, I can actually get down there to cut my own toenails and apply one coat of a neutral polish to make my piggies somewhat presentable in sandals. No basecoat followed by two coats of polish and a topcoat applied by a professional once a month. Easy peasy.

Most of the time now I wear cotton knit athletic shorts I buy at Walmart in the U.S. for $6.96 a pair. I own about ten pairs in different colours, mostly forgiving black though. They have an elastic waist with a drawstring, and they permit me to polish off half a container of Kawartha Dairy's pralines n' cream or maple walnut ice cream without feeling 'the pinch'. Fitted tank tops under sleeveless blouses or tee shirts have replaced bras, and I honestly don't know how I'll ever adjust to wearing a bra again.

I survived going seven months without having my highlights touched up and six months without a haircut. I'm delighted that situation has now been rectified, but I saved a lot of time and money at the salon. Women formerly accustomed to weekly blowouts and monthly root touchups have saved even more. Boomer gals are now emerging with healthier, natural gray hair that doesn't require expensive multi-tonal professional highlights every few weeks.

My collection of stylish leather handbags has been resting peacefully in their dust bags in the front hall closet while I throw an efficient Roots messenger cross-body bag over my shoulder when I make a no-more-than-necessary trip to the grocery store. My purses and I do miss each other though. I've been living in the same pair of comfortable sandals for several months now and no one seems to object or have even noticed. My extensive inventory of makeup and personal care products may soon be past their best-before date before they come out of seclusion. Once again, who cares?

This glamorous Housewife of Mississauga now spends most of her afternoons blissfully reading books and magazines in the comfort of my backyard LaZgirl under a shady gazebo with a cool drink by my side. That's about the only throwback to my former life as a trophy wife. I've spread weekly laundry chores out over three days now, so I don't over-exert myself by trying to do it all in one day. And I've convinced my husband that getting take-out is a fun and economical adventure, so cooking chores are minimized.

As I sit here in my stretchy shorts, braless and makeup-less, contemplating my comfortable good fortune, I'm aware that I'm not alone. The hosts of the women's programs on television that I PVR for evening viewing are in accord. They're loving the extra time with their children, even though they're not crazy about the home-schooling thing. Women of all ages are now learning that slowing down and relaxing standards a bit can leave us feeling less frazzled and much happier. We do miss getting together with friends and dining out, but damn, on the whole, this slower lifestyle is quite lovely.

We absolutely do miss spending time with family and friends, but we're slowly expanding our isolation bubbles to include a few more people who are proven safe. There are obvious downsides, but I think we're right to focus on the positive aspects of these major lifestyle changes. I've used the time to work on this book. I've learned how to use the UberEats app. I've saved a shitload of money by not hitting the mall for several months and I'm loving having time to myself without having to explain my lack of ambition. My friends are also indulging in hobbies, trying new recipes, and appreciating the simpler life as well.

Future challenges

I've heard no complaints from my honey that his trophy wife has obviously let her standards plummet. Has he even noticed? I've managed to sneak the emergence of the new me past him in increments and he's still nice to me, so I guess the slow transformation worked. He's not trawling the dating sites yet. It's made me reassess all the time and money invested over the years in maintaining a public presentation that now seems superficial and perhaps even unnecessary.

We have to view life as it unfolds in the future now as different from what we previously enjoyed. We'll have the eternal conflict between what looks good and what feels good. Ideally, we would prefer both, but I have a feeling comfort will reign. I'm also confident many women will in the future opt for a new perspective with obligation taking a back seat to 'sparking joy'.

I'll still cheer on his golf games, compliment his cooking, dress as well as I can for an old boomer, and laugh at his jokes but my duties as a trophy wife no longer end there. As we've both aged, we're being called on more often to refresh each other's memory, to pick up the slack if one of us isn't feeling well and to help each other over those increasingly more frequent bumps on the road. Between the two of us and the art of interdependence, we'll get through.

Will trophy wives become a thing of the past? Not likely but former trophy wives like me will be placing a higher value on our available time and how we choose to spend it. I vote for choice not chore. I'm also a happy wife and you know the saying: "Happy wife, happy life". Who could ask for more?

To nap or not to nap? There is no question

I am a world-class napper. One of the best. A friend once said I could sleep on a clothesline. My mother had to register me in morning kindergarten so I could still have my afternoon nap. And the habit stuck—to this day—and I'm now 72. Churchill, Kennedy, Eleanor Roosevelt, and me. We're all committed nappers. And the recent restrictions and self-isolation have allowed me to indulge with impunity.

We're learning a lot about ourselves during this enforced lockdown. There's so much time now for self-contemplation which is a luxury most of us have probably never enjoyed in our entire lives. Navel-gazing has its advantages. Haven't you ever been struck with a brilliant idea or inspiration just before you drop off to sleep at night? Or perhaps while you're idling in a traffic jam? That's why I keep a pen and notepad on my bedside table and in the console of my car. Fresh ideas need space to germinate and now is the perfect time to unleash our imagination.

Many of my boomer friends have commented on how they're enjoying the slower pace being enforced on us by house arrest. For the Type-A's it's been an adjustment but they're appreciating the extra time they now have for hobbies and simply taking time to smell the roses, peonies, or lilacs that are blooming at this time of year. Retirees, particularly retired baby boomers are known for being almost as active and involved as we were when we were working fulltime. Just try to organize a ladies' lunch or a

Shhh! We're creating, or regenerating, or something.

47

golf game and it's evident we all have busy schedules and the effort resembles the old saying "like herding cats".

I spend a lot of time these days playing around on my blog. My friend Perry has discovered digital art while another friend is finally doing all the reading that she never had time for previously. Terry has become a master sourdough baker. When we have time on our hands, our brains are allowed to run free which does not happen when we're constantly busy. After working all morning on the computer, I have my lunch and I find my eyes are tired after all that earlier computer work. So, I sit down in my backyard La-Z-girl to read and dang, before you know it, I've nodded off. No guilt involved. Just like in the old days when I was in kindergarten, I need a nap in the afternoon; it's a genetic flaw that was very inconvenient when I was working.

Allowing ourselves the time needed to recharge our batteries and let our minds wander is a practice I endorse wholeheartedly. As we get older, it's a delicious luxury we've earned. Leave the late nights working, partying, or whatever to those much younger than ourselves. We did it in our day and spent most of our lives sleep deprived. The pandemic is forcing the entire world to re-evaluate our natural circadian rhythms and acknowledge our limitations and natural inclinations. We're going to notice many lifestyle changes when this thing is over and I'm hoping that one of the outcomes is a less negative connotation associated with our natural need for sleep.

They say more sleep even encourages weight loss, but I can't vouch for that as I've put on five pounds this summer, which could have something (a lot) to do with my increased intake of Kawartha Dairy ice cream at this time of year. I think I'll just sleep it off and maybe the feeling and the pounds will go away. It's nice to do something I'm really good at and have an aptitude for. When we come out the other side of this crisis, hopefully, we'll all be happier, more aware of the damage we're doing to our planet, a bit smarter, a bit chubbier, and finally, well-rested. That's OK too.

Thoughts on a room of one's own

Spoiler alert: this is not a book review on Virginia Woolf so relax and enjoy some thoughts on serenity. Woolf did, however, know what she was talking about when she penned her famous story about the importance of women having their own private space in the home. Hers was devoted to writing and reflection. She recognized and advocated for financial independence and privacy in women's lives. When she was alive in the first half of the twentieth century women were considered second class citizens. Many could not vote, work outside the home, have their own bank accounts or divorce their husbands (yikes!).

Twenty-first century women have much to be thankful for, although we still have a long way to go. Woolf would be pleased to see the progress we've made but, time has only confirmed and reinforced her vision. Experts suggest it will be another one hundred years before women have full equality.

Now that baby boomer women are retiring, *a room of one's own* has taken on practical dimensions. In fact, my own special room is literally ten feet wide and eleven feet long. It contains bookshelves loaded with years of loved books. There's a comfortable off-white twill sofa for reading, a computer desk and chair for working on my blog, memory-evoking pictures on the walls including a street map of Paris and a shadow box with a rose from the bouquet my husband gave me on our first Valentine's Day together.

My own personal space.

"My room" also has a cream and taupe rug covering most of the dark hardwood floor and of course, there's a wee little dog bed for our Yorkshire terrier. A lovely wide window looks out over my husband's gorgeous hydrangea bushes, a linden tree and a blue spruce we planted the year we moved in. My little room is a genuine slice of feminine heaven and I spend several happy hours in there every day.

Not only do we boomer gals need our own space, but so do our husbands or partners. It's an equal opportunity arrangement. The high-tech digital age means laptops and televisions are now allocated to individual members of the household. In the case of retired people like ourselves, we each need our own space for working on our computers and I've discovered the secret to a happy marriage is separate televisions; one for news, weather and sports (his) and one for HGTV, PBS and other women-friendly channels (hers). Consequently, my honey also has a room of his own with his LaZboy, television, desk and computer. It's a happy arrangement.

When weather permits (this is Canada, after all), my favourite private space of all is sitting outside in the shade surrounded by flowers and trees in our back yard. I can listen to the birds, feel and smell sweet, warm breezes and maintain a sense of peaceful balance. I can read my books and even tip back in my cushioned faux wicker LaZgirl from Canadian Tire and have a delicious snooze. Life is sweet.

Virginia Woolf's understanding of the value of quiet time and private space is as relevant today as it was nearly one hundred years ago. Women still need private space and financial independence. The only difference today is technology. And we have to be careful that we don't let technology encroach too much. Do you have a favourite or special spot in your house where you can read, paint, write, knit or simply *be?* Perhaps it's a corner of your livingroom, bedroom or kitchen. Maybe it's a spare bedroom. I hope you are lucky like me and have managed to carve out your own private space.

It's time for a refresher from Miss Manners

Globe and Mail columnist David Eddy recently printed a letter from a reader who was frustrated and disappointed that she never received a thank you note for a shower gift. Eddy advised politely addressing the issue with the gift recipient by

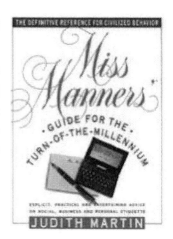

gently letting her know you would have appreciated a thank you note. This should be done in person, but an email is also acceptable. And it wouldn't hurt to remind the recipient that they *"should probably send one every time they receive a gift"*.

I am frequently disheartened at the dearth of manners in many young people today. Baseball hats at the dinner table and failure to offer your seat to a senior or pregnant woman on the subway are just unacceptable. It's a parental failure for not teaching basic manners for sure but that doesn't excuse people for not taking the time to thank gift-givers for wedding, shower, birthday and graduation gifts. **If your parents didn't teach you basic manners, you can easily learn by observing others who** *did* **get proper instruction when they were growing up.**

My girlfriends and I have had this same discussion many times and since it seems to be an ongoing issue.

Thank you for your thank you

When someone takes the time to tuck a cheque or gift card for a slice of their hard-earned income into a birthday card which they've gone to the store to purchase, put in the envelope with a stamp they've also purchased and walked it to a mailbox, how difficult can it be for the recipient to email a quick note or email saying, "Thanks so much for your birthday gift. I'm saving for a new bicycle and your cheque helps bring me closer to my goal."? After all, young people spend hours a day texting.

With the convenience of email there's no excuse for not taking a few seconds to thank someone who has done something kind for you or remembered your birthday with a card enclosing a cheque or gift card. And when a friend has taken the trouble to shop for and prepare a lovely meal for you or hosted you over a weekend, a thank you is meaningful. It doesn't have to be elaborate; it doesn't even have to

Hosting a dinner party or barbecue can involve considerable time, effort and expense. As a guest, be sure to follow-up with a thank you.

be a fancy card. A simple email will do the job.

When I was still working, I always took the time to send a note of thanks for corporate gifts that I received at Christmas but as someone who also *gave* corporate gifts, I know that unfortunately this wasn't the general practice in business. Boomers are now aunts, uncles and grandparents which means we're frequently the giver not the receiver and we appreciate the appreciation. Am I right? David Eddie and I think so.

Mondays are the most wonderful day of the week

Mondays come with multiple benefits. Not only because I'm retired and no longer have to get up at the crack of dawn and go to work but also because Monday is change-the-sheets day. When we're retired, it's often those simple rituals that give us enormous pleasure.

I'll never understand how people can wake up in the morning and go to work or start their day without making their bed. The only thing lovelier than sliding into nice, smooth, cool sheets at the end of the day is when they're freshly changed. In our house, that happens on Monday. When I change the sheets, I hang the freshly laundered ones outside to dry; screw the local bylaws. It's environmentally

I love to hang my laundry outside to dry.

friendly and they're hung below the fence line where the neighbours can't see them.

There's nothing more delicious than sliding into a freshly made bed with crisp cotton sheets that have been air-dried and the pillowcases ironed with a spritz of lavender linen water? I even cheat and change the pillowcases mid-week to rush the experience. Is it a boomer broad thing, or am I the only peculiar one? My friends and I even have an acronym for it: *Clean Sheets Day.* My friend Margaret loves the experience so much. she immediately hops in and has a snooze on CSD.

I've yet to meet a man who understands our pleasure. My mother always loved CSD and my father was oblivious. My husband doesn't get it either. Maybe it's because we're usually the ones who do the laundering and changing so we're true aficionados of the ritual. Oprah gets it; her sheets are changed every second day, which is particularly pleasurable when you have staff to do the work. The only downside I'm finding is that as I get older and my back gets weaker, it's becoming harder to pull and lift the heavy corners of the mattress to tuck in those fitted sheets. I need Oprah's staff to give me a hand, or better still, to do it for me.

The reward will come tonight around 10:30 when I slide into bed, propped up with a good book in my hands, snuggled up with my honey and my little Yorkie, and a smile of satisfaction on my face. It's a well-earned and delicious pleasure. Sweet dreams mes chères.

Is your clean house making you fat?

Every time I come across a new angle or theory on the science of weight loss, I get a little excited thinking maybe there's some minor tweak I can make with minimal effort in my lifestyle that will give me back the body I took for granted in my twenties. The business of weight loss is a multi-billion-dollar industry built around feeding our insecurities about how we

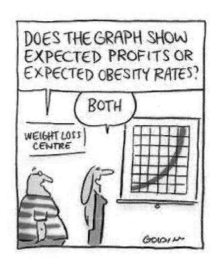

53

look. The health and wellness industries throw out the bait and reel us in.

It's not complicated. We are a privileged society. There is so much food available, much of which is unhealthy, that we overeat and don't work it off. Menopause throws the final wrench in the works making it impossible to stay trim without constant effort and vigilance.

University students are familiar with the *freshman fifteen (pounds)* just as boomer women are familiar with the *meno fifteen . . . or twenty, or thirty* that happens when we hit fifty-ish. Four years ago I spent an entire winter attending Weight Watchers, losing ten pounds, only to put it back on again. I'm lucky compared to those who work harder to lose even more and pack it all back on. We spend an inordinate amount of time, money and emotional energy on weight issues. What a waste of resources.

We're so brainwashed about the evils of consuming carbs that enjoying a simple piece of toast with jam can bring on paroxysms of guilt and shame. I love *ACE* bread and only allow myself to enjoy it toasted for breakfast as a treat on weekends. But, as we all know, cheating is a slippery slope. As soon as bread is declared an all-inclusive health food I'm going to eat nothing but toast a least three times a day, for the rest of my life. In the fickle world of health advice, it *is* a possibility. I keep hoping. Living on vegetables and protein alone is never going to work. I try not bring things like ice-cream and cookies into the house, but sometimes a gal's just gotta have a hot dog.

Then, a few days ago I read in the newspaper that household cleaners have been proven to affect the gut flora in children. When small children are exposed to high levels of the chemicals in cleaning fluids, the good gut microbes are lowered. According to the Canadian Medical Association Journal, the gut flora of 757 infants and children up to three years old exposed to cleaning chemicals resulted in higher BMI (body mass index) readings than those exposed to ecofriendly cleaners.

Naturally, this information leads me to conclude (not scientifically, of course) that the reason I'm overweight is because I've been exposed to too many chemical cleaning products for more than 70 years. So, that knowledge combined with the inevitable, irreversible menopause fifteen means I'm wasting my time and money trying to lose weight through traditional commercial health and wellness methods. Either I stop cleaning or I risk decreasing my gut flora and I'll get even fatter. I think the evidence is pretty clear. Don't clean. Stay thin. Wouldn't you agree?

When does too clean become a messy problem?

Being confined to quarters during the pandemic has forced me to confront the various large and small jobs that need to be done around the house. When I dig under the kitchen or bathroom sink, I'm shocked and appalled at the number and variety of cleaning products I have, most of them in plastic spray bottles. The other day, I threw a fit and gathered all of them together in one spot, pulling everything from the kitchen, bathrooms, laundry room and basement. This is just a sampling of what I had—and I am not making this up:

- Bathroom, tub and tile cleaner, two bottles
- Glass cleaner, Zep, Windex and Hertel
- Granite cleaner, three bottles
- Bona wood floor cleaner
- Bona tile floor cleaner
- All-purchase cleaner, Fantastic, and Hertel
- Toilet bowl cleaner, three bottles of Lysol brand
- Ceramic stove top cleaner, Barkeeper's Friend and Ceramabrite
- Zep Stainless steel cleaner
- Zep Leather cleaner for hubby's LaZboy
- Spot cleaner for laundry, Shout and PC brand
- Carpet cleaner, Zep and Resolve
- Sanitary wipes, various brands
- Disinfectant, Lysol
- No-name Ammonia
- Murphy's Oil Soap
- Wood furniture cleaner
- Brass and silver cleaner
- Distilled water for floor steam cleaner

- Spray starch, two cans
- Laundry detergent, Persil, Arm & Hammer, and Eco-Max
- Oxi-Clean laundry booster
- Downy fabric softener, which I never use
- Febreeze, two bottles, and I don't use it as I don't believe in artificial air and fabric fresheners
- Clorox bleach, two gallon-size bottle

Are you as shocked as I am? And that doesn't even include our inventory of things like cans of Raid, ant traps, bug spray and guy stuff like Armorall, car wax, Goo-Gone, Miracle-Gro and other garden products. Bear in mind, I did not have just one bottle of these different products. Multiple bottles of more than twenty *different* kinds of items were distributed among kitchen and bathroom cupboards as well as the laundry room and basement. And, I like to keep separate bottles of the required product at its specific location which means each bathroom

must have it's own supply so I'm not continually running up and down the stairs. Consequently, I have enough bottles of cleaning products to successfully give Highclere Castle a thorough spring cleaning and still have plenty left over for the Queen to do Buckingham Palace.

If I were a truly environmentally conscientious person, surely a single bottle of vinegar and water and a box of baking soda would do the job for most of these chores. I'm horrified at the excess. The overflow and attendant storage issues were driving me crazy so after collecting everything together in one place I started to cull my inventory. First, everything had to be sorted according to what surface it was intended for (see above summary). Then, partial bottles were combined and unused products were separated for disposal later at a proper hazardous waste disposal location.

When I pulled everything out of the laundry room cupboard (which is more like a pantry), I then thought it would be a lovely idea to remove the four original painted builder's shelves and redo the entire space, installing multiple clean, white melamine adjustable shelves so I could arrange the contents according to size and product category. When I ran this idea by hubby . . . well, let's just say he was not even a tiny bit supportive. *"You'll just fill it up with more stuff."*

I've now filled a giant IKEA leakproof bag with bottles of cleaning products to be taken to the hazardous waste disposal site. I hang my head in shame and have made a sincere promise to never let it come to this again. My remaining products have been redistributed and I'm pretty sure I've learned a lesson here. Some people collect art; others collect fine jewelry; I've chosen to collect a wealth of cleaning products.

I must confess, I found the entire purging process so daunting I had to spread it out over three days for fear I would get overwhelmed and just give up. Pacing yourself when it comes to nasty jobs has its advantages but it meant my sins were visible for all to see on our dining room table and on the floor for three days. Now, I keep opening the door of the cleaning supplies cupboard just to admire my brilliant work. It does feel good.

In the near future, my next project is to attack my far-flung supplies of light bulbs. But, don't worry, I'm not going to subject you to a blog posting about the scintillating experience of sorting my light bulbs. You would not believe how many different kinds are required though to keep a house illuminated. We have kitchen lights, chandelier bulbs, halogen bulbs, special ones for special fixtures, tri-lights, outside bulbs, clear bulbs, frosted ones and, of course, low-wattage fluorescents—after all, we must be energy

conscious. I think I'd better have another talk with my husband about that cupboard renovation. I don't see how we can avoid it and hopefully he'll see 'the light'.

What's next?

Now, I know what you're thinking. So, she purged her cleaning cupboard and has plans to do her light bulbs next. Big deal. I know a lot of my readers have accomplished far more during their weeks of isolation but cut me some slack. I'm a lazy, old lady and it takes me a while to rev up and get in gear. As they say, the journey of a thousand miles begins with one step and my first step was tackling Mr. Clean. At this rate, I should be able to attack the basement by 2026.

Don't buy into the multi-tasking myth

Science is now confirming what we've long suspected. Multi-tasking is not only an overrated virtue but can in fact be counterproductive. Women in particular have been brainwashed to think we should be able to juggle work, home, community and social activity balls simultaneously and efficiently without dropping a single one in order to be deemed successful mothers, wives and human beings. Well, it's all bull crap. Multi-tasking only results in an outcome that is less than it could or should be. Let's not fall for the multi-tasking myth and instead allow ourselves the time and space we need to properly manage and in fact, enjoy our lives. Here's my suggestion.

Feeling uninspired? Take a nap

Leah Eichler's Women@Work column in The Globe and Mail was a source of inspiration and affirmation better than most I've read in a while. Eichler maintains that we often get our best ideas when our brains are off duty. Haven't you ever been struck with a brilliant idea just as you're about to drop off to sleep or when you're walking the dog through the park? According to Eichler we should allow ourselves more down-time to allow these bursts of inspiration to emerge. Research has shown that we need quiet time for our brains to arrive at the state of zen conducive to new ideas.

I agree wholeheartedly with this philosophy. For that reason, I keep a pad and pencil on my night table and another in the map pocket of my car so I can write down these flashes of genius when they happen, or at the next red light. Fortunately, I'm very good at zoning out. And to think teachers used to yell at us for not paying attention. Just think of all the earth-shattering discoveries and inventions they probably killed when we were daydreaming in school.

Multi-tasking and "busyness" are considered virtues in today's world of 24/7 cell phones, e-mail and texting but these activities are ultimately counterproductive. Thomas Edison would regularly sit on his boat dock holding a fishing pole and line in the water, with no bait. He needed time to think. Bill Gates used to isolate himself at his cottage to free his mind for creativity. Gordon Lightfoot would check into a hotel and stay in his room for days to be free from distractions so he could write songs. And, Winston Churchill is well-known for his afternoon power naps that freed his mind from the stresses of trying to save the world from destruction.

When I was working, I always found the activity and noise inherent in daily office life to be distracting. My best ideas always came when I was doing some non-work-related activity. I needed my head to be free of clutter and my brain to be in a happy place to be truly productive.

This is my idea of being productive.

So, with that in mind, please excuse me while I go take a nap. There are major world problems that need solving and I'm pretty sure I'm just on the cusp of finding the key to cold fusion right after I summon up that Nobel-prize-worthy literature bubbling away in there somewhere. Maybe checking into a Four Seasons Hotel in Bali with the scent of fragrant blossoms and the sounds of surf outside my window would help. It certainly can't hurt.

There must be intelligent life beyond weed

Will the never-ending news about the legalization of marijuana in Canada ever stop? I'm sick to death of the monopolization of every form of radio, television, internet and print media for weeks focussing on nothing but the pros and cons of our newly legal recreational and therapeutic weed. I'm sure it's a fascinating subject to many people but I've had enough of the over-reporting. It's like watching O.J.'s white Bronco all those years ago.

I think I finally understand the difference between THC (tetrahydrocannabinol) which has mood elevating effects and CBD (cannabidiol) which is primarily used for medicinal purposes, although I had to Google it to be sure. As someone who stops after a glass or two of

Oh Canada!

wine (which I enjoy enormously but had to curtail because it gives me an instant hangover), I really don't like my brain operating beyond my control. Just a personal preference not shared by many people, but I am what I am.

The chemical analysis and application of various strains of weed and its attendant effects on human beings has been discussed, analyzed, explained and debated by so many sources for so many weeks lately I should be an expert by now but mostly I've tuned out. Being a non-smoker means that when my ailments require me to look at its medicinal properties, I'll probably opt for the gummy bears or brownies. I have no objection to getting a little help with pain or sleep issues, but getting high is just not on my radar. For those individuals who feel the need to self-medicate or alter their mood, that's none of my business. We all have different ways of getting through life.

Canada's liberal attitude toward marijuana, gay marriage and other social issues is to be commended. Our prisons are full of recreational users who probably should not be there. Baby boomers came of age when it was still illegal to be homosexual in Canada. It was finally decriminalized in 1969 although persecution in the military and police forces continued for another twenty-five years. I'm not qualified to present a case for or against illegal drug use but I am proud that Canada is finally eliminating the criminal aspect of using recreational weed. The end of liquor prohibition didn't result in America descending into Dante's inferno and neither will the legalization of marijuana. There will be problems for sure, but it's up to us as a society to manage the inevitable bumps in the road and over time that will happen.

Now that simple possession of marijuana is legal in Canada, maybe our nightly news can once again return to its regular, unending reporting of murders, stabbings, wars, robberies, car accidents, rip-off scams, political disasters and other everyday events. Can you believe, I'd almost welcome it. It's time to move on, with a little help from our friends.

What's with boomerang kids? Then, now and still?

We've all read about the 30-year-old man whose parents took legal action to evict their large so-called adult child from the family home once and for all. A few years ago we met a couple who resorted to selling their home and moving into a small condo in a last-ditch effort to ditch their immature, dependent son. It worked. Oh, that it should come to this.

While most baby boomers can't imagine living with our parents a day longer than absolutely necessary, it seems we're the generation that launched the unlaunchable generation. A much smaller proportion of boomers went to university than today's young people, not only for economic reasons but also because there was not as much emphasis and insistence upon post-secondary education when we graduated in the sixties and early seventies. When we finished high school we considered ourselves launched and headed off to the big city to get a proper job, earn money and begin our lives.

The high proportion of young people today still living with their parents past the age when they should be off on their own got me thinking about why this has become so 'normal'. Let's take a look at why *we* were so anxious to cut the cord and today's young people are not.

Real life is not easy. The parents of boomers, also known as The Greatest Generation, lived through the Great Depression and many were veterans of World War II. They knew genuine hardship and made sure we appreciated every single advantage we had growing up. Everything was hard-earned and nothing was taken for granted. They instilled these values in their baby boomer children while

61

simultaneously offering us a better life than they had. Helicopter parenting was unheard of. I clearly remember one day during my working years when four people in our office (including two Vice Presidents) were working on their kids' school projects. How does that teach young people about hard work, responsibility and accountability?

Freedom. We had to be home for meals and frequently had to help prepare those meals and hand wash the dishes after. We had multiple chores to do around the house for which we were most certainly not paid. If we were disciplined by a teacher, we got it again when we got home. Parents defended the teachers not their precious misbehaving children. Parents were clearly our parents and not concerned with trying to be our friends. By the time we finished high school, we were anxious to be free of parental restrictions and go out on our own. It's called growing up and I don't see how this can be construed as a bad thing.

Economic responsibility. Weekly allowances were just enough to get us into the Saturday matinée and perhaps buy a comic book on our way home. When we ran out of money, the supply dried up. We had to collect pop bottles for extra pocket money. When we were old enough we got after-school or weekend jobs, babysitting, cutting grass, waitressing, whatever we could do to earn extra spending money. Today's young people just ask for money and it's handed out freely. How does that teach fiscal independence and responsibility?

We learn from our mistakes. Despite our parents having high expectations, boomers were given plenty of latitude to make mistakes. We hurt ourselves; we made bad decisions and had to deal with the consequences; we were accountable and often had to make restitution for our mistakes. That's how we learn to become responsible adults. Our parents knew that protecting us from physical and emotional hurt (within reason) was not character-building. They were there to pick us up and get us on our way again, but they made sure we learned the lessons we needed to learn from our mistakes.

Gifts are for birthdays and Christmas. It's shocking to see the volume of toys and games children today have at their disposal. Boomers received toys and gifts on birthdays or Christmas only, and they were modest by today's standards. A bicycle was special. Many of us did just fine with hand-me-downs. My own two-wheeler had been owned by two girls previous to me before my father bought it from a neighbour and repainted it for my birthday. Monopoly and Scrabble were high-end, expensive gifts. How is it possible to truly appreciate a gift when a child already has everything? I understand some parents are now discontinuing the distribution of loot bags at children's birthday parties because they can cost parents up to $200.00 in total and children are so jaded, they usually toss the contents anyway. Material consumption is way over the top for everyone, including us old boomers.

Your first home does not need granite countertops. How many boomers grew up in a 1,000 square foot house with one bathroom for a family of five, one phone and one black and white television? When we left home, we often shared a room in a boarding house or packed three girls into a one-bedroom apartment to afford the rent. By the time I'd rotated through a series of spartan accommodations over a period of several years when I started working, I was thrilled to finally be able to afford my very own walk-up bachelor apartment on Vaughan Road in Toronto. It had a claw-foot tub in the ancient bathroom, no countertop at all in the itty bitty kitchen, just a big, deep laundry sink, and I had to walk several blocks with my bundle buggy down to St. Clair Avenue once a week to do my grocery shopping and go to the laundromat. But it was *mine* and I loved it. Even when boomers got married, we didn't expect to buy a house immediately. We lived in a cheap apartment while we scrimped and saved to accumulate a minimum down payment on a starter home 'way out in the burbs. No granite countertops. No ceramic flooring in the kitchen and bathroom. No air conditioning. When I got married the first time, we didn't even have a clothes dryer in our first home because we couldn't afford the full complement of appliances. I hung clothes to dry in the basement for the first three years we were in our new (town)house, and I was in my thirties.

Money is not fairy dust. It must be earned not sprinkled from above. Having skin in the game always makes the outcome more meaningful. When parents and grandparents keep bankrolling young people after the age when they should be launched, they're enabling dependence.

The boomerang didn't come back. Returning to our parents' home after we left was not an option. There was no safety net because our parents made it clear we were grownups and we were expected to fend for ourselves. Once we left, we were off the payroll, permanently. And we were usually still teenagers. That forced us to get our shit together and get on with life.

How much support is a young person really entitled to?

I once read an essay in The Globe and Mail written by a young woman who felt universities should be providing much more support in terms of mental health services and guidance for students transitioning into the working world. She felt lonely, isolated and disillusioned living in her tiny studio apartment within walking distance of Fifth Avenue in Manhattan where she got her first job. The more I read her essay, the angrier I became. First of all, it's the parents' responsibility to instill independence in young people, not that of the university. This young woman graduated with no student debt; she spent holidays with her parents in Maui and there was no mention of having worked summer jobs or internships. Clearly, she was one of the entitled and ill-prepared for the real world. The comments from readers that appeared under her column were unanimous in telling her to grow up. Life is not easy and the sooner you realize that the sooner you develop coping skills.

Every generation has its own identifying characteristics. The Greatest Generation lived through the Depression of the thirties, worked hard, fought in World War II and hatched baby boomers. Boomers discovered rock n' roll, the sexual revolution and amazingly, the digital revolution. Gen X piggybacked on and benefited from the freedoms introduced by boomers. Then, along came millennials who are often maligned for being entitled and spoiled. No doubt, many do qualify for this distinction but not all. Each generation tries to improve on what they grew up with.

Young people who are independent, resourceful and prepared to start life with less than their parents spent their entire lives working for are more likely to succeed and become better citizens. Life truly is not easy and baby boomers themselves have been responsible for enabling boomerang kids and grandkids. Have we created a monster that's forever going to need constant feeding and nurturing like the thirty-year-old whose parents needed the courts to boot him out? I'm not sorry I won't live long enough to see how much longer this false foundation will stand up.

2019 Super Bowl vindicates this non-fan of football

Let me be absolutely clear right up front; I have zero interest in and no knowledge or understanding of football. In my opinion it is a violent, concussion-inducing game right up there with cage fighting. Any time I've tried to watch a game I'm bored to tears within four minutes watching overpaid fat guys run a few yards and fall down, or more often, get knocked down, then, get up, only to run and fall down again. I can think of four hundred things I'd rather be doing with my time than watching such masochism.

My husband has the polar opposite attitude toward football. He loves it and in an ideal world he would watch it on television non-stop all day every day. He's been known to get up in the middle of the night when he can't sleep and watch a prerecorded college game. He even prefers to watch the Super Bowl alone on his own TV with no distractions so he can concentrate and focus totally on the plays. So, you see we're not on the same team when it comes to football. I have no objection to him watching football until his eyeballs fall out as long as he wears his headphones and doesn't try to involve me.

The 2019 Super Bowl was a turning point, however. He made a tactical error that I plan to capitalize on for the rest of his life. After the third quarter of the big multi-bazillion-dollar game between the Los Angeles Rams and the New England Patriots, he emerged from his man-cave and declared that it was the most boring football game he'd ever seen. *"There was no offense; just defense and at the end of the third quarter the score is only 3/3."* Obviously, there had been no blood and guts, no questionable calls, no brilliant plays and in general, no excitement. He complained that even the much-anticipated commercials were boring. I'm sure the companies that invested $5.2 million for their 30-second slot would be thrilled to hear that. Things picked up only slightly at the end of the fourth quarter and as we all know the Patriots won again! Yawn.

The only conclusion I can draw from this experience is that I was right all along. I was better off watching Masterpiece Theatre where the blood is fake and the suspense is guaranteed. It's my intention to milk this vindication of my attitude toward football until our ashes are resting side by side on a quiet hilltop far from big-screen televisions. I knew all along I was right; it just took the 2019 Super Bowl to prove it.

What do you do when your dongle dies?

The first time the word dongle came up in conversation was a few months ago in relation to my Firestick streaming device. Prior to that I didn't even know I had a dongle. And I giggled like a little boy when he hears the word 'boobies', or that old sixties joke about the angle of the dangle. Anyway, I'd like to think I've matured a bit since then, but apparently not.

I heard the word dongle again this week when I took my laptop in for service. It's actually the little slug that plugs into your computer's USB slot that sends signals to your wireless mouse or keyboard if you use one. (I'm still not sophisticated enough to use the touchpad or touchscreen on my laptop.) The girl at the computer store referred to my dongle when she snapped it back into the base of my mouse before turning if off. You're never too old to learn new things or expand your vocabulary.

Anyway, the point of this story is really about how totally incapacitated I was without my laptop. As a blogger it is as essential to my daily routine as a pot of tea with my morning paper or brushing my teeth. As soon as I've finished both of the former, I head into my sumptuous (!!) office to start work on my BOOMERBROADcast blog. I love doing it and can't wait to get at it each morning. So, when the geeks told me they would need four days to bring my laptop back to life after heaven knows what plague struck it, I was devastated. It felt like an amputation. I kept making regular phone calls to check on its progress and was soooo relieved when I was able to finally bring it home safely.

The absence of my laptop reminded me of how strongly and perhaps inappropriately attached I am to it—I'm sure those of you who are fused to your smart phones will understand (which I'm not, she said self-righteously). I stumbled around the house the first day alone and lonely wondering what to do with my time. Then, on the morning of the second day, my brain spontaneously rebooted and reconnected within itself. I wrote out by hand (in cursive, no less) an old-fashioned "To Do" list on a piece of paper and put it on the kitchen counter. That old system still works. By noon on the second day I'd completed a huge pile of ironing while watching the Today Show on television, made my honey a giant freezer bag of his breakfast muffins, did a couple of loads of laundry, prepared five pounds of ground beef and vegetables for dog food and even managed to get showered and dressed before noon. I was understandably rather proud of myself.

In other words, I was productive, genuinely productive in a real sense not virtual. And, for what it's worth, I was disappointed to see that Jenna Bush has been chosen to replace Kathy Lee Gifford to co-host with Hoda Kopke on the Today Show. For some reason I can't stand Jenna Bush and will now have to find a replacement show for ironing days. (*And*, I strongly suggest you watch the video *Pet Fooled*; you'll start preparing your own dog food too. It's available on Amazon. Shocking stuff about the commercial dog food business.)

That temporary burst of productivity reminded me of just how much time I "waste" on the computer every day doing my blog, scouring FaceBook, emailing and otherwise fooling around in the digital world. It makes me wonder how much more I could accomplish if I also gave up evening television watching. I'm a captive of technology with nothing but a spreading waistline and sore back to show for it. I love blogging but should I channel more time toward more active pursuits? It seems to me that my laptop has become my personal dongle and without it I'm useless and unproductive. I'm open to suggestions and perhaps you have personal dongles of your own that require addressing.

The perils and pleasures of being a helicopter pet parent

This is really embarrassing to admit but the other day my honey and I had an actual disagreement about the intelligence of our dog, a 3½ pound 9-year-old female Yorkie called Sassy. (I truly dislike the name she came with, but she'd been named when we got her.) I like a name that denotes gender and one that's easy to yell so I wanted 'Stella' (think *Streetcar Named Desire*). My husband couldn't come

up with anything better that we both liked, so 'Sassy' stuck. I liked my last dog's name, "Gracie". It was always fun to sign Christmas cards, "*Lynda, George & Gracie*" (you have to be a certain age to appreciate that). She'd been returned by her previous owners who found her energy level unsuitable to their lifestyle.

She was a dismal failure at puppy school. She's never been motivated by food or treats (the primary training tool) so when all the other puppies were joyfully dancing and bowing to their masters' commands, my dog preferred to simply sit there looking cute. Intractable. An embarrassment. There was another Yorkie in puppy school who could do everything but her owner's income taxes, so my dog's obvious shortcomings weren't breed specific.

The other day she walked within five feet of a field mouse on the street and didn't even see it, completely disregarding the noble heritage of her Yorkshire Terrier working ancestors who were bred to catch rats in the coal mines in Yorkshire, England. That's what initiated our conversation about her dubious doggie I.Q. She can fetch a ball but refuses to "give it up", preferring to shoot it under the couch or coffee table instead. That requires creaky old me or my creaky old husband to get down on all fours and retrieve the ball with a yardstick. I'm not sure that's what they meant when they said dogs ensure we get our exercise. She can "Sit" but only for three seconds when offered a treat. Then, she ignores the treat and walks away (see what I mean about not being easy to train with treats). Sometimes she carries the treat around for a few days. Or it might turn up a week later in my husband's shoe or in our bed. She loves stuffing treats down between the sofa cushions so we have to go mining for them (is that the coal mine genes at work?). I can put food down for her at any time during the day and it'll sit there for hours before she decides to partake.

Being a pet parent is a responsibility not unlike the more serious kind. Pets require food, in some cases expensive special food with special price tags only available from the vet. After seeing a horrifying documentary about the pet food industry called *"Pet Fooled"*, purchased and shown by a member of our local dog park, I've given up on commercial dog food (with the exception of some dental crunchies, from the vet of course) and cook my own with meat and vegetables. Some of us spring for doggie daycare and regular boarding which can run into hundreds of dollars before the week goes by. And those vet bills can be heart-stopping. But boomer pet parents take it all in stride. They're our fur babies. We love them with stupid devotion that I only wish all animals could receive.

If you've ever been to Florida you'll regularly see seniors pushing their pets around in specially designed pink and purple pet strollers that allow them into restaurants and malls. You can't leave a pet in a hot car and those strollers make sense. I've also seen older, ailing pets enjoying a blissful walk in the Florida sunshine pushed along in their luxurious strollers by their equally ailing senior pet parents.

Non-pet owners love to poke fun at those of us who dress our dogs up. Especially when you have a petite little one, it's so much fun to dress them up in seasonal attire. In nearly forty years of owning little dogs, I have accumulated a pet wardrobe that includes a Roots baseball jacket, duffel coats, a golf shirt, faux Chanel-styled hoodie, Valentine's and Christmas outfits, a Halloween pumpkin, a lady bug and a particularly cute muscle shirt imprinted "Security".

Even larger dogs who spend a lot of time indoors need supplementary winter coats. Raincoats make sense in keeping pets dry. There's nothing more unloveable than a smelly wet dog when you return from a walk. And the boots prevent painful burns on the pads of their feet from winter salt on the sidewalks. They also prevent pets from licking the salt from their feet and incurring digestive problems, which of course could bring on more of those expensive vet bills.

Then, there's the cost of grooming. I'm quite capable of doing a half-assed job of grooming myself but it's never as thorough and lovely as what the professionals do. I hate having to pay $70.00 to get a 3.5 lb. dog groomed but I have to admit those groomers earn their money. It takes a long time to bath and blow-dry, followed by trimming, ear and other orifice cleaning, nail clipping and fine-tuning. I once took a one-day grooming seminar with a friend which gave me an even greater appreciation for the work performed by the pros. So, I give her a bath and mini grooming every couple of weeks. When Sassy's too embarrassed by her appearance to go out in public, then we take her in for a spa day.

Boomers love their pets. Most of us grew up with at least one dog or cat in the family. Back then, however, our un-neutered or un-spayed dog probably slept outside in a doghouse and the cat roamed free and vulnerable to every danger lurking in the neighbourhood. We were emotionally imprinted at a young age by such canine heroes as Lassie, Rin Tin Tin, The Shaggy Dog and who can forget Old Yeller. Now that we're retired and don't have to worry about leaving a pet home alone all day, we've once again become enthusiastic pet parents, but with a difference. Now we're over-the-top  devoted to our little ones and we don't care what other people think about our pet-fancying ways. On the plus side, other boomer parents understand because they probably have a fur baby too. We're all kinda crazy about our pets.

There's a reason pet therapy is so widely encouraged in seniors' residences and nursing homes. The health benefits are scientific and well-documented. Having a pet lowers our blood pressure, gets us outside for a bit of walking exercise and bending exercise fetching balls from under the sofa or coffee table. Pets give us something to think about besides ourselves and the lovin' just never ends. They do make it tricky when we travel and the pain of losing a pet is colossal and overwhelming, but the benefits far outweigh the disadvantages. My friend Terry once gave me a coaster the says "A house is not a home without a dog". So true.

Several years ago, when Murphy, my 15-year-old Maltese passed away, I thought I'd take a break from doggie parenthood, but the house felt like a tomb. No one waiting for me when I got home, jumping around wanting to go for a walk; no one to snuggle with when I needed some lovin'. I lasted a month, then I went and adopted Gracie, making my life complete again. When Gracie was nearing the end we adopted Sassy and there was a year's overlap. I must say having the replacement pet already in place helped ease the pain of losing Gracie, even though the replacement isn't nearly as obedient, quiet or well-behaved as Gracie was.

Which is how we got into the discussion about whether Sassy is a bit dim or just smarter than we give her credit for. To her credit, she is a brilliant at making herself invisible when I turn on the taps in the laundry tub in readiness for her bath. She can disappear into the teeniest little remote corner of the house which sends us on an endless search, again, more exercise for us up and down stairs. When I tell her I need a hug, she dutifully walks over and positions her body so I can pick her up. Like typical helicopter pet parents, we're stupidly overjoyed when she successfully uses her overnight pee pad in the laundry room. We think it's nothing short of genius.

I'd always wanted a Yorkshire Terrier. After three Maltese in succession, I figured I had time for one more dog before I go to the 'home' and I wanted that dog to be a Yorkie. A Morkie (Maltese-Yorkie cross) would have been even better but when we saw the ad in the paper for a Yorkie who had been returned by her previous owners, we did the deed the same day. But, as time goes on and I do the math, I figure Sassy may not have to be my last dog after all. There are so many  senior dogs in shelters who need a home. I'll be in my 80's when Sassy reaches the end of the line but an older dog would absolutely fit the bill if I can still manage it. After all, a house is not a home without a dog, even one whose level of intelligence is a secret. Or are we just overthinking it like all helicopter parents.

It's time up and time out for my cell phone

You'd better sit down before I say this as I don't want the shock to induce a coronary issue in any of my readers. *I rarely use my cell phone.* It's true. Survival in today's world *is* possible without the electronic appendage that's become so vital and addictive in everyday life today. I have a 'lite' phone plan from Zoomer Wireless (affiliated with CARP) that costs only $18.31 per month including taxes. I could text if I knew how. It takes messages  if I knew how to set my voice mail and retrieve messages. It allows me to access WiFi in public places if I knew how to do it. The thing is, the only person who ever calls me on my cell is my honey and by the time I hear it ringing deep in my purse, I've missed the call and I have to call him back which I actually know how to do, *if* I remembered to charge it *and* managed to figure out how to turn it on.

It's with a great deal of impatience and annoyance that I watch the rest of the world unable to function without their phone constantly clamped to their ears. I go nuts when people pull out their phone at meals and I must confess I'm not exactly polite when I ask them to put it away and enjoy the company of the people they're already sitting with. *"But it's my grandson"* they say when taking a call during a girls' lunch. Unless your grandson is on life-support and the power just went off, then *IT CAN WAIT*. I'd like to think I'm worth at least an hour of your time.

Years ago when cell phones finally came within the financial reach of everyday people like you and me, I was a late adopter of the technology. Then, one cold, snowy night in December 1995 as I was heading north of Toronto on Highway 404 beyond the reach of service stations and habitation, it occurred to me that I could have a problem if something went wrong with my car. So, I purchased a cell phone, one of those huge contraptions the size of a brick. Bell Canada offered a special "Emergency" plan for $5.00 a month which suited me fine and gave me piece of mind when driving alone beyond city limits. As time went on, I updated my phones but still rarely used them.

Now I have two phones; one for Canada and a wonderful little flip phone that I bought at Walmart in Florida for $14.98 for when I'm in the United States. I purchase two-year pay-as-you-go cards for only $149.00 from TracFone at Walmart that give me more airtime than I'll ever use in my entire lifetime. Unbeatable. (Canada has a lot to learn from American cell phone plans.) And that includes voice mail, unlimited texting, camera and all the usual features. My phone card is expiring in a few weeks and now I must make a decision to let it go, renew it or investigate something new and improved. I've banked thousands of unused minutes on TracFone and the price is right but trying to figure out and compare different phone plans causes more stress than I can handle. And it involves math, which I'm not very good at. My CARP plan more than meets my needs in Canada.

I'm just an old lady who wants to be able to use her phone in Canada and the United States without all the fancy features. I just want to be able to call my honey if I have a problem when I'm out. And I do not want to pay more than $20.00 per month. My friends all know I'm not cell phone friendly and call me on my land line at home, which I will *not* get rid of because I do not want to tote my phone around on my belt or in my pocket for the rest of my life and when I go to the bathroom. My life is peaceful and my friends will never be interrupted by my phone pinging when we're enjoying a cup of tea and a good gossip. Unfortunately, the reverse is not true, *"Oh – I just have to check that"*. I don't need a phone to wake me up in the morning; an old-fashioned clock does the job to perfection. And apps? Don't need 'em; don't use 'em; don't want 'em.

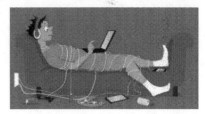

Maybe I should just pull the plug.

My husband loves his cell and talks to his buddies on his cell more often than the land line. The downside is because he's not technologically inclined and requires the constant services of our friend Mike to sort out technical issues. I'm feeling so guilty about the amount of time required of Mike that I think we should put him on the payroll. I abdicated all I.T. support a couple of years ago when computer issues threatened our marriage. Since then, peace reigns on the domestic front.

I've written before about how frustrating it is when our electronic thingies never work the way they should and have penned polite blog postings to Bill Gates, but the problem persists. We need our computers, cell phones, Wifi and other goodies, but I sure wish they were cheap and simple. Our monthly telecom bill costs more than our mortgage payments used to be. Apparently, there are ways to disconnect from the greedy clutches of the cable and satellite companies but I'm not willing to risk the transition. Missing my favourite channels or programs just once might be enough to bring me to the breaking point. It's a fragile line. They're coming to take me away, ha ha, is closer than we think, thanks to all these technical challenges. Or, I could just opt out altogether which is sounding more appealing every day. Using public pay phones, if I could ever find one, would save me a ton of money and a lot of stress. There must be a better way.

What's your binge-worthy substance of choice?

Some of us (including me) binge on ice-cream or cookies. Others may binge-watch television sports or Downton Abbey. The beauty of streaming and *'On Demand'* is that we can now watch what we want, when we want and that's pretty wonderful. For those of us who binge on snack foods, packagers offer individual 100-calorie serving sizes of snacks and treats which theoretically makes it easier to *not* binge, but that's a fool's game. We just eat several packages. Who's kidding who? I must confess to binge-watching a few television shows that I discovered after they've already peaked. But the chief culprit of my bingeing is reading. When I'm into a good book, the goings-on in the rest of the world cease to be.

Unfortunately, my level of productivity in household chores is inversely proportional to the skill level of the author I'm currently reading. In other words, when I'm reading a good book, nothing else gets done. Sometimes it's better if I don't pick up a new book when I've finished another one. That allows me to drift aimlessly around looking for things to do around the house. And, as we all know, one chore often leads to another. We must keep going before we lose momentum. After I've washed the kitchen floor, I'm thinking I'd better haul out the ironing board before I run out of 'steam'.

I've just lost the last few days of my life to another book. I even managed to stay up 'way past midnight reading in bed, *just the next couple of pages . . . just a couple more pages.* It's a slippery slope. It's unbelievably easy to waste away a complete day when the weather is above 70 degrees (F) and I can park myself in the backyard in my outdoor La-Z-Girl. I read, nap, read, nap. Then, before you know it, it's dinner time and I have to come into the house and pretend I've had productive day.

But the evidence is clear. The grocery shopping didn't get done. Dinner is something microwaveable that includes as many healthy food groups as I can fake in one package. The kitchen floor is still sticky. The dog is begging to go for a walk. The only sign I've done anything all day is my eyes are tired from being focused on the pages of a book for hours at a stretch, and definitely not from cleaning the bathroom or vacuuming the floors. And, I'm pretty sure all that time I spent on FaceBook doesn't qualify as productive.

Now that I've finished the latest Kate Atkinson novel, I'm facing a dilemma. Should I crack open another book or should I attack some of my household chores? There's a basket of ironing, which I actually don't find to be a chore when I set up in front of the TV and watch my PVR'd shows. The dog needs to be walked; that's good for both of us and the weather's fine so that's not a chore either. The kitchen floor needs to be washed. I have some sewing alterations to do but that involves going down to my sewing machine in the basement which is not likely to happen in the next couple of months, what with the dog needing walking and all. And I'm terrified to face all those shelves of crap we've accumulated in the basement that should be sorted and disposed of. Scary prospect. Best to avoid the basement. If I can restrain myself from starting another book, I might actually get something else done.

I do multi-task sometimes, although at my advanced age I try not to exert myself too much. In the evenings I read books and magazines while I binge-watch my TV programs. Apart from my regular PVR'd shows like *Baroness Von Sketch, The Social, CityLine* and *The Marilyn Denis Show*, I'm currently working my *"On Demand"* way through *The Loudest Voice*, the story of Roger Ailes of FOX TV fame. I've already exhausted *Fleabag, Broad City* and every British drama, comedy or crime show that managed to reach our Canadian airwaves. My husband pretty much has a monopoly on all the sports channels which he could watch 24/7. How he can tell one football game from another is a mystery to me.

I had to put a stop to binge-eating ice-cream. I would stand at the kitchen counter eating it directly out of the container until I felt sick. I'm paying for that slip with an extra ten pounds that will not be easy to shed. Reading is much more virtuous although not entirely non-fattening as it involves sitting on my ever-expanding derrière for lengthy periods of time. But reading is free (I download most of my books from the library), mind-expanding, doesn't disturb the neighbours, is pollution-free, and sooooo satisfying. During all those years in the working world, all I wanted to do when I retired is sit in a comfortable chair and catch up on all the reading I never had time for. And that's pretty much what I'm doing . . . living the dream. Have book . . . will binge. What is your substance of choice?

Chapter 3

Aging

10 reasons why I love being an old lady

As we celebrate Canada Day on July first, I found myself thinking about how we won the lottery being born in this country. Canada is now 154 years old and I'm approaching 74. We're growing old gracefully and joyfully. We have so much to be thankful for and, the freedom to grow old gracefully and peacefully.

When I woke up the other morning, I rolled over and squinted one sleepy eye open to check the time: 8:12 a.m. As I was lying there, I found myself contemplating what I would be doing if I weren't retired. I'd be sitting at my desk in a suburban office building, vetting and culling a gazillion emails, sipping a cold mug of tea between urgent phone calls, each one presenting a new problem, and wondering how on earth I was going to get everything done to submit that  proposal to its destination by 3:00 p.m. Then, reality settled in and I snuggled down for another few minutes of blissful dozing. I'm an old lady and I'm retired.

There's a lot of negative thinking around aging these days. Ageism is considered a form of discrimination with all sorts of unpleasant connotations. While it's tempting to focus on our aches and pains and being on the descending bell curve of life expectancy, on the whole, we're the luckiest people in the world. I found myself contemplating this when I read a piece in the paper about how the baby boomer demographic bulge is going to strain our social services. It's an old and worn out refrain that I have no time for. We've contributed throughout our entire lives and we're still contributing.

I'm fully aware of how great life is and how lucky I am to be part of it. My day starts with reading the morning paper (the old-fashioned, hard-copy kind; I'm trying to support print journalism) while I eat my breakfast and consume two large mugs of strong tea. So far so good. In normal times when I'm not self-isolating I might have a late-morning hair appointment. I'd grab some sushi at the food court in the mall afterward while I people-watch and pass bitchy judgment on the good and bad fashion choices of fellow shoppers. Sweet. I'd pick up some groceries on the way home, walk the dog, have supper with my honey, then read and watch my PVR'd television programs. How is that not a perfect day? The only way I'm able to live this blissful life is because I'm retired and to be retired you have to be

a) old, or

b) young and extremely rich.

I'm definitely *a)* and will never be *b).*

I've never understood the eternal quest for youth. It's the focus of all advertising and the ultimate goal of many people who have lost it. I wouldn't want to go back even one single day in my life as it just gets better every year. We have so much to be thankful for. The most important thing is that we're still here to enjoy life. Being an old lady comes with so many extra benefits I think it's important to remind ourselves how lucky we are. Despite being currently confined  to quarters, here just a few of the things I love about being an old lady:

- I don't have to go to work every day. I'm the boss of me and there's no one to tell me what to do. No deadlines, sales quotas, reports to be submitted or working late nights and weekends doing something I'd rather not be doing.

- Being an old lady means I'm pretty much off the radar for sexual assault or discrimination. I'm invisible to predators, except perhaps purse-snatchers and unscrupulous boy scouts trying to help me across the road.

- Lovely discounts at movie theatres, certain restaurants, and retail outlets—when they reopen.

- Public transit is cheaper. While Toronto Transit Commission charges slightly less for seniors, the Mississauga Transit Authority (where I live) charges seniors only one dollar, one mere looney to ride their buses. How's that not a good thing?

- It's wonderful to no longer have to deal with the missteps, mistakes, angst, stresses, and challenges of being young. No more mortgages, worries about car payments, promotions, relationships, or life choices.

- I've accepted that my waistline is long-gone and will never return. I recently sent thirty-four lovely leather belts to charity and sighed with relief that I no longer have to waste my time on situps that will never change a thing.

- Being the boss of and the last word on the use of my time is one of the biggest advantages of being an old lady. I can be productive on any given day if I wish, or I can sit and read a book all day if my heart desires. We now have the time to pursue hobbies, community work, or do absolutely nothing.

- Interestingly, I'm also relieved that I won't live long enough to see the results of the damage currently being done to our planet. I'm doing the best I can in terms of recycling and being environmentally conscientious but that's all I can do. It's pretty much out of my hands.

The best time in life is now

- No apologies. I've earned the right to my opinions, my feelings, and my principles. If you don't agree, it's not my problem.

- My circle of friends is tried and true. We've withstood the test of time, divorces, job loss, health issues, and life's normal stresses. We've been together for a long time and will be together for whatever time we have left. That may be the best gift of all.

Aging also comes with some unexpected advantages which came as a nice surprise. When I'm having telecom problems (which happens far too often) and I'm forced to contact someone in a call centre who's barely old enough to vote, I've mastered putting on a frail old lady voice that is guaranteed to get the sympathy and patience I need to get my problem solved. *"Hello? I'm a senior so you'll have to be patient with me, and please speak up."* Works every time. Admittedly, it perpetuates the ageism negative stereotype. Never mind that I spent more than forty years in a senior management position in the corporate world. I call it being resourceful.

There are just so many advantages to aging and other than unpredictable health, we're a pretty lucky bunch a' boomers. Every morning I wake up and say a silent thank you to whatever forces are guiding me through life. We live in a caring democracy here in Canada, a country with universal health care, among caring people and we've put most of life's crap behind us. If I don't watch the news on television any more than necessary, being an old lady is the best thing that ever happened to me. I consider it a blessing and a gift.

Can baby boomers literally outgrow jeans?

One size does not fit all, so, why isn't there a size that does fit me?

As if I weren't feeling insecure enough already after a recent closet purge to get rid of things that didn't "fit and flatter", I foolishly went shopping for new jeans this week. The jeans and general closet purge preceded my recent

big bra purge (by that I mean quantity not bra size, obviously). Embarrassed and frustrated with a closet full of jeans that no longer fit, tops that made me look pregnant and sweaters that only flattered my lumps and bumps, I trucked bags of cast-offs to charity bins and the consignment shop. That left me with only two pairs of jeans that were marginally comfortable and not too embarrassing to wear out in public. A trip to the mall was needed to remedy the situation. (Doesn't that solve pretty much any existential crisis?)

Buying new jeans can be every bit as painful as trying on bathing suits, which I gave up on a long time ago. The process can involve visiting different stores and, lo, even different malls in different area codes in search of the perfect fit for the less-than-perfect body. I've always had the best luck with NYDJ (Not Your Daughter's Jeans) as I'm only 5'3" and their petite and ankle-length sizes usually fit me perfectly. Not this time. I was looking for a mid-blue colour (not too pale and not too dark as the only two remaining pair I have are light blue and dark wash), no holes in the knees or thighs (boomers understand why), a nice ankle-grazing length for summer and also with summer in mind, softly distressed and not too heavy. I also prefer the high waisted style that does a better job of corralling muffin-top than those ridiculous designs with a five-inch rise. NYDJ didn't have just what I was looking for so I had to cast further afield which is a terrifying prospect. Who else makes jeans for boomers who aren't 6 ft. tall and weigh 94 lbs? Was I asking for the impossible?

I started in Hudson's Bay Company at Sherway Gardens in Toronto. I didn't want to invest in expensive designer jeans because I was casually considering a frayed hem which will probably be out of style next season or more likely, within the next ten minutes. The Bay has a wide range of brands and sizes, many of which are conveniently on sale at this time of year to clear out current inventory in preparation for next week's fickle trend. No luck. I'm always on the

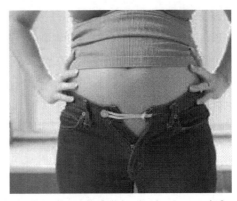

Help! What do full-bodied women do?

cusp of being current, but not quite there. I also learned that Top Shop is unaware that there's a large portion of the population that is not size 00. Not one single person I know has a 25" waist with a 32" inseam and I know a lot of people.

So I went to my favourite store, Nordstrom which tends to carry more high-end merchandise. Shopping for jeans calls for desperate measures. The only ones that came close were Frame but at more than $300.00 the fit was only so-so. If they don't feel marvelous when I try them on, they're doomed to languish in my closet unworn. If I've learned nothing else about clothes' shopping over the last sixty years, it's that if I don't absolutely love an item immediately, don't buy it. I have a mantra I repeat when I'm in the fitting room: *"If in doubt, "DON'T!"*. That's saved my bacon many times, preventing me from committing serious fashion "don'ts". Meanwhile, I'm trying not to recall those cute little 27-inch-waist jeans with the snappy red zippers at the ankles, that I once purchased for my once lean young body at Bayview Village many years ago.

Leaving Nordstrom, I hit every store in Sherway Gardens that carries jeans. That included The Gap, the Levi's store, ZARA, Mendocino, Andrews, Dynamite, Eileen Fisher, Eagle Outfitters . . . and on and on and on. My feet felt like clubs and my self-esteem was totally crushed. Most of the children working in those stores had no understanding or sympathy for my plight, like it's *my* fault I'm old, fat and frumpy. Their day will come. Just wait 'til menopause hits *them* and I hope they remember how cavalier they once were about me being unable to zip up their stupid, skinny jeans. I ventured into stores I didn't even know existed until I went hunting for a new pair of inexpensive, fashionable jeans. I'm now very familiar with the millennial world of disposable clothing. Not that their clothing lines were able to offer anything remotely appropriate.

Even the Levi's store which has wall-to-wall, floor-to-ceiling shelves stacked with jeans of every style, colour, cut and uncut, still couldn't find a pair that fit my boomer body. What they did have, however, was a seamstress sitting at the centre of the store in front of a very scary looking commercial sewing machine that could embellish my jeans or jean jacket with any type of logo, sparkle, fringe or embroidery I could dream of. The girl operating the machine wore black lipstick with a lip ring piercing her lower lip, purple, pink and black spiked hair and a tight tee shirt that made it easy to calculate her bra size, if she had been wearing one. Her false eyelashes were thick and heavy enough to scrape the mud off your golf shoes. And, the store's piped-in music was selected specifically to scare off weird interlopers like me, which it was successful in doing.

My excursions to find the perfect replacement jeans also made me an expert on retail dressing rooms. They are all consistently poorly lit, and frequently lacking in hooks for my purse and the clothes I'm wearing. Rails are great for what I bring into the change room already on hangers, but unless there are hooks, I'm forced to drop my clothes on the floor. And, the floor of every dressing room is crawling with dust bunnies and questionable fungi, particularly close to the baseboards, which are, well, close because most dressing rooms are . . . close. And, not many change rooms have a chair or stool to perch on when we're trying to put our shoes back on, which would be a much-appreciated amenity for boomer bottoms. And if you're shy about all that cellulite and overflow being visible to passers-by when you're stripped down to your frillies, then take the jeans home to try them on because those ring-topped curtains never quite completely close to give you privacy during your darkest hours.

After three separate excursions to the mall and trawling dozens of stores, I finally circled back to Hudson's Bay because that's where my car was parked. I made a last-minute detour into the lingerie department in a vain search once again for suitable nightgowns. No luck there either, although I purchased another sports bra, the only kind that seems to offer any degree of

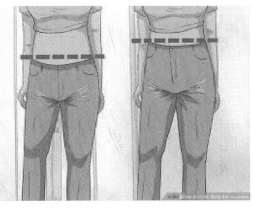

High waist fit helps with muffin top

comfort. As I was approaching the elevator, I thought I'd pick up that white linen Ralph Lauren blouse I saw on sale earlier in the day (as if I need another white blouse!!).

To get to the change room, I had to pass through the BCBG Maxazaria section that was all but abandoned (they've closed a lot of their stand-alone retail locations). Everything except the striped blazer I liked was on sale, including their jeans. I'd never considered that brand as a suitable candidate for this body as most of their fashions are for wisp-thin gals with a social life far beyond my level of experience.

The nice lady with the Polish accent who was working the change room check-in desk complimented me on my choice. Lifting up her blouse to show me how well BCBG's jeans fit her trim, young body, I should have felt reassured but of course, felt even fatter. She ushered me into an adequately sized change room with a hanging rail, stool, and hooks (!!!), where I tried on a pair of soft jeans in what is usually my size. Too big! Thank you vanity sizing.

By then, nice Polish lady had disappeared (as we all know, Hudson's Bay Company only employs one sales person per store in the suburbs) so I had to grab my purse and waddle back out into the store in my ill-fitting jeans to find another size. After two more tries and managing to lock myself out of my own change room, I finally found a pair that were soft, sufficiently contained all my floppy bits without pinching and actually were almost perfect. All I have to do is cut six inches off the hem.

Even though they were on sale, they still cost more than I would have liked to pay, but it seems body dysmorphics like me have to settle for and be happy with whatever is *close* in terms of fit. I'll be damned if I'm going to buy jeans with pregnancy panels. I'm not *that* big, yet! What on earth do truly full-bodied women do?

So, just when I was beginning to despair of ever finding a simple pair of everyday jeans that fit me and were available in my native province, Lynda now has a new pair of jeans. After I chop half a foot off the bottoms, I'm going to try a do-it-yourself version of a frayed hem. I never like the way altered hems on jeans look (regardless of what the alterationist says is a fool-proof European stitch-job). I've marked the line; I'm going to stay-stitch the new line on my 52-year-old cast iron Singer sewing machine, just the way the real raw-hem jeans are done, chop off the excess fabric, carefully hand pick and fray away the bottom hem to create that perfect look so that I can wear them proudly before they go out of fashion on Tuesday.

Remember the olden days when shopping used to be fun?

When you see me struttin' out in my new jeans, be sure to compliment me. I'm physically and emotionally exhausted from the experience and could use some reassurance that my efforts weren't in vain. All those young millennials cruising the streets and malls in their perfectly fitted, just-so-perfectly distressed jeans on their perfectly firm little bottoms have my future to look forward to. Rest up all you young Ava's, Sophia's, Harper's or whatever trendy new name you have these days. Someday, you too will lose your waistline, be unable to walk in stilettos and suffer hot flashes for twenty years longer than you expected. I should probably feel ashamed about taking pleasure in the sadistic knowledge that they too will someday mourn the loss of what they so take for granted today.

There was a time when I also thought I'd be able to wear mini-skirts and high platform heels until death do us part, but alas, time catches up with us all. Maybe this is nature's way of telling me I should no longer be wearing jeans. Naw! Boomers practically invented jeans and made them part of everyday fashion lexicon for eternity. I refuse to be beaten by a generation of consumers who is completely unaware that  we boomers are the generation to thank for this solid wardrobe staple.

We've grown from being offered only one choice of stiff, dark blue denim Levi's in the sixties that we had to wear sitting in the bathtub full of hot water and salt to start to break them in and bend to our individual body shapes, to zillions of different styles, washes, manufacturers and colours, none of which fit us or are appropriate. We must rise up and demand our due, preferably with a high rise. I love jeans. I deserve to wear jeans. I will not be wedged out by built-in obsolescence and a nuclear wedgie. Welcome to the Age of Nefarious mes chères.

Have Baby Boomers gone to ground?

There was a time when I simply couldn't understand why my parents' generation didn't like to drive after dark, or why they preferred to stay home and sleep in their own beds. Look at all they were missing—nights on the town, travel and weekends away with friends. Then, I totally got the driving after dark thing a few years ago when I found my eyesight was just not as sharp as it used to be when I went out at night. The solution was to plan our nights out carefully, so we didn't have to drive too far, if at all. That was the first step on a slippery slope.

I'm now developing a greater appreciation for sleeping in my own bed. Much as we love traveling, nothing is sweeter than crawling into our own bed when we get home. We just returned from a few days visiting Washington, D.C. for some sightseeing and our room at the Hyatt Regency couldn't have been better. They had spent the last four years renovating the hotel and everything was perfection. The elevators in the lobby atrium were glass so we could experience our ascent and descent; the furniture and decor was all fresh and new; the bathroom was large and well-appointed and the floor was slightly heated which felt wonderful on our sore feet after a day of walking miles. The sheets were smooth and delicious to slide into at the end of the day. The pillows felt like down and there were four of them. Even the television was huge, just like at home which pleased my honey enormously. Despite these comforts, it was so good to get home.

Air travel comes with its own special set of horrors which make overseas travel particularly gruesome. If one of the unions has not declared a last-minute work-to-rule or full-on strike, then weather delays keep us stewing in the airport holding area for hours on end. If we do manage to get on our flight at the scheduled time and we can't afford to fly business class with the elite, then we're jammed into teeny tiny seats with our knees touching our chins while munching dry ham and cheese "snacks". Who among us hasn't been trapped on a full plane upon arrival awaiting jetway clearance or waiting for the lightning to stop before we can disembark.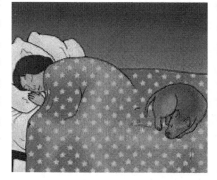

Americans are known and (rightly) mocked for insisting on American food like burgers and fries when traveling in Europe, but I always take a zip-lock baggie of my own Canadian brand of Red Rose tea when we travel, so who am I to judge. We like things that are familiar, and this trait only becomes more entrenched as we get older. That's not to say we don't like some adventure and travel, but we're starting to feel the impact of being away from our home comforts. This insight has made me much more understanding of my parents' preference for staying home and not visiting me in their later years.

Even staying overnight with close friends can be fraught with challenges. There's a hilarious sketch on *Baroness von Sketch* on CBC that pokes fun at the numerous rules imposed by cottage owners on their weekend guests. *"Don't flush. If it's yellow, let it mellow. No shampoo allowed; it causes algae. Keep the door shut to keep the blackflies out."* And the list goes on. It just makes you want to be in your own home, in your own bed, with your own bathroom on familiar ground. We all try to make our visiting guests feel at home when they come to stay and go out of our way to provide hotel-like amenities, but we know from experience that there's no place like home. And the older we get, the sweeter it is.

Are our senior citizens really OK?

Unfortunately, we tend to judge people without knowing their background story. In fact, my entire blog, *BOOMERBROADcast* is a form of judgement. I did it again this week, at the grocery store. I'll give you the details and let you be the judge.

It's harvest season in Ontario, the season for juicy, fresh beefsteak tomatoes, peaches and no end of wonderful local produce. Shoppers are checking out with bushels of Roma tomatoes, cucumbers, beans, and seasonal fruit for preserving. It truly is the most wonderful time of the year for fresh food.

As I was standing in the produce section husking corn into a giant bin in the middle of the floor, a small, very elderly, very frail gentleman approached. He was probably in his nineties and his face was sweet and kind looking. His grocery tote was a hand truck he'd brought with him with a single reusable vinyl grocery bag propped open on the base.

He was wearing worn, comfortable shoes and socks, a short-sleeved plaid shirt and beige shorts. His shorts were held up with striped suspenders and where one of the suspender's clips was broken, he'd used a bit of twine to tie the suspenders to the belt loop of his shorts. This simple piece of twine touched my heart as it reminded me of how resourceful and practical his generation is—those who grew up in the Depression. It's so different from the obscene consumerism of subsequent generations.

For a few minutes I was transfixed as I watched this stooped gentleman pick three ears of corn and place them in his vinyl shopping bag. An Asian woman standing nearby helped him dig through the bin to find some nice ones.

Suddenly, I found myself contemplating his entire back story in my imagination. Where did he live? Did he live alone? Did he drive himself here? Did he walk, pushing his hand truck? How does he manage in winter? Particularly in a large city it's so easy for these vulnerable people to be forgotten.

Because he was buying groceries, he obviously does not live in an assisted living facility. Perhaps he lives in a nearby apartment or maybe he's still living in the same little bungalow he bought in the 1950s and is unwilling to leave. Does he have children? Do they visit him and help him out? Is his wife still alive or did she pass a few years ago? Is he lonely? Does he need help? So many questions swirled around in my head for the few minutes I observed him.

I found myself thinking of my own father who is 94 and lives in the most wonderful assisted living residence I could imagine. He's happy, healthy, well taken care of, and is mentally as sharp as ever. His residence overlooks the Trent Canal in front and Ranney Falls on the Trent River behind the building. It's an idyllic environment and he's surrounded by kind, caring people and fellow residents he's known for decades.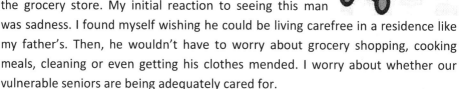

My dilemma concerns my judgement of the elderly man in the grocery store. My initial reaction to seeing this man was sadness. I found myself wishing he could be living carefree in a residence like my father's. Then, he wouldn't have to worry about grocery shopping, cooking meals, cleaning or even getting his clothes mended. I worry about whether our vulnerable seniors are being adequately cared for.

But perhaps I'm wrong to cast judgement. Maybe he's living the life he chooses, independent and busy with the simple rituals and routines of daily life. Perhaps my concern is misplaced and he's happily living his best life. I wonder if and how my husband I will be coping when we're in our nineties, which isn't that far off anymore, and if we make it that far. Once again I found myself casting judgement on someone I knew nothing about, however, sympathetic my intentions. I'm still thinking about him, days later. I can't get him out of my mind, wondering how he's doing. Is he OK? Are they all OK?

Today's lesson for Boomers. . . 1 + 1 = 1

Math has never been my strong suit. I'm a consistent 20% tipper in restaurants because it's easier to calculate 20% than 15% in my head (and because I was a waitress a long time ago, so I appreciate the value of tips to servers). But, as baby boomers age, we realize that it's easier to get through life with two people than it is with one. I was single for ten years before I married for the first time and spent seventeen years between husband number one and number two, so I've had a total of twenty-seven years of experience being single and on my own. And I've come to the conclusion that as we round out our third quarter, as The Beatles so eloquently put it, *"we get by with a little help from our friends"*. And that includes husbands, partners, neighbours, family members and even pets. They all help us get through the day. They filled the void during all those times I was on my own and continue to do so. The much-maligned phrase uttered by Tom Cruise in *Jerry McGuire,* "You complete me," is suddenly not so corny.

I've written before about the downside of certain aspects of aging. Being forgetful or absent-minded is natural. It's rather like defragging our hard drive. Our brain must dump old data to make room for new input. Regrettable but understandable. But my honey and I have recently experienced too many memory faults and error messages to write them off as simple updating of our ROM.

Just last night we were sitting at dinner and couldn't figure out what year we moved into our house. Was it five years ago or eight? The mental exertion soon proved too onerous, so we moved on to dessert.

One day when I was checking out of a big box store, I got caught with twelve items in my cart and only eleven items on my bill. I'd picked up two bags of pecans and accidentally only rang up one. I naively thought I was intelligent enough to handle the self checkout but obviously I over-estimated my abilities. To make it worse, just as I was standing there sorting out the issue with the checker at the door, while the lineup of impatient shoppers grew even longer behind me, I hear *"Hi*

Lynda". My friend Jeannette happened to be passing by just in time to witness my embarrassing shakedown by store security. Two lessons emerged from this experience:

- I am incapable of managing self-checkout without supervision.
- Henceforth, I will always check out with a cashier because,
    - they not only do a better job, but,
    - I am saving a job.
    - Self-checkouts and other self-serve functions deprive someone of a real job and that's not good for anyone.

Last week I mentioned to my husband that the windshield washer tank in my car was empty. When I kept pushing the lever, nothing happened. He was inappropriately smug and a tad too condescending when he informed me later that I'd been pushing the wrong lever.

And the list goes on. I gathered some girlfriends recently to watch a Christmas movie and swill wine, but my television froze. Nothing worked. A couple of days later when the cable guy came out, it was a loose connection on the back of the receiver, *which I had already checked, several times*. He was very understanding, under the circumstances (dealing with an old lady).

But the pièce de résistance came earlier this week when my laptop computer died. It's only eighteen months old and when I bought it I also purchased every warranty and service package available to humankind for just such occasions. I checked the power outlet to make sure it was working, even moving it to an outlet in the kitchen to double-check. I changed the battery in the mouse and double-checked that the mouse was 'On'. I  couldn't even reboot, which usually solves most problems, because it wouldn't turn on or off. I pushed the laptop's On/Off button multiple times with varying degrees of pressure and lengths of time in futile attempts to achieve ignition. No luck. Like Monty Python's parrot; it was *dead. Not resting. Not asleep. Definitely dead!*

So, I called Microsoft and the nice man informed me I might have a faulty display driver and suggested I take it to the Microsoft store where they would address my problems and perhaps replace my laptop. I was thankful for my brilliant foresight in purchasing those expensive warranty and service contracts. The next morning, I made a forty-five-minute drive to the store. When I explained my situation to the little boy working there, he laid a nice protective pad on the counter, placed my dead parrot on the pad . . . and . . . *TURNED IT ON*. It worked!!! Heaven only knows why I couldn't do the same thing pushing that little button; maybe my laptop just wanted to go for a nice long car ride and be fingered by someone with a gentler touch. Even my technically challenged husband now takes great delight in offering to turn my computer on.

As I said earlier, I'm not a math whiz; in fact, I'm a complete ditz but when it comes to numbers. Fortunately, my husband is amazing, so he helps me. But he's not good with the English language, written or spoken so I'm always available to bail him out with spelling and pronunciation issues. It's the perfect yin and yang. We support each other's shortcomings.

Watching my parents as they grew older, I began to appreciate the value in having someone alongside to help shoulder the load. Now we're in the same boat. What one can't do, the other usually can. We muddle through. My friend Terry showed me how to use the timer on my oven; Gail's our social convener; her husband Mike's our go-to I.T. guy. I'm the source of new Britcoms on television. When we're feeling discouraged or in need of a little moral support, who do we call? Our friends.

The challenges of aging aren't what John Lennon and Paul McCartney had in mind when they penned *"I'll get by with a little help from my friends"* but even then they understood the depth of meaning in the words to *When I'm Sixty-Four*. So far, he still needs me, still feeds me (twice a week when it's his turn to cook), and still sends me Valentines. Mine for ever more. The reciprocal shortcomings of two people added together equals a whole in any equation. That's not just science; it's life. Maybe Jerry McGuire wasn't so stupid after all.

10 signs that baby boomers have finally hit that perfect sweet spot

Creaky joints, back pain and stiff shoulders are a way of life for many boomers as we now enter the third period of an unpredictable and tough game. Bumps, bruises and the odd metaphorical concussion over the years have taken a toll and we now rely on our innate skills of playing the game like pros to get us through each day. It takes a little more effort to hoist ourselves up from our LaZgirl chair and leaping up stairs two at a time is a distant memory. When we reflect on our younger working days with stressful jobs, families and little to no time to ourselves, we wonder how we had the stamina. The answer is simple. We were young.

That's not to say this stage of life isn't without benefits. Many years ago when I asked my Aunt Lois to describe the best and happiest time in her life she unhesitatingly answered "When your Uncle Ron and I first retired". That's the stage most baby boomers are at right now and speaking from personal experience, I couldn't agree with her more. There's no place I'd rather be than *now*. There are so many benefits:

- We're finally our own "boss of me". No more daily grind, going to the workplace in overpacked subways and buses or sitting in traffic jams on overcrowded highways.
- Seniors discounts all over the place, at certain retailers on special days of the week, movie theatres, public transit. Even the fee-hungry, greedy banks give us free chequing, just for being, you know, *old*.
- OAC (old age pension) and CPP (Canada Pension Plan), lovely little automatic deposits into our bank accounts every month, after a lifetime of payout. Keeps us in wine.
- Time management is now purely a matter of personal choice. We're no longer subject to the tyranny of report deadlines, sales quotas or production schedules. We can now choose if and when we want to golf, play tennis or go to yoga classes. This includes the ability to say "No" without the accompanying guilt.

- We can toss the Spanx and stilettos because we're no longer beholden to the latest fashion fads. We finally know what works best for each of us and can opt for comfort.
- We're financially comfortable. As my friend Margaret likes to say, *"I have enough."* We realize that relationships are the true foundations of happiness. With close friends, a roof over our heads, a warm bed and assurance of three squares a day, we're in heaven.
- No longer sleep deprived, we can stay in bed as long as we like on cold mornings and grab a few zzzz's in the afternoon if we feel like it.
- Even though we occasionally forget where we left our keys or why we entered a room, we're considerably and blessedly smarter and wiser now. No more worries about making bad choices in romance, fashion and lifestyle. We've finally sorted things out and disposed of most of the crap in our lives.
- Thanks to the movement started all those years ago by Tommy Douglas, we have universal health care. And because we're Canadian, we don't have to sell the car or mortgage the condo to pay for a hip replacement or refill our cholesterol and gout meds.
- Our #metoo days are pretty much behind us and that's a good thing. No more competing for jobs, recognition and attention from the opposite sex. At our age, most boomers are now well beyond the scope of predators. *We* know we're fantastic and that's good enough for us.
- Every day is a gift and we're now the best we'll ever be. This is the best perk of all. As Mary Pipher said in a recent New York Times article, *"Many of us have learned that **happiness is a skill and a choice.** We don't need to look at our horoscopes to know how our day will go. We know how to create a good day."* Let's just do it.

Our music has stood the test of time. And we can still dance to it. I'm constantly amazed at how much I'm enjoying this stage of life. We've earned an ice advantage, there's no pressure to score. Post-menopausal women over the years have often described their lives after menopause as being the best but I think they predated it a bit. It's actually when we retire that we hit the real sweet spot. Keep your stick on the ice ladies. As baby boomer women we are now playing the best game of our lives. And it's oh soooo sweet.

93

When you're retired, every day is Saturday

Productivity is a relative term.

Type A personality types who must be constantly busy and productive must also be constantly exhausted. Or maybe I just wish that so I don't feel guilty about not being as virtuous as they are. Much as I wish I could be like them, that's not the way I was engineered. My mother had to register me in morning kindergarten so I could nap in the afternoons and unfortunately, the habit stuck. I still love to nap in the afternoons. It was inconvenient when I was working (!!) but now that I'm retired I am free to doze, not entirely without guilt but it helps if no one else is home to make me feel like I should be doing something productive. I guess I'd describe myself as Type D-minus. Having nothing on my agenda and lots of time to devote to it is my idea of a perfect day.

Life wasn't always a week of Saturdays which is why I appreciate retirement so much. During all those years of getting up in the dark, driving to work in the dark, driving home in the dark, preparing a meal, doing chores and never getting enough sleep I only dreamed of the schedule I enjoy today. Sometimes at work, I'd be so totally exhausted I'd feel like my head was going to thump down on my desk. It was everything I could do to keep my eyelids from slamming shut. Sleep deprivation is a common affliction among working people and we're made to feel guilty if we aren't giving our jobs one hundred and ten percent. I think millennials have turned their backs on that attitude, which is another topic for another day. It was different for boomers and even more so for our parents, The Greatest Generation.

Retirement has afforded me the time to be my own boss, a well-earned luxury and a privilege. Spending a day in my own home doing whatever I want is a complete and utter joy. Most of the time I don't even put the radio on as the news or a talk show that focuses on political or social conflicts only spoils my tranquility. Daytime television is verboten unless I have a pile of ironing to do. Then, I set up the ironing board in the living room and iron while I watch one of my favourite PVR'd shows. I read voraciously; I compose my rants for ***BoomerBroadcast.net***; I sit in the yard; go for a walk; putter about the house; generally, I live my best life.

That's not to say I'm anti-social or inactive. Not at all. Lunches with girlfriends are great fun. We now have the time and energy required for entertaining at home from time to time. Attending seminars on subjects of personal interest, visiting friends and indulging in hobbies are all part of retirement life. Even having the luxury of being able to go grocery shopping on a quiet Tuesday morning is an utter joy. There are always new sights in the city to see, new movies to check out or author readings to attend. Many boomers are dedicated volunteers, contributing generous, unpaid hours to various community services.

But there's nothing quite as delicious as a day *chez moi*. Too many of those days would, of course, be sad but that's not what we're talking about. I've spent considerable time and a little bit of money getting my home to be a place of complete comfort and joy. My boomer gal pals have also created colourful, creatively decorated homes that they too enjoy and enjoy sharing with friends. We're nesting and loving it.

Now that I'm in my seventies (*Yeoww!* That number still blows my mind), I've become philosophical about my time left. It could be 20 years, which will fly by far too quickly, or it could be 20 minutes. As we've watched some of our friends cope with illness and others pass away, we have a greater appreciation for the time we're enjoying now. Every day is truly a gift, wherever and however I choose to spend it. And for that, I am profoundly grateful.

You CAN teach an old boomer new math. Or maybe not.

The problem began when I couldn't answer the simple skill-testing question to enter a contest. Penguin Random House Canada ran an online contest to win a free book and here's the skill-testing question required to enter: *(6 x 4) / (4 – 2)*.

I stared, I pondered, scratched my gray roots, and for the life of me I couldn't figure out what the */* symbol in the middle of the equation meant. Was it a typo? Did they mean to insert a multiplication sign, a minus sign, or a division sign? I contemplated contacting Penguin to advise them about the typo but got lazy and forgot about it.

When another contest came up, I was puzzled to discover they hadn't corrected their previous error and I began to wonder if I was the only person who had spotted it. Had no one else entered the contest or was I the only stupid one?

Math has always been anathema to me. Ask me to write an essay in English class in school and I would light up like a Christmas tree. Such joy. But sit me down in front of an algebra problem, a physics equation or a column of numbers and my eyes would glaze over, I would feel faint and my stomach would knot up. Math phobia is not a myth; it's a real thing.

This contest obviously needed much bigger brains than mine to find a solution, so I emailed my professional sources. My husband's daughter and one of his sons are both C.A.s, and a friend's daughter Beth is a teacher so I ran the equation by all of them. A big math problem calls for big brains. My sources very gently informed me that yes, indeed, there is a new math symbol for division, and it's represented by that **/** symbol between the two parts of the equation. The ÷ sign is going the way of the flip phone (which I proudly still own and use). Obviously, pretty much everyone in the entire world has a better grasp of math than I do. C.A. Daughter went on to further explain the new symbol:

Think of it as a fraction symbol . . . which basically is division. So, while not the division symbol it is equivalent to being division . . . so yes, they are teaching a different symbol and using the keyboard. We also use * as multiplication...

$$6 \times 4 = 24$$

$$4-2 = 2$$

$$\underline{24}$$

$$2$$

as a fraction is equivalent to 12/1...or 12 as a whole number, . . . so, your answer is 12.

I kinda don't really understand that last bit and I'm not sure what a 'whole' number is, but I get the gist. And now you tell me that the * symbol could also mean multiplication? This is getting way too complicated. You see, as I mentioned above, my eyes have already glazed over and my brain has shut down at the sight of so many numbers swimming before me. But I'm pretty sure that somewhere in there she gave me the answer to the skill-testing question to enter the book contest. Thank you, Susan.

Every day the world is getting harder to decipher. First, they changed the words to *Oh Canada*, our national anthem. The original version that I sang my little heart out to thousands of times in school were changed to something I stumble over every time I'm called on to belt it out at public events. And now that they frequently sing half of it in French, I'm reduced to mumbling. I'm sure that's why I've never been called on to sing the national anthem as a soloist at Blue Jays games.

Does the alphabet still start with "A" and end with "Z"? Canadians have started pronouncing the last letter of the alphabet as *zee,* not the proper English Canadian *zed.* And now universal math symbols are changing? Next thing you know they'll dispense with teaching  cursive writing in school. *Whaaaat?* Tell me it's not true. I need *some* old-school lessons to still have merit. Otherwise, I'll start feeling like the obsolete old crone that I am.

I'd better run. I have to fill in that contest entry form before they change the rules . . . or I forget the rules altogether . . . or more importantly, before I forget the answer Susan gave me. Either way, my mind is slip-sliding away. I really want to win the book from Penguin Random House Canada but when I do will I still be able to read it? I'll keep you posted—in cursive, baby boomers' secret code, just to mess with the minds of those millennials who keep changing my math symbols. It's becoming a bridge too far for this boomer brain.

Gone with the waist. And frankly my dear, I don't give a damn!

Today I officially acknowledged that I will never again in this lifetime have a waistline. Menopause is irreversible and I have decided to part with thirty-four beautiful leather belts worth more dollars than I care to contemplate, that will never fit this old boomer body again. I rounded them all up for consignment (the better ones) and the charity bin. I did keep half a dozen on the off chance I'll get a parasite or the plague and manage to get skinny again. Over the years I've collected every width and style of belt ever invented. I've kept them all in case they ever came back in fashion, or, miraculously my waistline returns. It's time I faced facts. And you know the saying . . . *"If you've worn it once, it won't work again."* The clothing manufacturers always manage to tweak reincarnations of various fashions so that our old pieces never quite work. And that includes belts.

We hang on to old things for various reasons. This morning during my belt purge I came across a sturdy 4-inch long kilt pin that my mother wore in her wool skirts when she was a teenager. She later used that same huge safety pin to secure me and then my brother under the blankets in our crib when we were babies, to keep us covered and warm. Imagine getting that one past Child Services and safety vigilantes today. That old pin is definitely a keeper though and now that I've found it I can see it being put to use on one of my many shawls. It could still help keep me tucked in and warm.

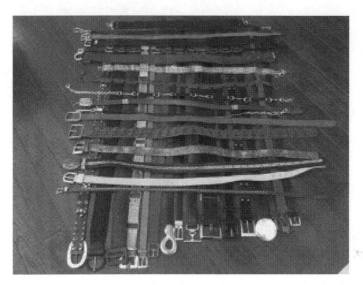

I hope my old belts find a forever happy home (well, at least until menopause hits the new owners)

My dad mentioned the other day that he still has the Waterman fountain pen he bought himself when he started high school in Cobourg, Ontario in 1939. When he shared this discovery with one of the ladies at the seniors' residence where he now lives, the next day she produced an old bottle of ink, still in its original box to go with his pen. He's understandably reluctant to try filling the pen as the internal reservoir has probably deteriorated beyond use and he'd end up with a big mess . . . which we used to use blotters for. Remember those? Please tell me you don't still have some.

We recently celebrated an Oktoberfest dinner with our friends Mike and Gail. Mike's mother was born in Germany and they inherited a wonderful collection of original beer steins from the old country which we put to use sipping (??) wine at our dinner. It's hard to part with our heritage, especially when it can be upcycled to today's lifestyle. Another friend with a German mother didn't have the same attachment to her collection of Hummel figurines and I completely understand. I also have my mother's original roller skates made in 1930 with the leather strap, cast iron wheels, and the original key on a dirty string worn around my neck.

I have regretted getting rid of certain items over the years. It's difficult to know what to keep and what to let go of. Will I regret getting rid of those belts? I hope not and perhaps some pre-menopausal young woman will enjoy them as much as I

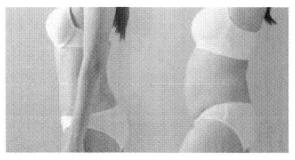

Before menopause . . . and, after menopause

did once upon a time. B'bye belts. Hello spandex.

The other day I watched a young woman trying on jeans in a department store. She had the cutest little bum and before I could stop myself I said aloud, *"Ahhh. I remember when I used to look like that!"* She laughed and replied that her parents and in-laws were pressuring her to have a baby so she knew her cute bum days were limited. That's nothing, though, compared with what menopause does to a woman's body. Ugh! When I was young, I never honestly thought my body would lose its waistline as I aged. We all thought those tight tummies and firm upper arms would last forever. Like those lovely leather belts, I miss my waistline but as they say, focus on your assets. We're alive; we're healthy and we're surrounded by loving friends and family. That's plenty for me. With or without a waistline. Belted or unbelted.

Despite what they say . . . you really are OK, Boomer!

There's a lot of buzz these days about a new expression aimed at trivializing the opinions of baby boomers. Generation Z (born between 1995 and 2010) is apparently getting sick and tired of being derided and put down by our generation. They think we're old and irrelevant so they've coined the phrase "OK, Boomer" which infers a dismissive *"Whatever!"*

Many boomers and others have taken great offense to this expression as being insulting, ageist and discriminating. I'm not sure I agree. In my opinion, I think Gen Zs are just being who they are—a generation of young, inexperienced, somewhat naïve individuals who are doing exactly what we boomers did at the same age.

Remember our days of *"Never trust anyone over 30"*? It embarrasses me now when I think about how self-righteous and confident in my ill-informed opinions I was when I was in my twenties. Our lack of real-life experience resulted in some bad decisions and what I now realize were horrifying opinions I had back then. Having just burst out of our teens and entering the working world, we were full of confidence in our young, independent adult status. That is precisely why the military loves to recruit young people; they think they're invincible.

We've all encountered university students who presume they alone have a definitive grasp on global, business and domestic affairs. They think that now that they are educated, full of book-learnin' and ready to solve the world's problems, they can climb the corporate ladder as quickly as possible and correct the mistakes of earlier generations. Thank goodness for that! Otherwise, we'd never have any fresh ideas or insights. And we old boomers are tired of it all. We've paid our dues. We're happy to hand over the reins and watch others make their own mistakes in an effort to get it right.

We made a difference, in our day

Can baby boomers honestly claim they left this old world in a better state than when we entered it? On the one hand, we have all kinds of new tech gadgets that collectively simplify and complicate our lives. Our marches and protests back in the sixties and seventies did make a difference in civil rights, women's rights, the Vietnam War, abortion and various other social issues, but we didn't finish the job. Living life simply got in the way. And now those fragile gains are being compromised, particularly for our sisters in the United States.

When we got married, had children, built careers, and acquired mortgages, we shelved our idealistic plans for world peace and a safer, cleaner planet. We were too busy worrying about careers, car payments and saving for our Gen X, Y and Z children and grandchildren to go to college and university. We got sidetracked and now things are in a terrible shamble.

The standard of living now is better for us than it was for our parents, The Greatest Generation, but that's not a world-wide pattern. Without going into all the sad details, we have a lot of 'splainin' to do. Crime is down. Cars are safer and we're better educated but now we have mass shootings, political instability and environmental problems unheard of when boomers were young.

Gen X'ers, Ys' and Z's will make a lot of mistakes too. That's how we learn and improve. Who among us hasn't dusted off the old "back when I was young" song to remind the younger generations how much easier they have it than we did? Our parents did it to us and Gen Z'ers will, in turn, do it to their offspring.

I find the OK Boomer lament to be a bit amusing. Inside its message is the subtle suggestion that we screwed up and it's someone else's turn to set things right. We once thought we knew everything and now realize wisdom does, in fact,

We shouldn't give up. There's still a lot of work to be done.

come with age and experience, both of which we now have in abundance. As we aged, so did our intelligence and emotional quotients.

But who's going to listen? Did we listen to our parents? Few of us did. Each generation must learn 'on the job', and the X, Y and Z'ers will too. In fact, I hope they learn faster than we did as there seems so much more to be done to set this old world straight again. It's pretty much beyond our control now. To some extent, our votes count, but only when the good candidates win. That doesn't always happen. So, we have to continue involving ourselves in the right causes.

As we grow older each new generation thinks the previous generations are irrelevant. In many ways we are. That becomes painfully evident every time we try to fix our computer problems, reprogram our thermostat, or try to get a new smartphone working (speaking from personal experience). But, making mistakes and being wrong is how we learn and grow. I personally have not been confronted with *OK, Boomer* yet but I'm sure it's being silently articulated every time I regale the younger generations with comparisons between their life experiences and how it was for us Boomers all those years ago.

The bottom line is, we may be right but younger generations bring a lot of intelligence, hope and fearlessness to the table and for that, we should be thankful. And, while there are some of us who may consider *OK, Boomer* to be a slur, or ageist and discriminating, the younger generations must be forgiven. They will learn, just like we did, and still are. And that's OK with me.

1 – may be the loneliest number, but 70 is definitely one of the scariest

One of my girlfriends recently celebrated her 70th birthday and it got me thinking about my own 70th milestone. As one of the older members of my baby boomer group of friends, I was among the first to hit the big 7-0 . . . and it affected me profoundly. Hitting 30, 50 or any other big number really had *no* effect on me as every year of my life that passed just seemed to be getting better. There really wasn't a downside.

But the day I crossed the threshold to 70, the world shifted on its axis. Somehow, I realized I could no longer overlook or deny the passage of time. I'm now officially everything those ageist clichés imply. I'm *elderly, senior, old, retired, a pensioner.* I am a new-to-me demographic with all kinds of connotations that tend to be more negative than positive, although not necessarily true.

There is a lot of negative thinking around aging. Ageism is a form of discrimination with all sorts of unpleasant implications. While it's tempting to focus on our aches and pains and being on the descending bell curve of life expectancy, on the whole, we're the luckiest people in the world. I found myself contemplating this when I read a piece in the paper this morning about how the baby boomer demographic bulge is going to strain our social services. It's an old and worn out refrain that I have no time for.

I've now reached a point in life when *function supersedes form*. Comfortable clothing and shoes have now replaced the latest fashion. Instead of worrying about whether all the trappings of my physical life are coordinated and aesthetically pleasing, I've opted for comfort. My La-Z-Girl chair is probably the world's best invention since the Guttenberg press. The fact that it's ugly is not important. My decorating gurus would not approve, but it elevates my tired feet, supports my wonky back and provides the perfect landing spot for my lazy brain when I fall asleep reading.

There's a reason birthdays are celebrated. They're a gift, a reward for another year of being part of this vast universe of life. But turning seventy is a sobering reminder that the gift of life now has a time limit. This recently hit home with me personally when a few days before Christmas I fractured my hip. That's something that only happens to old ladies, right?

About ten years ago, I had both hips replaced. That experience alone made me so glad I reside in Canada where we have universal health care, and I was taken care of without cost. So, when I heard a loud *snap, crackle, pop* in my left hip as I went to turn around in the shower, I was afraid I'd broken something that would have grave consequences. Fortunately, the fracture did not require surgery (like a broken rib, they leave it to heal on its own) and with the aid of a walker and time, I'll gradually heal. My artificial hips are still intact and structurally sound.

That incident was a reminder that as boomers, we now must "act our age" and make sure we conduct our lives in a way that is conducive to longevity. We have already installed grab bars in the shower and followed up with the doctor about bone density issues. Many of us no longer drive at night and we only partake in sports with minimal risk of personal injury.

Whoever thought we'd come to this? While we do not have to orchestrate our lives around "being old", we do have to become more cognizant of our limitations. We now come home from parties at around the same time we used to depart for a night out. We're opting for pickleball and guided coach tours instead of downhill racing and backpacking around Europe, arch supports instead of stilettos, and a night of cards instead of drinking ourselves blind with the gang at the pub.

Simple pleasures now provide as much enjoyment as expensive vacations and designer shoes used to. We enjoy our everyday routines and rituals, our friends and family, activities we choose that have not been foisted upon us against our will. As we move into our final decades, we celebrate everything that we've experienced in the decades prior and look forward to in our years to come.

Boomers now get to determine what kind of day we're going to have when we wake up in the morning. We have the wisdom, the experience, and the intelligence to chart happiness in the context of our own lives. If anything, turning seventy reminds us of how truly blessed we are. After all, we're in great company. Don't you agree? "One" may be the loneliest number but we're not alone. We have an entire demographic to see us through. Rock on mes très chères.

High maintenance has taken on a new meaning for baby boomers

Baby boomers have finally reached that age and stage in life we've all dreaded — when a major topic of conversation has now become our various ailments. It's sad but unavoidable. We're wearing out, getting rusty, past our best-before date. Our maintenance costs have risen dramatically, and we require more frequent tune-ups to keep the old girl running efficiently.

In the olden days, a high maintenance woman was considered to have expensive tastes in fashion, beauty products, and personal care. High maintenance for baby boomers today, however, looks a little different. Not only do we still require the mandatory regular mani/pedi treatments, salon hair colouring that costs more than we care to divulge, and regular rotation of our wardrobe pieces, we have added new categories to our personal maintenance programs.

Remember when we always coloured our own hair from a box? *Nice n' Easy* or Clairol's *Frost n' Tip* were affordable, easy solutions to getting the California look we wanted. Then, gray started creeping in and with menopause our hair became fragile. Drugstore boxes of hair colour exacerbated the damage, so professional intervention was required. Add more to the maintenance budget.

There was a time when we did not need expensive moisturizers, neck creams, retinol, exotic serums, or eye creams formulated with rare oils leeched from the underside of fairy wings or distilled from captured baby tears. After a quick scrub with Dove or Dial soap, some Bonne Belle 1006 and a swipe of Cover Girl foundation, we were good to go. Maybe a bit of

I'll have the works please.

Nivea Creme or Noxzema at night for some of us. Now, we employ every combination of ingredients on the periodic table of elements in our attempts to eliminate wrinkles, lighten age spots and bring back the 'dewey' skin we once took for granted.

Today's maintenance costs also include yoga or zumba classes, dental implants and veneers, waxing, exfoliating, peeling, massages, and for some boomers, injections, fillers and more extreme medical intervention. We're signing up for CPR classes. Our skincare and body treatment products cost the equivalent of a European vacation. Is it worth it? Absolutely. Unless we take care of ourselves, we won't like ourselves and that's a much bigger issue to deal with.

When boomers gather together these days, have you noticed how the topic of conversation soon switches to how we're feeling? Tragically, there's not a single one of us who doesn't have a friend or family member affected by cancer. We're experiencing high blood pressure, high cholesterol, gout, A-fib, arthritis, fragile bones, hearing problems, cataracts . . . and the list goes on. It's impossible to ignore what's happening to our old bodies. These issues have replaced more superficial problems like weight gain and hair loss.

Even though we swore we wouldn't be one of those people who talked about nothing but their aches and pains, it's becoming unavoidable at our age. We really do care about how our friends are feeling and reminiscent of the days when we couldn't understand why old people didn't like to drive after dark, *now we get it.* We're living it. We share helpful hints and health tips we've Googled and support each other during health setbacks.

Golfing, tennis, powerwalking, pickleball and other hobbies and sports activities keep us moving but we injure more easily and have to pace ourselves. A shoulder or knee injury could put us out of commission or, worse, require surgery to correct.

My age really hit home the other day when I went to the hairdresser. Before I sat down in the chair, I first had to remove my glasses, then my hearing aids, and park my cane (I fractured my hip just before Christmas). I was totally at the mercy of the stylist . . . I could not hear, could not see and could not stand up.

Boomers are rather like old cars. We're past-our-prime classics. We still have a solid chassis although with a few nicks and scrapes in need of touchup or buffing. We may have a lot of miles on our old bodies but we still have some life left to go before we crap out. Oil changes are more frequent; the exhaust system is probably not up to current environmental standards, and our transmissions take a little longer than they once did to shift into gear, if they ever do. We require more frequent inspections and trips to the shop for maintenance issues but we're still willing to throw a bit of cash at the old buggy to keep 'er hummin'.

So, the next time you're tempted to ask me how I'm feeling, you might want to reconsider. My reply could take awhile. I hate that it has come to this, but as John Lennon paraphrased, *"Life is what happens when you're busy making other plans,"* and time has caught up with us.

There is a bright side, though. We're the healthiest generation of seniors *ever*. We're the most affluent, the best educated, and the most active. There's every indication that we will enjoy the longest, best senior and retirement years of any generation so far in history and that's worth celebrating. So, on that thought, let's just say I'm feelin' goooood! How about you?

Chapter 4

Remember when?

Do you remember those Friday nights on the town as boomers?

The other night I rewatched Ron Howard's iconic movie *American Graffiti* which perfectly captured what life was like for teenagers on a Friday night in the early sixties. Every time I see that movie I can connect each one of the characters with someone I knew and grew up with in real life. We all knew a Steve and Laurie (played by Ron Howard and Cindy Williams) the perfect couple, the sexually precocious Debbie (Candy Clarke), and a nerdy Terry (Charles Martin Smith) trying to score.

Bob and John (Harrison Ford and Paul Le Mat) were the ultra-cool guys everyone wanted to ride with but knew we were forbidden by our parents. One of the coolest guys in our town, when I was growing up, was a big guy who drove a hot rod, and oddly, his nickname was 'Bunny'. I was definitely not one of the cool, cute ones like Cindy Williams's Laurie, so I occupied a spot as a bystander rather than a participant in *Paradise By The Dashboard Light*.

In the early sixties, I worked as a carhop on the weekends at a tiny drive-in restaurant behind the bowling alley in our small town. That put me front and centre to witness all the comings and goings of the Chevy Belairs, Oldsmobiles and Pontiacs cruising around on Friday and Saturday nights. There were also a lot of old Ford and Dodge farm pickup trucks and a few VW bugs—the originals. Working as a carhop didn't generate a lot of tips from fellow high school students but it was an invaluable experience as life goes.

The first year (when I was 14) I made 65 cents an hour and a year later got a raise to 75 cents an hour. We'd work until 1:00 a.m. on Friday and Saturday nights when the restaurant closed. Then, we'd spend the next hour washing dishes by hand, cleaning the single unisex washroom, scraping the grill, washing the floors, and generally cleaning up for the next day's business. And we didn't get paid for that final hour of cleanup. I kept that job until I left home at seventeen.

When I was growing up in the fifties and sixties, small-town life was considerably different from today. A couple of times a year our family might make a big trip to Peterborough, thirty-five miles away to buy a new spring coat or Sunday shoes. But most of our shopping was done locally at the stores in town. Even though our town had a population of only 3,200 at the time, in the fifties and sixties we had a vibrant downtown. There were several jewelry stores, multiple family grocery

Vintage carhop (me) at a vintage car show, reliving the good old days.

stores, a couple of small department stores, several hardware stores, ladies wear shops, pool rooms, restaurants, two professional photographers, and shoe stores. We even had an Eaton's and Simpson's catalogue order pickup office. The shops closed on Wednesday afternoons to give the shopkeepers some time off to compensate for being open Friday nights and Saturdays.

Friday nights were always special though, particularly in the warm summer months. Being a rural community, the farming families came into town to do their grocery shopping and pick up a few things in the shops. Just like in *American Graffiti* cars would cruise up and down the main street, go around the block, and back around again, often parking in front of one of the shops to watch the "action" and enjoy an ice-cream cone. With the car windows rolled down, people passing by would stop and get caught up on the latest news or share a few words.

We had packed churches in every denomination as churches often provided much of the social life for boomer kids in a small town. The church basements were ground zero for weddings, Brownies, Girl Guides, Scouts and Cubs, strawberry socials, Rotary Club lunches and other community events. Everything was prepared by volunteer women from the community.

Back then, Friday nights on the town were our Facebook, Twitter, email, and dating sites. We knew everyone and we often put extra effort into what we wore to look extra smart for the Friday night stroll. *"Put yer nylons on, dear; we're going to town."* Local baseball games at the high school field attracted crowds of local people and eventually, a lot of them ended up at the drive-in where I worked.

Except for Canadian Tire, Stedman's and the IGA, none of the stores or restaurants in town during the fifties and sixties were chains or franchises. I never had my first taste of pizza or Chinese food until I left home at seventeen and moved to Toronto. Local restaurants and shops were all small family businesses, just like the little farms that surrounded our community. We all had a vested interest in supporting these businesses as they were the people who provided our food, our medicines, supported our various churches, and their kids attended our schools. The father of one of my school friends even went so far as to insist his family only support businesses owned by veterans. They only bought their meat from a butcher who was a veteran, got haircuts from a veteran and gassed up their car each week at a veteran's gas station. The Second World War had only been over for a few years then and loyalties were strong.

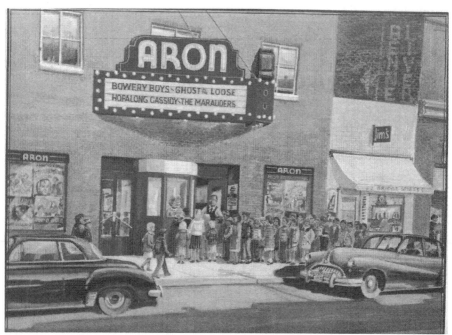

I spent many Saturday afternoons in the Aron theatre as a kid and a few Friday and Saturday nights when I became a teenager. It was next door to Jimmy Quinn's barbershop where I also had my hair cut in the days before salons became the norm for kids. Jimmy once cut my hair so short I looked like a boy and wore a camp hat all summer until it grew out.

Our town had (and still has) an independent movie theatre, now run by volunteers, mostly boomers who treasure the memories. In the fifties and sixties we caught the latest westerns, Bowery Boys and Annette Funicello movies on Saturday afternoons. We'd throw popcorn at the screen during the exciting parts and all the boys would boo if there was a kissing scene. My 25-cent allowance covered admission (10 cents), a bag of popcorn (5 cents), and a trip up the street for an Archie and Veronica comic book (10 cents) after the movie. Our noisy group of neighbourhood kids would emerge from the theatre around 4:00 p.m., blinking as our eyes adjusted to the bright sunlight.

It's not a myth that our only instructions were to be home by the time the streetlights came on. The main switch for the streetlights back then was located at the fire hall and managed by my grandfather who worked as the night watchman in the fifties. He often fell asleep on the job and my grandmother would have to phone him and remind him to turn the town's streetlights on. Back then, boomers pretty much ran free from an early age. Our mothers took us to our first day of kindergarten; after that, we walked with the rest of the kids on the street and eventually by ourselves. We attended school with most of those same kids from kindergarten until we finished high school.

Fortunately, one of the greatest assets to our town has survived all these years— the bakeshop. It's now a third-generation business and still serves the best cream-filled donuts, jam cookies and other goodies from the original owner's recipes created decades ago. My mother worked behind the counter there on Friday nights and Saturdays in the sixties. In fact, Dooher's Bakery was voted "Sweetest Bakery in Canada" for the last three years. Well done!

My father once sent me downtown in the mid-fifties to the hardware store with some loose change and an empty brown whiskey bottle with a cork in the top. He gave me instructions to get it filled up with coal oil (they sold it in bulk in those days) for cleaning something in his workshop. By the time I got to the store I'd forgotten what I was supposed to get (I was only 7 or 8) so I just handed Mr. Vice the money and empty whiskey bottle and told him my dad wanted it filled up. Being a small town, Mr. Vice knew who I was and called my Dad for more specific instructions. Imagine that scenario today. The police, child services, and who knows how many other agencies would be alerted and my poor dad would probably still be serving time. As they say, it takes a village, or in our case, a small town.

The downtown I grew up in doesn't exist anymore. Storefronts are empty. Parking is a snap as there are hardly any cars anymore on the main street. It's a sad sign of progress. Every family now has a car and many have multiple cars so it's easy to make the 40-minute drive to a larger urban centre for a visit to Costco or Walmart. Tim Horton's has replaced little family hamburger joints and churches are closing. Socializing is done impersonally, online and if someone is deemed not cute

113

enough, you just swipe right. Steve and Laurie now have trendy names like Mason or Madison.

Years ago I saw the play *"The Trip to Bountiful"* at the Fairview Theatre in Toronto. It's about an elderly woman who lives unhappily with her son and daughter-in-law. She knows she's reaching the end of her life and all she wants to do is return to the hometown where she grew up, where all her best memories reside. When she finally gets there, nothing is the same as she remembered but she sees only its beauty.

I have no illusions of returning to my own "Bountiful" but there is always a gravitational pull to where we were born or grew up, isn't there? Baby boomers had the wonderful experience of growing up in times of great change, strong family values, and amazing historical events, both bad and good. Much as we enjoyed our liberation when we left home and started lives on our own, we always feel nostalgic about those amazing years growing up in the fifties and sixties. And the music was and still is, in our opinion, the absolute *best*.

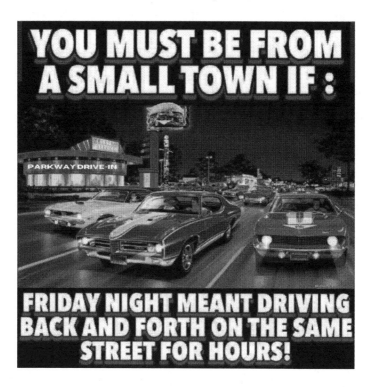

I sometimes find myself wondering how I'd fare as a young person if I'd been born a few decades later in today's world. The entire world is a vastly different place now, which is a natural and logical progression. I only hope today's children and young people remember their childhood to be as well-rounded and colourful as we remember ours. They have their share of problems like COVID-19, Trump, school shootings, and terrorism to deal with. But we had the Cold War, Vietnam, Diefenbaker, and polio. Every generation has its pandemics, its wars, its stupid politicians, and its very own joys. There's no place I'd rather be than here and no time better than now, retired and happy to be alive. Thanks for the memories.

Does anyone know where Lake Ontario went?

A recent visit to Chicago dramatically reminded me of what is missing in Toronto— *our Lake Ontario shoreline*. When the great Chicago fire leveled their downtown in 1871 the city displayed great foresight and generosity when they decreed it illegal for private builders to monopolize the Lake Michigan shoreline. Consequently, Chicago now enjoys an incredible twenty-seven-mile long park that ensures the lake is forever accessible to its citizens.

While I don't advocate setting fire to downtown Toronto to get rid of unsightly buildings and planning blunders, I do think our city planners need to rethink what's happening to our waterfront. We're literally losing sight of it. Ugly high-rise condos are obliterating our view of Lake Ontario and the problem is only going to get worse. It's difficult to stop a moving train but short of land-filling a new shoreline even further into the lake, what are our options?

I used to love glimpsing the sparkling lake from Lakeshore Boulevard as I passed along the south side of the Canadian National Exhibition grounds. Even the grotesqueness of Ontario Place obliterating our view of Lake Ontario was alleviated by the whimsical faux farm silos which always made me smile.

Toronto's shoreline has no green, no vistas and few public spaces.
In the sixties, boomers used to catch the ferry to the Toronto Islands at the foot of Yonge Street. Back then, the waterfront in the harbour was still visible as we lined up at sunny outside turnstiles and paid our 25-cent fare to hop aboard the Sam McBride. The Toronto skyline was defined by the Royal York Hotel and the old 32-storey old Bank of Commerce Building on King Street West. I could see Lake Ontario from my room on the south side of Willard Hall on Gerrard Street.

Driving east or west on the Gardiner Expressway through downtown Toronto these days is like negotiating a slow train through a concrete jungle. We go nowhere, see nothing but faceless buildings and otherwise have no clue we're a stone's throw from one of Ontario's beautiful Great Lakes. The view may be spectacular from offshore, but from landside, sadly, there's nothing to see. I know progress is inevitable and we can't undo the damage that has already been done to our waterfront views. It's a shame our city managers have allowed this to happen. I just wish they'd had as much foresight and courage as Chicago did in 1871.

Where's Lake Ontario? It is hidden from view by ugly condos.

November 11, 1918. A celebration of two anniversaries.

On the same day that the Armistice ending The Great War, WWI was signed on November 11, 1918, my English grandmother married my grandfather, a young Canadian soldier in Folkestone, England. *"It all started on The White Cliffs of Dover,"* he used to say at noisy family Christmases. That date forever has an extra special meaning for us on Remembrance Day.

Grandma loved to tell us about how all the church bells were ringing, and people were dancing in the streets when they walked out of the photographer's studio after their wedding. She thought everyone was celebrating her wedding but in fact, the Armistice had been signed while they were in the photographer's. She was engaged twice previous, once to an Englishman and once to another Canadian, before marrying my Canadian grandfather. Both of her previous fiancées and a brother had been killed in France. In 1919 she left England behind and boarded a ship bound for Halifax with hundreds of British war brides sailing to join their new husbands in Canada.

My great-grandmother was a widow with sons who had enlisted for service and she was left at home with three daughters, the eldest being my grandmother who was in her early twenties at the time. Tens of thousands of young men enlisting to train and fight in The Great War (WWI) resulted in a shortage of barracks. One day an army officer knocked on the door of their terraced house and asked how many soldiers my grandmother's family could accommodate. Her mother's reply, "Probably two or three". My grandmother described how the Major asked to go through the house and then informed her mother that they would be taking **seventeen soldiers** into their home. They received a stipend for housing them and providing meals.

What would your reaction be if a military officer showed up at your front door and told you he was going to billet a dozen soldiers in your home for an indeterminate length of time, and you had to provide meals and laundry service for them? And you had no choice in the matter. Families willingly accommodated them One hundred years later, billeting

soldiers in private homes seems unimaginable. But it was a widespread practice during the First World War and every family did their bit. She described how some of the young men were illiterate miners from the north of England who had never been exposed to such things as how to use table cutlery and basic hygiene such as bathing and brushing your teeth. She and her sisters enjoyed the social life which included going to dances with all the soldiers.

Later on in the war, as the various allotments of soldiers were rotated out to cross the channel, their house was requisitioned to provide accommodation for Belgian refugees, women and children. My grandmother had many amazing stories about these experiences. Now that she's gone and I'm older, I can think of so many more questions I wish I had asked her.

This touching painting depicting bloodshed hangs in a Canadian war museum we visited in 2014 in Dieppe, France.

We recognize November 11th with special reverence. Our own family includes many veterans who served in both wars, including one uncle who was captured during the Japanese siege of Hong Kong in 1941 and served four years as a Canadian prisoner-of-war in Japan. As a baby boomer, we all grew up with friends and schoolmates whose fathers, uncles, cousins and grandfathers served overseas. Remembrance Day services were and remain very personal.

Watching the news on TV today about the horror of the ongoing wars in this tired old world and the living conditions of other innocent citizens in regions of conflict, we need to always be thankful for being born in Canada. Hopefully an army officer will never knock on our doors and tell us we have seventeen soldiers moving in. We welcome new Canadians. We live in a peaceful country and for that we can be eternally grateful. Remembering one hundred years ago today. Happy Anniversary Grandma and Grandpa . . . and thank you for everything.

Step right up and behold the wonders of the season

When I walk into a department store during the Christmas season I feel like a mouse standing in front of a trap loaded with lovely fresh Gruyère, wagging my cute little tail with a sense of anticipation and a teensy bit of caution. My nose and my credit card are twitching, my ears are perked up taking in the cuddly Christmas music and my belly is calling out for gratification. I want all the cheese and I want it now.

The cosmetics department is strategically positioned at the entrance to every store because that is how their marketing gurus bait us as soon as we walk in the door. It's particularly hazardous during the holiday season because everything is festooned with sparkles, sequins, tulle and ribbon unlike any other time of year. And what girl can resist bling? Visions of sugar plums dance before our innocent, unadorned eyes.

Speaking of eyes, have you tried the latest bedazzled glittery palette of eye shadows? Electric turquoise, sparkly bronze, shimmery green, deep sea iridescent blue; they're all on display and irresistibly packaged with a bonus highlighting apricot blusher in a clever little compact resembling an evening clutch. With a little leopard motif. And if I spend just $65.00, I can score a travel case loaded with *more than $400.00* worth  of products for a mere $85.00 extra. By my calculations, that's a savings of $315.00? How can I resist? The fact that the travel case and most of its contents are of no use to me is irrelevant. I'm smitten. Hooked. Sucked in. But not quite.

Then, there's perfume. The bottles enchant me; the fragrances rarely do, which is why the fragrance companies hire top designers to create new, glamorous decanters that gullible people like me can't resist. And at this time of year, they'll toss in a cute purse-sized atomizer and a lovely bottle of matching body lotion exquisitely packaged in a gilded gift box with pink and gold grosgrain ribbon. My heart is screaming *"Load up"* while my brain says, *"Whoahh girl! You already* *have #$%^too many bottles of perfume and you're running out of spaces to put them."*

Due to my advanced age, I've been down this road before. Over the years I've learned to resist the cosmetics sirens calling my name. I even have photographic evidence to remind me of my previous falls from sanity. The only solution I've found to avoid these seasonal promotions is to avoid department stores altogether until mid-January. I should be able to accomplish this because in our world of over-abundance and rampant consumerism, my family and friends have reached a "No Gifts" agreement which suits us just fine. I may not be sporting the latest fluorescent yellow eye shadow or be wearing a debt-inducing glamorous new sparkly outfit this season, but that's OK. I just wish January would hurry up and get here before I make a grab for the cheese, which will just leave me feeling constipated and hating myself. That would not be in the spirit of the season at all.

How does he love me? Let me count the ways

With Valentine's day on the horizon, it serves me well to remember that I am a very lucky girl. Every day my honey demonstrates his love in so many ways I can hardly count them. Today, for example, he took me out to lunch, treating me at a restaurant where they offered a two-for-one special, until the 25th of the month. He didn't even ask me to pay my share and we had enough leftovers to bring home for dinner. That's *four* meals for the price of one. He's so thoughtful like that. I'm always overjoyed when I don't have to cook dinner and, as a bonus, there were only serving dishes to wash up after, no pots and pans.

Sometimes he takes me to the movies too. And because he knows I don't like to share my goodies; he lets me buy my own popcorn and Diet Coke. To show my appreciation, I often order the larger size popcorn, so I'll have some left over to bring home for him to munch on while he's watching football. Which brings me to another example of his devotion. He watches television with wireless headphones, so I'm not subjected to endless excruciating hours of listening to football, baseball, golf, hockey, car auctions and old westerns. What a guy!

Even our little Yorkie prefers lavishing all her love and attention on my husband rather than me. So, in order to prevent me from feeling neglected or left out, he allows me to be the full-time dog-walker to ensure I get my share of quality time with her. In our nearly twenty years together he has never once walked the dog and if that's not a clear indication of his love and consideration for me than I don't know what is. He gets his own quality time though when she marches back and forth on his back in bed at 6:00 a.m. while he's still sleeping and sticks her tongue in his ear to remind him it's time to go outside. You see, life has a way of rewarding the love.

When I do the laundry he allows me to keep whatever loose change I find in the washing machine after I've washed his golf clothes. It's mine to blow however I wish. Same thing for the coins I find under his giant La-Z-Boy when I move it to vacuum. He's incredibly generous that way so I usually take my haul and head straight for DQ and treat myself to a blizzard or 'buzzard' as he calls them. If that's not love, I don't know what is.

When he stops at Costco on the way home after a morning of golfing to pick up his bushel of Chicago popcorn or his favourite fruit danishes, he usually springs for a hot dog and Diet Coke which he brings home to me for lunch. Sometimes it's Five Guys' fries and Diet Coke for a bit of variety. He always makes sure to surprise me with these little gourmet treats.

During a discussion once about our impending and eventual respective deaths, he announced that if I weren't on the scene, he'd be living on a boat on Marco Island in Florida. You have to agree; that's quite a sacrifice he's made on my behalf (knowing I want nothing to do with living on a boat). The guy's just overflowing with love for me. We're the perfect yin and yang.

As we celebrate Valentine's Day we are reminded that sharing your life with another person includes daily demonstrations of mutual love and affection. It always warms my heart to wake up in the morning and find the tea already made and waiting for me in the pot on the kitchen counter, with three bags because I like it strong. He makes sure my car is always gassed and washed.

More importantly, receiving the love of another person means appreciating what they bring to our lives in less obvious ways. He's kind when I'm grumpy; supportive when I'm feeling beaten; he listens to my complaints, celebrates my joy; helps me make it through my days and nights. When I count the many ways he demonstrates his love for me, I feel like I hit the Valentine jackpot and for that I'm thankful every day of the year. What does your Valentine do to show his or her love? Are you as lucky as I am?

Love takes many forms and has many faces

The approach of Valentine's Day has caused me to reflect on the value of love in our lives. I'm no expert on love but during the ten years before I married husband #1 and the seventeen years I spent as a single person between husband #1 and husband #2, I've had a lot of time (27 years) to reflect on the pros and cons of being single and on my own versus being married. There are plenty of arguments on both sides and we're wise to focus on the positives regardless of our current status.

Being single means doing your own thing without compromising. You can eat whatever you like, whenever you like, or not at all if you prefer. You don't have to fight for the blankets in the middle of the night and you can spend your money however you wish without having to justify the cost of those shiny new red shoes. You can pick up and go wherever you like on vacation and it can include all the shopping you can cram in without someone complaining. On the other hand, it's wonderful to share a vacation with your soulmate when you're going to visit a special place you both enjoy. Sipping delicious wines and marveling at spectacular sunsets is always more satisfying when shared with someone special.

As we get older, boomers appreciate the difference between being *in love* with someone and *loving* someone. *In love* is that surreal, heady state we enter in a new relationship when we're savoring the euphoric high, while we're not quite sure where the relationship is going. We can still have that feeling after many years of being with one person. A girlfriend recently commented on how her heart still skips a beat when her honey comes into the room and they've been together for more than thirty years (second

There are many ways to say I love you.

123

marriage for her too). That's wonderful—being *in love* with the person you love.

Loneliness is one of the major downsides to being single. Much as I appreciated the benefits of being on my own, there were many times during my single years when I was reminded of how lovely it would be to have someone looking out for you, sharing the ups and downs of everyday life. Many boomers are now single again having lost partners in recent years. This is when loneliness can be most acute.

Once, I dropped a coworker off at her home after we'd been away for a couple of days at a meeting. Her partner had a bag of her favourite fruit (papaya) waiting so it would be there when she returned home. That simple, caring gesture said so much.

Another time when I was working late at the office one of the guys I worked with called his wife as we were leaving a meeting. She was sick and he wanted to see how she was doing. *"I'll be home soon honey. Go to bed and I'll make you some tea and something to eat as soon as I get home."* That caring tugged at my heartstrings. Incidents like that reminded me of lovely it is to have someone who cares when you're sick, when you're tired, or when you're stressed. I was single at the time, living alone and often worried that I could be dead for days before anyone would notice. The buzzards would be circling my bed before my presence would be missed.

Regardless of whether we're sharing our lives with someone special or living successfully as a single person, it all comes down to perspective. There are pros and cons to both situations but the fact that we're still here to enjoy each new day is a gift in itself. So many of our friends and family members have departed too early and sometimes we must remind ourselves that we are so fortunate to have each other, whoever that *'each other'* might be. As The Beatles said so well, *"We get by with a little help from our friends"* and as we age, we have a greater appreciation for what that means.

Friends become family and are an essential part of the love we give and the love we receive. In fact, friendships are often more enduring than our relationships with a husband or wife. Ideally, we get both in one package but more often we get our love from a variety of sources. Ultimately, it really is love and kindness that make the world go round. When we celebrate Valentine's Day this year, let's celebrate *everyone* who brings joy and love into our lives—not just partners and spouses, but also friends, acquaintances, relatives, and even kind strangers. We get what we give so let's give generously.

Let's discuss the 'C' words . . . competition, comparison, and confidence

When I was born, I was missing one significant component in my DNA strand—***competitiveness***—which is somewhat essential for getting ahead. Consequently, I'm happy to settle for less, which can be a good thing and a bad thing. Lacking a competitive streak meant I never cared if I got high marks in school, never cared whether I hit a home run in softball, or never worried when others earned many more badges in Brownies

and Girl Guides than I had. I did my best (or some approximation of my best) and soldiered on.

That trait (or lack thereof) carried on into my adult life and resulted in me being less aggressive in the business world than I wish I'd been (although I did rather well in spite of myself). I'm also a dead loss in sports because I simply don't care about winning or scoring. Count me out when everyone else gathers around the table to play cards or board games. I have zero motivation to win and would much prefer to retire to a corner and read whatever book I'm currently into. I do like the concept of Scrabble though because it's about words (which I love) but hate counting up my points and keeping score because that involves math which is anathema to me.

Seeking to win and enjoying competition is a healthy state of mind. Without competition, we'd have no Olympics, professional and organized sports, contests or motivation of any kind. Competition keeps marathoners training, keeps beauty queens squirting spray tan and hair spray, race car drivers pushing that accelerator, and politicians lying and deceiving. Our heroes can motivate us to try harder, do better and generally improve ourselves.

I don't really consider a lack of competitiveness to be a serious shortcoming but there's another 'C' word that can be very destructive and that's *comparison*. Comparison is the death of confidence. We've heard many variations of that expression and in my experience, it has proven to be true. When we compare

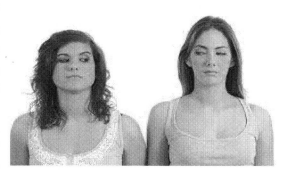

Comparison is the death of confidence.

ourselves to so many of today's media heroes, we feel sucker-punched, knowing we can never be as beautiful, as fast, as rich or as talented as they are.

The fashion and beauty industry must be the worst offender in setting us up for feeling like losers. On the bright side, there's an ever-so-slight change happening now to present women in a more realistic light in the media. Fashion and beauty magazines maintain no one would buy their products if we weren't confronted with an image of perfection that can be achieved only with whatever they're peddling. I do not agree but they really do not care what I think.

I'm encouraged by pictures of Helen Mirren, Diane Keaton, Maye Musk and Ali McGraw displaying their earned signs of aging well. I recognize I'll never achieve their beauty but I find them inspirational and even aspirational without being deceitful. Who among us can relate to pictures of anorexic teens with perfect skin, bodies and hair? That only serves to make us feel *worse*, not better about ourselves

It's always a good idea to feel motivated to try harder, whether this applies to our fitness, eating habits, state of mind or our appearance. But comparing ourselves to unattainable standards in anything can be soul-destroying and depressing. Knowing I will never be as beautiful as Jane Fonda doesn't discourage me from admiring her intelligence, her energy or her approach to how she presents herself.

There was a particularly funny episode of Frankie and Grace where Fonda dramatically pulled out her hair extensions, wiped off her makeup and yanked off her false eyelashes to demonstrate that we all need a little help, even those who appear to be so perfect.

The crucial C-word to incorporate into our everyday lives is *confidence.* Remember how confident we felt when we were little girls? Up until the age of about 10 or 11, we felt we were absolute perfection, invincible and undaunted. Then something happened. Was it peer pressure, hormones or life in

general? Whatever it was, we need to recapture that feeling of self-esteem and confidence that we enjoyed as little girls. Some of us regain it after menopause when we're finally free of the pressures of competing in the working world, mating and mothering.

European women exude confidence regardless of their comparative beauty, size or visible assets. That's why they all appear beautiful. They walk with purpose and style. They too have fashion magazines and media influences that could erode their confidence but they choose to ignore comparisons with the perfection of youth and instead celebrate their innate beauty.

Helen Mirren and Diane Keaton are my personal style talismans. Even though they're both thin, which I'm not, I love the way they each dress confidently, according to their individual and personal tastes. Helen Mirren loves colour and high fashion. Diane Keaton leans more toward neutral colours in a quirky combination of tailored basics tweaked in unexpected ways. Each of them has chosen to be true to herself and present with confidence. By the time baby boomer women have reached the age we are now, we pretty much have a handle on what works and doesn't work for each of us. Finding inspiration for our demographic can be a challenge although I've found several websites and blogs by boomer broads that I can relate to that fill that need. Heaven knows, it is not in the pages of Vogue or other fashion mags.

Amy Schumer's message is spot on.

The other night I rewatched an Amy Schumer movie I really enjoyed because it brings the confidence message home. *I Feel Pretty* is about a young single woman named Renée whose self-confidence takes a 180-degree turn when she falls off her exercise bicycle and sustains a head injury that completely alters her self-image. Instead of seeing herself as ordinary, plump and somewhat invisible, she suddenly awakens to a perception of herself as everything she always wanted to be—slim, fit, funny, and brilliant. Even though she looks exactly the same as she did before her fall, her behaviour is profoundly different when she *perceives* herself as beautiful. It's all a state of mind. I highly recommend watching this light-hearted movie.

Women are often criticized for not supporting other women in business and I have *never* found this to be the case. During my 40+ years in the corporate world, I always found other women to be unfailingly supportive. We're sisters in the struggle for equality with men in salaries, promotions, recognition and responsibility. One of our greatest challenges is to ignore the unfair comparisons, accept the challenge to compete with men and do it with complete and utter confidence. So, of the three C-words—competitiveness, comparison, and confidence—**confidence** is the C-word I like best of all.

How to survive a man cold

Every woman knows what it's like when your husband or partner has a man cold. They require all the care and attention of a newborn.

When my friend Gail's husband gets a cold she dusts off her black mourning dress and prepares for the worst. While it's tempting and seemingly easier to just divorce the old boy, I have some startling news. Women get man-colds too. In fact, I'm just recovering from one and thought I'd share my coping strategy.

I have to preface this piece by saying that I'm not a wimp. I have a high pain tolerance (with a double hip-replacement to vouch for my stamina) but when it comes to the common cold, as soon as I get one I'm totally incapacitated. When I feel that familiar thickening in the back of my throat that signals an oncoming cold I turn vicious. That's because I know I'm going to be totally immobilized; can't function; can't move; can't do anything but get myself into a horizontal position and stay there for three days. Even my brain ceases to function.

Recalling the old days when I was working for the telephone company in the sixties and I didn't get paid for the first three days of an illness, I would drag my ass into the office in a state of near-death, passing my germs to everyone near and far and prolonging my recovery by several days. I couldn't afford to miss sixty percent of my weekly paycheque. A friend once told me when she was raising young children, she dreamed of being able to check into a hotel when she was sick. Illness doesn't excuse mothers from still having to feed the family and doing all the chores being a mother entails. Booking into the local Hyatt for a couple of days of isolation and recuperation in a quiet, calm hotel room, with room service would be the perfect solution. The good news is now that we're retired, we *can* opt out of life and feed our recovery.

I should also mention here that when I'm sick, my husband is the perfect nurse. He's kind when I'm sick. When *he's* sick, I'm *not* kind. I curse him for getting sick and go to extreme measures to avoid any kind of contact, generally eliminating him from my life until he's better. Florence Nightingale I am not.

Here's the secret

My experience has proven that the best way of dealing with a cold is **two or three days in bed with lots of soup and liquids**. Retirement allows us that luxury. When you feel a cold coming on, do not try to fight it as you'll lose. Your body needs every ounce of strength to get rid of the demon and that can only be accomplished by going to bed and channeling all your energies toward recovery. It works for me and puts me back on my feet and living the retirement dream after only three days of bed rest. If I try to push through and keep up my normal routine, the cold only hangs on and keeps me miserable for at least a week. Trust me. My remedy works. And on the fourth day, I did riseth from the near-dead and resumed my life, and you can too.

My past is now officially an historical site

The Maclean-Hunter Building at University and Dundas, where it all began for this boomer.

You know you're old when the once-modern building where you landed your first job has been designated an historical site. On Monday, July 5th, 1965 I walked into the shiny marble lobby of the Maclean-Hunter Building at 481 University Avenue in Toronto to begin my first full-time job. Bell Canada leased space in the building and they'd hired me to start work as a clerk-typist, beginning the week after I finished high school. I was 17 years old and wore a pink and white gingham dress and new white high heels purchased specially to start my new job. The day before, my parents dropped me off at the door of Willard Hall, 20 Gerrard Street East, a four-storey boarding house operated by the Women's Christian Temperance Union, where I would live for the next two years.

I had arrived from small town Ontario, in the first wave of baby boomers to be released into life as adults in the big city. Willard Hall was full of eager boomer girls like me. We'd all left our small-town homes to take jobs as secretaries, switchboard operators, clerks and stenographers for Bell Canada, Ontario Hydro and various insurance companies. Some, like my room-mate Liz wore the traditional white gloves issued by "Manpower" as they began temporary work while awaiting a permanent position.

I remember that day in July 1965 so clearly. Sitting at the reception desk in the lobby of the Maclean Hunter building was an attractive blonde woman wearing a smart navy-blue uniform. She was official-looking and seemed to know most of the people entering the lobby, greeting suited businessmen, women and couriers with a smile and "Good morning". Her demeanor screamed big city and professional and I wanted to be just like her, very Doris Day. I took the elevator to the fifth floor where I met my new boss and was introduced around the office. My job was to provide clerk-typist services to half a dozen managers in the Buildings, Vehicles and Supplies Department of what was then called The Bell Telephone Company of Canada. My salary was $55.50 a week, more money than I'd ever seen in my life, much better than the sixty-five cents an hour I'd been earning as a carhop in high school. A year later when I moved to Bell's office tower at 76 Adelaide Street West, they still employed white-gloved uniformed elevator operators.

Very quickly I made friends with another new hire, also named Linda (but with an "i") and we soon became known as *The Linda's*. We took our breaks together, shared office gossip and generally became attached at the hip. She was my new BFF, if that acronym had existed back then. Linda was a city girl from Scarborough and I had so much to learn about sophisticated Toronto ways from her. In the evenings, she took modelling classes at Patricia Stevens Modelling School which

Bassel's Restaurant on Yonge St. at Gerrard was where all the Willard Hall girls would go for coffee and a smoke.

131

absorbed most of her wages. Linda introduced me to my first compact of blusher, a major beauty revelation for this young girl from the country.

Linda and I ate our lunch in the Maclean-Hunter subsidized cafeteria on the main floor of the University and Dundas building. We paid a nominal amount to load our plates with the daily special, always ordering mashed potatoes and gravy because we were both skinny and wanted to put on weight. Imagine that! That same cafeteria dispatched coffee carts throughout the building mid-morning and mid-afternoon each day when we would enjoy a hot styrofoam cup of tea and a butter tart wrapped in cellophane. All those mashed potatoes, gravy and butter tarts have since more than done their job to my great chagrin.

In the sixties, Chinatown was still located on Dundas Street between University Avenue and Bay Street. At the age of eighteen I experienced Chinese food for the first time in my life, sharing the ubiquitous "Dinner For Two" with Linda one day at lunchtime. The menu combo remains fixed in my memory: fried rice, chow mein, sweet and sour spareribs and egg rolls. Authentic Asian or what! I loved to browse the exotic items for sale in the shops along Dundas Street but will never forget my horror the first time I saw dead, roasted Peking ducks hanging in the windows of butcher shops.

There was an office tower at 20 Edward Street behind the Maclean-Hunter building that housed Edward's Books and a drug store on the main floor. We loved going into the drug store on our lunch hour and spritzing ourselves with the tester perfumes that we couldn't afford to buy, coming back to the office reeking of fake lilacs or the high-class *L'air du Temps*. Living at Willard Hall, I was able to walk the back streets behind The Hospital for Sick Children to get to work, saving money on subways and soon familiarizing myself with downtown Toronto. Back then,

Toronto was much smaller, only a million people, and our weekends were spent cruising "The Village" to observe the hippies on Yorkville Avenue.

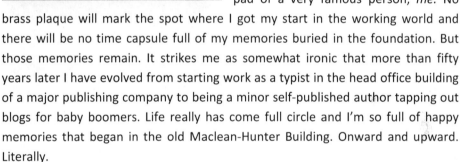

The new and improved United Building proposed for 481 University Avenue.

481 University Avenue is now slated to be gutted. The façade will be saved for its historical value while the inner building will be demolished and replaced by a 45-storey tower housing condos and commercial space. Renamed *The United Building* it will replace the old Maclean-Hunter Building and wipe out any trace of the launching pad of a very famous person, *me*. No brass plaque will mark the spot where I got my start in the working world and there will be no time capsule full of my memories buried in the foundation. But those memories remain. It strikes me as somewhat ironic that more than fifty years later I have evolved from starting work as a typist in the head office building of a major publishing company to being a minor self-published author tapping out blogs for baby boomers. Life really has come full circle and I'm so full of happy memories that began in the old Maclean-Hunter Building. Onward and upward. Literally.

"You've got mail" is now a ping to be ignored, not a pleasure to be savoured

Call me old-fashioned but I love getting mail, the kind now referred to as snail mail. If a day goes by that I don't get a magazine or something personal in my mailbox, I can get downright cranky. Is it because my life is so utterly lacking in excitement that the mail is a big deal to me? Even my little dog jumps up and down spinning with excitement when I announce, *"Let's go get the mail"*. She understands.

Yesterday I was thrilled to find my mailbox stuffed with magazines, mail order catalogues, a couple of personal envelopes and even (praise be!) an envelope that obviously had a cheque enclosed. But my joy soon turned to disappointment when, upon closer examination, I realized the mail carrier had mistakenly put our neighbour's mail in our box. Our neighbour was the recipient of all this wonderful bounty. I was tempted to score a couple of the mail order catalogues for myself thinking she wouldn't miss them, but honesty prevailed and I reluctantly stuffed them into her mailbox.

Remember when we used to regularly get newsy letters, written by hand in loving cursive with a fountain pen? As kids we had pen pals in England who sent us letters on those thin blue airmail forms, telling us all about their lives far across the ocean. Even Christmas and birthday cards are rare these days as people either don't

Letters to and from overseas were essential for morale and saved for sentimental value.

bother or they opt for e-cards. Email has totally replaced hand-written letters. Will the love letters from war veterans of today have the same cachet and impact when they're lost in the ether of email or Skype? Somehow the old sentimental letters our fathers, uncles and grandfathers wrote home from overseas in fountain pen or scratchy pencil seem so much more meaningful, more enduring and more historically significant because they were written by hand, addressed, stuffed into an envelope with a stamp to be saved in a book, slipped into a mailbox, then bundled and tied with a ribbon to be saved by the recipient.

I was saddened and disappointed to learn that many people now object to "Amber Alerts" because they also land in the middle of the night. So many people now sleep with their phones by their bedside that it's become impossible to even have a peaceful night's sleep without feeling the need to be connected via electronic devices. Other than doctors and firefighters, who among us is so important that they need to be 'on call' during the night? If keeping your phone alive while you sleep means Amber Alerts disturb you, then shame on you.

Our addiction to personal electronic devices means we now get mail 24/7. That familiar ping announces the arrival of requests from friends to meet for lunch, a reminder that we have a dentist appointment at 2:15 tomorrow and less welcome notices such as bill payments due or worse, overdue. Mail is no longer fun. It's something to be given the once-over, reviewed, culled, acted upon or dumped. Another time-consuming chore in an already busy day.

We have a "No Junk Mail" sign posted on the mailbox on our front porch which greatly lightens the load in our paper recycling bin each week. That means most of what lands in our mailbox is the real thing and I look forward to receiving it each day. Sometimes there's a hand-written thank you note from a friend or a birthday card when it's time for the annual celebration. Most often it's statements, announcements, promotions and printed material that actually qualifies as junk mail but the marketers were able to circumvent immediate disposal by enclosing it in an envelope with a first class stamp. Their trickery works as I open each one and read it before tossing into recycling.

Imagine the thrill of receiving a hand-written love letter.

My passion for print publications like magazines ensures my mailbox has regular deposits of good stuff though. A couple of years ago I received a three-page hand-written letter from someone (another baby boomer) I stayed with on an American army base in Germany in 1968 when I was travelling around on a Eurail Pass. I've kept that letter in my desk ever since, a relic of times gone by when people actually hand-wrote letters. They're so rare and so precious now, they're like collectors' items. I'm afraid to part with it in case I never get another one in this lifetime. Even wedding invitations are now getting the electronic treatment. No more embossed cards to be saved in a scrapbook.

I still buy little boxes of illustrated note cards at the stationery store in hopes that I'll have an excuse to write and send one to a friend. I take special care when selecting and mailing (by snail mail) birthday and anniversary cards to the special people in my life. I can't help feeling they enjoy receiving them as much as I do, a little ray of sunshine in a gloomy pile of flyers and junk. Much as I appreciate and enjoy receiving instant photos and news from friends by email, I'll always save a little spot in my heart for the old-fashioned kind that the nice letter carrier from Canada Post drops into the mailbox on my front porch every day around noon. It could be a letter, a card or even a cheque. Whatever it is, it's special because it was delivered personally, by hand. Still.

Who's your old lady heart throb?

For me, it all started with Elvis and peaked during his 1968 television special.

Elvis Presley was my first and most enduring celebrity crush. What began when I first watched him on The Tommy Dorsey Show and then on Ed Sullivan was signed, sealed and delivered when I saw him in *Love Me Tender*, *Jailhouse Rock* and *King Creole* at the Saturday matinée in the fifties. By the time *G.I. Blues* and *Blue Hawaii* came out in the sixties, my feelings for Elvis were enshrined for eternity. I knew the words to all his music, including pauses to take a breath and those little vocal riffs that made his music special. The first LP I ever purchased was *Elvis' Golden Hits* which cost four weeks' allowance. I still have it, and all his other records. Even though his later movies were dreadful and embarrassing, I remained loyal and faithful. When he kissed Hope Lange or Juliette Prowse in a movie, it was really me he was kissing.

When The Beatles came on the scene, I was as crazy a Beatles fan as anyone and had their posters up all over my room. But I still kept a special place in my heart for Elvis. My favourite Beatle was not the popular and overtly cute Paul or cerebral John, but I preferred dog-faced Ringo. A definite pattern in my celebrity worship was taking shape. I seemed to prefer the guys who were not conventionally pretty boys. I was attracted to the ones who were a little bit bad, a bit off.

For that reason, Frankie Avalon and Fabian were not my choices of heartthrob. Ronnie Hawkins, Eric Burdon and Burton Cummings were much more appealing. Mick Jagger was never my cup of tea either (too effeminate) and I preferred Phil over Don of The Everley Brothers. Michael Caine's east-end London working-class accent canceled out

We all had a favourite Beatle. Mine was Ringo

his pretty blond looks and I kept a large black and white poster of his Harry Palmer character hanging over my single bed for more than a year in the sixties.

As the years went on, my crushes evolved. Musicians were replaced by movie stars and other high-profile celebs. For the same reason I didn't fancy Frankie Avalon and Fabian, I never had crushes on Robert Redford or Brad Pitt. Too pretty.

Then, I saw Liam Neeson swinging his kilt in the 1995 movie *Rob Roy* and I fell in love forever. I think he's still my most enduring crush. Gerard Butler rings my chimes and I've even developed a taste for younger men after watching Jason Bateman starring in *Identity Thief* with Melissa McCarthy. I also enjoyed him in the HBO series *Ozark,* and can confidently confirm no one wears jeans better than Jason Bateman.

Now that I'm "of a certain age", I've noticed my fancies are less about looks and more about brains. Bill Maher will likely always have a little piece of my heart and one of his guest panelists, Van Jones makes my pulse go pitter-pat. Gorgeous smile and a fine mind. Despite the 22-year age difference (he's that much younger than me), I'm pretty sure we could make it work. I've had a little crush on Corey Booker, not only because of his looks but mainly because of his integrity. And what boomer broad doesn't love Daniel Craig and those gorgeous blue eyes? He's my friend Margaret's favourite. Prince Harry is awfully darned cute too.

In canvassing my boomer gal pals, my friend Perry confessed her love for Kris Kristoffersen and I have to wholeheartedly agree. Brains *and* beautiful blue eyes but a bit of a bad boy. It's too bad Anderson Cooper is gay as I think we'd make a great couple.

C'mon. He's awfully darned cute, isn't he?

In the age of #METOO we're now dealing with the issue of having to separate the man from his music/art. I was never a great Michael Jackson fan but those who were and still are must be struggling with the moral dilemma of supporting a musical genius who was also a predator.

We've always known that men have 'romantic' thoughts about female celebrities but I was surprised when my friend Mike named Katy Perry has his special girl. Obviously, he has a discerning eye. My husband and another friend Keith have a thing for JLo which was slammed home when they saw her pole dance in the Superbowl half-time show. They're still recovering. She seems to be in a class all her own and captures all men's hearts and other parts.

Celebrity crushes are harmless and probably even a bit healthy. Many years ago a friend commented, *"It doesn't matter where you get your appetite as long as you come home for meals,"* and based on my informal survey of friends, it seems we still have a healthy appetite for fantasy love interests and different tastes. That's normal. We're not dead yet. Do you have an old lady celebrity crush?

Chapter 5

Mind, Body, Soul

Do you remember your multiplication tables?

Something unsettling happened the other evening after dinner as we were sitting under the gazebo in the back yard having a cup of tea. We were discussing the birthday party we'd thrown the day before for our little Yorkshire Terrier who turned nine.

Now, before you get all harsh and judgey because we threw a birthday party for our dog, keep in mind that under current physical distancing rules and lock-down, we're all getting a bit desperate and crazy when it comes to excuses to socialize. Our bubble is pretty small and we're working it the best we can. So, we invited our verified safe friends and neighbours (two couples) and their two dogs over for refreshments and, well, more refreshments. It was great fun.

Anyway . . . as we were discussing the excitement of the previous evening, my honey and I tried to calculate the age of our dog in 'people years'. You know the equation: one dog year equals seven people years or something like that. If Sassy is nine years old, then she must be . . . how many years is that? 9 x 7 = ??? We were stumped. Is it 72? Is it 54? No, it has to be more than that? We started counting back from 9 x 10 = 90, right? It took us several very long minutes to agree that the correct and final answer was 63. And it was a lot of work.

My husband is supposed to be the numbers guy in our family. I'm the word wizard. Between the two of us, we muddle through. When I can't count on him to provide a quick and accurate answer for basic multiplication, then we have a serious problem. He made a highly successful career out of being able to accurately estimate the real cost of hundreds of millions of dollars in huge construction projects *in his head,* with uncanny accuracy. I'm a known disaster at anything math related but I can spell just about any word accurately and pick up grammatical errors unflinchingly, much to the annoyance of my husband.

There's a reason baby boomers were drilled, and drilled, and drilled again in multiplication tables in school. In the days before pocket calculators and smartphones, we needed to know these things to get us through life. We even learned how to use a slide-rule. Basic math is a basic life skill. In fact, educators are planning to reintroduce this rote type of learning to grade-schoolers as the value of knowing these things is becoming increasingly more evident. It shocks boomers that young people today don't know how to make or count change because they didn't learn 'numbers' the way we did.

It's time to go back to basics.

Does the slippage of my husband's skill with numbers mean I'm now doomed to soon be unable to spell or pronounce words correctly? We have counted on each other to offset our respective weaknesses. That's what togetherness is about. The future is looking scary indeed. I suppose we could have easily Googled the answer to what is 9 x 7 but as boomers, that wasn't our natural default. We started counting our fingers and toes.

Perhaps I should make up some flashcards just like Miss McArthur and Mrs. Thompson used when I was in grade one and two. I'd have to verify the answers on Google though to make sure they were correct before I inked them in. Sheesh! Two apples plus one apple equals three apples. Maybe I can blame our brain fog on the pandemic. That covers a lot of excuses for why the world is falling apart around us.

Whatever the reason for our lapse, it's obvious we need to sharpen our math skills. Or did that information just evacuate our brain cells to make room for more unwelcome and unneeded COVID statistics which are overwhelming and depressing? Maybe, I'll just keep our little brain burp a secret tucked away with the rest of our lapses and hope no one will notice. After all, our entire generation is losing brain cells and the younger generation wouldn't even notice our mathematical errors because they can't calculate in their heads anyway. We'll just write their inheritance cheques in cursive and they'll have no idea what the numbers mean. Just like the rest of us.

When hearts not heads prevail

Emotion often trumps logic. That statement explains so much. Like why the Americans elected Donald Trump as their President. Or why the Canadian government is building temporary housing for asylum seekers crossing into Canada illegally at remote border points instead of turning them back to follow proper channels. Why should Canadians be spending tax money to house and support *illegal* immigrants when legitimate immigrants who follow proper legal channels often have to wait years? It makes no sense.

As many Britons are now realizing, Brexit was obviously an issue influenced more by feelings of nationalism than practicality. So many unexplainable outcomes are the result of human beings letting their hearts overrule their heads. It's why so many women fall in love with bad choices in men. I did. Once. When I was very young and stupid. Learned my lesson.

We know we shouldn't put that designer purse on our credit card because we *can't live without it*. But the smell of fine leather and the dreams of being transported into a rarefied stratosphere of pleasure overrules common sense. We can't afford to get the oil changed in the car but we can rationalize dropping the equivalent of a month's rent on a luxury consumer item. Those designer sunglasses cost more than groceries for a month but we slap down the old credit card despite the obvious stupidity of the purchase. Instant gratification beats logic.

Tattoos are cool and everyone is getting one. Do you still want to live with a faded, wrinkled, distorted picture of a rose after it's endured thirty years of wear and tear on your forearm? What seemed like a good idea at the time may not be as appealing down the road. A bad choice in hair colour grows out. Tattoos do not.

141

Men also are not immune to the pull of instant gratification in consumer purchases. It's mind-blowing how they can rationalize purchasing a shiny new truck or SUV without having the cash in the bank. In fact, I've

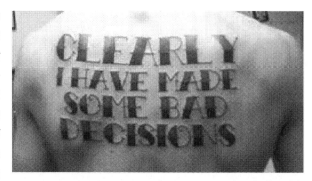

observed that men's toys generally come with a much higher price tag than women's. Vehicles, boats and electronics aren't cheap. The experts are right when they advise it's not always in our best interest to try and outbid someone with deeper pockets just because we can't imagine not owning *that* house. No one's immune. Men, women, governments, voters, corporations, even really smart people fall prey to the pull of the heart, often with disastrous results.

One of the greatest benefits of aging is the wisdom that usually accompanies it. Baby boomers have made more than our share of mistakes and bad decisions over the years and we've learned a lot. Hopefully, most of my mistakes are behind me. But, I'm still acknowledging the infallibility of the adage that heart generally trumps head, and the truth is when I look at the world around me, some things never change. It's mind-boggling, the eternal conflict.

10 things I wish I'd known for sure

I was going to title this piece *Things I wish I'd known when I was 20.* Then I realized the same wisdom applies at age 30, 60 or at any point in our lives. Knowledge is knowledge. It's all about whether you absorb it and make it work for you. I wish someone had told me these things (and I'd actually taken it heart) when I was 20. So, Gen Xers, Y's and Millennials, this is for you. Here are some things I've learned for sure along the road of life:

- **Things dry up as we get older**, skin, nails, eyes, vaginas, all our body parts. Appreciate your dewiness while you still have it. It won't last. That's why there's a multi-billion-dollar cosmetics and pharmaceutical industry to keep us lubricated and functioning.
- **Your hair is the best it will ever be**. As we get older, our hair thins, loses its shine and is never as luxurious and abundant as it was when we were twenty. That is why we have expensive salon treatments that become increasingly more expensive as we age.
- **Menopause symptoms are not a short-term inconvenience**. They can last for years. In my case, the hot flashes were never-ending and lasted more than 20 years. The accompanying weight gain is practically irreversible. Try not to beat yourself up. Millennials, Gen-X's and Y's, consider yourselves warned. You are not immune and this too *will* happen to you, no matter how many ab crunches you do.
- **Being assertive in business is a good thing**. If I learned nothing else after 40 years in the corporate world, it's ***take care of yourself first!*** Men have no qualms about asking for raises, a company car or an extra week of vacation. Boomer gals were raised to be polite, compliant and patient, hoping our rewards will come. Did not really do us a lot of good. Put yourself first.
- **Loyalty to your employer is not in your best interest.** I think most men understand the basic premise here but women tend to take some convincing. All those late nights working to meet a deadline, family time traded for priorities at work? Not worth it. Your tombstone won't read "Loyal Employee". See Item 4 above.
- **Manage and promote your personal brand**. We'd never heard of those things in the workplace when boomer gals were trying to get ahead or even survive in those last decades of the twentieth century. We were raised to believe that it is wrong to self-promote. It is wrong not to.
- **Catch that 5 lb. weight gain before it becomes 10 lbs**. or 20. Once you hit menopause you're screwed and it's nearly impossible to lose weight.
- *Financial independence = FREEDOM.* **Financial security is paramount.** It's tempting to spend, spend, spend when you're young and making good

143

money. But when you hit mid-life you might want to change careers or take a sabbatical. Financial security and ultimately financial independence equip you with **options** later in life. That cool car or those expensive shoes and purses you couldn't live without in your twenties are long gone and forgotten when you're reading your bank statements with enormous regret at fifty. Save, save, save. **It's only when you're financially independent that you're truly free.**

- **Be yourself.** You're a worthy, whole and valid person without changing your personality for the sake of someone you think you love. Love yourself first.
- **Be healthy. Everything in moderation.** A little bit of this; a little bit of that, without overindulging in all the things we like including wine, desserts, sugar, bad carbs, red meat etc. Taking care of our bodies will pay off as we get older. Smoking causes cancer, a raspy voice and zillions of wrinkles. Keep drinking under control, keep moving, stay curious and take care of yourself.

I'm not sure I would have listened to any of this advice when I was young but for what it's worth, here it is. Like most people, I did some things right and a few things wrong but overall, baby boomers are the healthiest, most financially secure generation ever. Was it our music? Our parents? Hard work? Whatever came together to create our generation, we have a lot to be thankful for.

Mirror mirror on the wall . . . what the hell happened to us all?

My friend Margaret had already purchased the 10X magnifying mirror before I could warn her about the consequences. As we progress along the aging continuum (how's that for euphemizing 'getting old'?) we often need help chasing down those errant eyebrow or chin hairs. Over time, we move from 5X to 7X and we're now at the 10X stage which can be truly traumatizing when we go exploring.

If you want to restart your sluggish heart or enact your own version of Edvard Munch's *The Scream,* then checking out your face in a magnifying mirror is guaranteed to get all your bells ringing. The reason our eyesight gets weak as we age is an earned kindness. We were never intended to see the resulting wrinkles, pitting and pigmentation we've acquired over the years. When we look in the (regular) mirror we hazily see pretty much the same face that stared back at us in our twenties, and that one was rather pretty. Why spoil the illusion by getting a magnifying mirror? In fact, they're so distorting it's impossible to cram your whole face into one full-size shot to apply makeup and we are forced to view our imperfections pixel by pixel. Downright horrifying.

Those pores and fine lines I keep working so assiduously on trying to wrangle with expensive lotions and creams appear like moon craters. Stray chin hairs look like birch trees in a field of dried grass. Tiny wrinkles become trenches. And, I've discovered, it's not just men who get unsightly nose hairs. It's best not to be confronted with the harshness of all that reality. I was much

happier and prettier before burdening myself with a magnifying mirror. Facing the truth in the mirror can be very demoralizing.

Makeup mirrors should come with a warning label. At the very least, they should have a decal affixed, like on the side mirrors of cars: *"Image may appear scarier than it really is."* It's too late for me and my friend Margaret but I'm warning you. If you're contemplating buying a 10X magnifying mirror DO NOT. Just slap on the spackle, paint those eyebrows somewhere in the middle of your forehead, add a slash of blusher and put on a great, big smile. It'll remove years. Face it; you're the best you'll ever be. You're still able to admire yourself so be thankful and celebrate it.

A rose by any other name wins by a nose

Scents touch a special chord, not only in our olfactory systems but also in our hearts and in our brains. We all can relate to a certain scent transporting us to another time and place. It's a magical transformation. The smell of certain things baking in the oven may take us back to our mothers' or grandmothers' kitchens. Being near water may remind us of all those carefree days as children swimming in the lake or nearby river every summer.

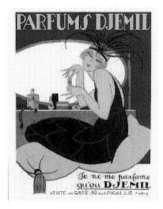

The fragrance of certain perfumes may transport us to memories of loved ones and ones we've loved. Whenever I open my late mother's jewelry box, the lingering scent evokes the inside of her house and memories come flooding back. Sometimes, people who have lost a special person, keep a bathrobe or favourite sweater that carries the scent of that person, to provide comfort.

Ever since the days of owning a single bottle of (cheap) *Evening in Paris* cologne purchased at the local five and dime store and proudly displayed on my bedroom dresser when I was a teenager, I've been charmed and affected by fragrance. I love the different moods each one presents. I adore the beautiful bottles and feel so feminine and uplifted when I spritz myself each morning. Over the years, I've accumulated a sizeable collection and even though many, if not most of my bottles are probably past their best-before date, I cannot part with them.

When I first started working for Bell Telephone on University Avenue in Toronto in 1965, my girlfriend and I used to go into the drugstore behind our office building on our lunch hour and spray ourselves with generous quantities of expensive perfumes we couldn't afford to buy on our clerk-typist wages. *White Shoulders* and *L'air du Temps* were always favourites. I'm sure there were many days when we came back into the office after lunch nearly asphyxiating our coworkers after we'd doused ourselves in lilac or lily of the valley perfumes of questionable quality. As they say, 'those were the days, my friend'.

There was a time in the '80s when blooming boomers were encouraged to adopt a 'signature scent'. Offices were awash in *Opium, Red Door, Obsession,* and *Poison.* One of the girls in my office came to work every day drenched in Cartier's expensive *La Panthère.* I've never been able to limit myself to just one fragrance. Some days

I was the in-store representative for Yardley of London at Eatons' College Street Store in Toronto in 1970.

I'm in the mood for floral; other days I lean toward citrus or spicey. Does anyone remember wearing *Shalimar* or Estée Lauder's *Youth Dew* in the sixties? Or Elizabeth Arden's *Blue Grass?* We were so sophisticated. When I worked in Eaton's College Street store's cosmetics department in 1970, we had people who came in purposely to buy giant bottles of *4711*. We also sold a lot of *Jean Naté,* Yardley's *Lavender* and *Chantilly* in the pink bottle. Remember them?

My favourite fragrance is called *Émilie* by French perfumier Fragonard. It is a blend that includes my favourite flowers, rose, and jasmine. I first experienced this fragrance in 2012 when I toured southern France with a group of ladies guided by decorating and style guru Kimberley Seldon. We toured the Fragonard factory in Grasse, France where we were able to see how they gather the blooms, then distill and manufacture the various fragrances according to which flowers are in season. I also once toured a small, second-floor perfume museum near the Opera House in Paris and thoroughly enjoyed myself.

After I originally purchased a tiny atomizer of Fragonard's *Émilie* and it turned out to be so amazingly beautiful, I went to the internet the following year to order more. A few weeks later, to my great delight, a more substantial bottle arrived in the mail, all the way from France. Sometime later, however, I was disappointed to receive a notice from them that they would no longer be able to send it to me as postal regulations forbid certain chemicals and liquids being sent by mail. I guess I'll just have to fly to France to restock. It's available on Amazon from third-party sellers but I've never ordered from them so I can't vouch for their authenticity. I did manage to pick up another bottle a couple of years ago when I was In France which should last me long after I go to the 'home'. I only hope my fellow residents will enjoy it as much as I do . . . cough, cough.

What seems to distinguish the Fragonard perfume from so many (and there are soooo many) available on the market today, is the purity of the fragrance. Perhaps it's just me, but whenever I try a sample of some new fragrance being launched, I find it inevitably leaves an unpleasant chemical smell on my skin, not the clear floral fragrance I'm looking for. So many perfumes today, even from the major perfume houses, contain so many synthetic ingredients that they all smell the same. And, as we all know, each one reacts differently with our individual body chemistry. Chanel No. 5 always smells like ginger ale on me while it is divine on a friend of mine.

Visiting Fragonard's perfume factory in Grasse, France was a once-in-a-lifetime treat.

One day when I was in the Hudson's Bay store's perfume department, a customer produced a small gold atomizer like the Fragonard one I bought in France, asking the sales associate to find something similar. Her daughter had bought it for her, also in France, and she wanted to replicate it. 'Good luck', I thought, as I meandered off.

I once read somewhere that Michelle Obama wears Cartier's *Délice* which has a delicate cherry essence. I couldn't get myself off fast enough to Holt Renfrew to spritz myself from the tester, hoping to capture just a tiny bit of her essence.

Even the scent of sheets dried outside in the fresh air is enough to send me into paroxysms of bliss. A whiff of fresh spruce can return me to the Christmas trees in my childhood home. Does the smell of wood smoke remind you of summer camping trips? The smell of Neutrogena soap always puts me in the hands of Dr. Cornish, an old dentist I had fifty years ago, in the days when dentists didn't wear latex gloves, and washed their hands for every new patient. The unique scent of old-fashioned ivory soap reminds me of time spent as a child at a friend's cottage.

Perhaps my aging nose has lost some of its sensitivity as the years go by. As my sense of smell diminishes, I pity the people fainting in my wake as I stroll down the street in a suffocating cloud of my floral scent du jour, oblivious to those with allergies or an aversion to fragrance. I absolutely adore fragrance and will never stop wearing it. For whatever effect scent has on our brains and hearts, I'm not going to deny myself.

Chapter 6

Food

Life without nuts would drive me nuts

With all due respect and a measure of sympathy for those people who suffer from nut allergies, I can't imagine life without nuts. I was contemplating this the other day as I chowed down on a lovely piece of carrot cake with cream cheese icing in the IKEA cafeteria. The nuts in their cake were ground a little finer that my personal preference but we all have different tastes.

Part of the fun of eating nuts is the satisfying crunch and the workout our teeth get when consuming anything with nuts. And, as an extra bonus, there's the protein value. Nuts make everything last longer because of the extra chewing required. It kinda forces us to eat slower and savour the experience. Then, you get to spend lots of time afterward picking the pieces out of your teeth and enjoying them all over again.

I don't think a single day passes that I don't consume nuts. A dish of almonds is a constant fixture on my kitchen counter for a protein hit and mindless nibbling throughout the day. I pour 'almond milk' on my cereal every morning and I simply can't imagine sipping a Timmie's steeped tea without a bite of their peanut butter cookie melting in my mouth. I purchase giant bags of pecans from Costco for various baking projects including the morning breakfast muffins I make for my honey (it's the only way I can keep him from eating packaged breakfast/candy bars).

Eating pumpkin seeds or sunflower seeds makes me feel virtuous. We'll just overlook the fact they're usually unhealthily oiled and salted. My honey always has a large jar of Costco cashews on the table beside his LaZboy for those all-too-frequent stressful moments when the Jays or Leafs are losing, which is usually.

A 'Tin Roof' sundae would just be a plain old chocolate sundae without the redskin peanuts.

So, a day without nuts would seriously impede my life. Just imagine:

- Dairy Queen's Peanut Buster without the peanuts. It would be a bust.
- Carrot cake without walnuts is just a boring vegetable.
- Brownies without walnuts don't even deserve to be called brownies.
- Tin roof sundae without Spanish redskin peanuts would just be a boring chocolate sundae.
- Peanut, almond and cashew butter would be non-existent.
- Christmas wouldn't be Christmas without Hello Dolly Bars, Pecan Squares, Fruit and Nut Cake, mixed nuts in a bowl with a cracker.
- What would Charles Schultz have named his famous cartoon strip? Beans?

I could probably survive a trip to Five Guys for a burger and their amazing fries even if they didn't have a bin of free peanuts, but it just wouldn't be the same. Their boiled, salted peanuts are absolutely *THE BEST* and someone else gets to clean up the mess. Any kind of ice-cream with nuts is beyond nirvana. Being able to crunch those big chunks of walnuts in Maple Walnut ice cream or the sugared pecans in Butter Pecan or Pralines n'Cream makes it last twice as long which is twice as decadent.

World War II might even have taken a different direction if General Anthony Clement McAuliffe hadn't uttered that famous word *"Nuts"* when challenged by German soldiers wearing allied uniforms in Bastogne during the Battle of The

Bulge. "Fooey" just wouldn't have had the same cachet. Donald Trump's already limited vocabulary would be seriously challenged if he couldn't refer to his each of his many adversaries as a "nut job".

I cannot imagine German chocolate cake without a bushel of walnuts.

Cashews are a gift from the gods. Pecans are nature's gift to baking. Almonds are unbeatable. Peanuts help the world go round and make sports, movies, chocolate bars and beer an infinitely more enjoyable experience. Nuts are a protein hit when we're feeling low. They're portable, not messy (unless still in the shell), easy to eat and relatively inexpensive to consume. As I reach for a handful of some kind of nut every day of my life, I feel sorry for those people with nut allergies. And I find myself wondering why nut allergies are so prevalent today. When boomers were growing up in the fifties and sixties we never ever knew a single soul with a nut allergy. School lunches were wall-to-wall peanut butter and jam sandwiches and peanut butter cookies. What happened in our food chain to cause this crisis? I blame Monsanto and other big-agra corporations for all our food-related problems.

If it weren't for nuts, what would we have to chew on? Raw broccoli? Tough red meat? Nothing quite does the job like nuts. Except when the person sitting behind you in the movies is chewing them too loudly. But, then again, I do the same thing when I'm chewing popcorn in the movies, so I'll have to overlook that one. I have a divine recipe for butter tart squares that calls for a couple of cups of raisins that I made infinitely better by substituting pecans. Much healthier, wouldn't you agree? Salads, baking, snacks, just about everything benefits from the addition of nuts. I'm so thankful I was born a baby boomer and avoided that nut allergy plague. Can't imagine life without them.

I'm on the rocky road to death by ice-cream

As soon as that container of French Vanilla ice-cream in my freezer is gone, I'm going to quit. This time for sure. It's the last remains of some flavours I stocked up on when we had company a couple of weeks ago. Understandable, right? I bought the French Vanilla to

I'll have one of each please . . . to go.

serve with fresh Ontario strawberries which have a life expectancy of only 24 hours, but the Black Jack Cherry, Heavenly Hash, Pralines n'Cream, Rocky Road, and Maple Walnut are just plain inexcusable examples of my character weakness. It reveals a clear and undeniable propensity for addictive substances but this time I'm truly committed to reforming my ways.

Ordinarily, I try not to buy ice-cream because I've been known to stand at the kitchen counter eating it directly out of the container until I feel sick. It's safest to not even have it in the house. But, like any alcoholic or addict, it's a slippery slope once you submit to temptation. I love ice cream. It's a genetic mutation inherited from my mother and her mother, my grandmother. It can't be helped so all I can do is try to manage it. Often, when I'd drop into Long's Restaurant for my after-school cherry Coke fix as a teenager, there would be my grandmother sitting in a nearby booth enjoying her ice cream in a cone-shaped stainless steel dish with a paper liner, before she began her mile-long walk home. You see, it is not my fault.

Then, today I found myself trying to find Spanish redskin peanuts at the grocery store to go with that boring vanilla ice-cream. They're the only kind of peanuts suitable for making a tin roof sundae, which is a chocolate sundae made with real chocolate syrup (*not* hot fudge), and only those special redskin peanuts on top will do. I can't find Spanish redskins anywhere, although they do have them at Dairy Queen because I regularly get them in my Blizzards.

All those ice-cream parlour treats boomers grew up enjoying in the fifties and sixties are going the way of rotary phones. Does the younger generation even know what a real 'soda' is these days? It's not a bottle or can of pop. The Americans generically refer to all soft drinks as soda. A genuine ice-cream soda is like a 'float'

(another anachronism) with a large scoop of vanilla ice-cream over a shot of flavoured sundae syrup topped off and mixed with soda water, whipped cream and a maraschino cherry. It's consumed with both a straw and a long-handled spoon.

I've heard that most of the machine-made milkshakes we are served these days aren't even made with real milk but are an edible oil product or a concoction made with dry milk solids, whatever that means. *Real* milkshakes are made with ice-cold whole milk, a generous squirt of flavour syrup and a couple of scoops of vanilla ice-cream, whipped in a green Hamilton Beach dedicated milkshake maker. Chocolate milkshakes are *not* made with chocolate ice-cream but with vanilla ice-cream and real chocolate syrup. Having worked in a hamburger place for three years in high school, I'm an expert on these things. I still remember the short-form codes we wrote on our order slips: CMS = chocolate milkshake; BMS = butterscotch milkshake, and so on. For an extra five cents, we'd throw in a fresh egg and whip it up in the milkshake too.

Considering my history in the biz and my own predilection for ice-cream, you would assume I'm pretty particular about which brands I consume. Sadly, I'm not, although I do prefer thoroughly Canadian private brands like Chapmans and Kawartha Dairy. It's so hard to know what crap goes into our food sources these days with all the preservatives, stabilizers and thickeners, so I try to read labels and be somewhat discriminating. On the other hand, I regularly go to McDonald's drive-thru to order their ice-cream cones which cost only $1.40 and leave an unpleasant aftertaste. I like them even better than Dairy Queen which costs four times as much. What the hell, I'm an addict and sometimes we just take whatever we can get our hands on when we're dying for a fix. I'm just an ice-cream slut.

Today, as I was checking out at the grocery store, I noticed the guy in the lineup behind me had a box of Haagen-Dazs ice-cream bars in his cart. I offered to take them off his hands if he didn't feel he could carry them home. When he told me his wife wouldn't approve, I was horrified to realize that he must have thought I was trying to pick him up and he was letting me know he was taken. That's how low we addicts will go to get our fix. We have no shame.

When was the last time you had a root beer, Coke or Pepsi float?

There probably isn't a 12-step program that I can take to break the cycle. Even as I've pledged to buy no more ice-cream, I find myself thinking, "but it's only August". My sick mind is reliving the satisfying crunch of those walnuts in Kawartha Dairy's special blend of maple walnut ice-cream. And as much as I love Chapman's Black Jack Cherry frozen yoghurt, I always feel sick after pigging out on it. Even with the overriding threat of a stomachache and the undeniable reality of the extra five pounds already registered on my bathroom scale, I cannot say no.

Don't even get me started on gelato. A few years ago when we were in Italy I was overjoyed to see counters with gelato of every flavour that stretched forever. The shopkeepers are still talking about that

Italy is still restocking after my visit a few years ago

weird Canadian lady who consumed so much gelato I nearly paid off their national debt.

Then, there's the issue of company coming on Labour Day weekend. It includes two grandsons (20 and 22 years old) who enjoy and would probably expect me to have ice-cream on hand. I'm thinking Rocky Road and Heavenly Hash for starters but who doesn't enjoy Blackjack Cherry? Maybe I should up my efforts to those find Spanish redskin peanuts and I should probably pick up a bottle of chocolate syrup, just in case.

Labour Day weekend is usually hot and it's also my birthday, a special occasion which absolutely calls for a sweet treat. Like I said . . . no strength of character. I can already feel my waistline growing and my arteries hardening. Did I mention it's my birthday that weekend? And you can't have a birthday without ice-cream . . . right? What's your favourite flavour? I should probably get some in just in case you pop by.

Do you use plastic drinking straws?

I'm probably not the only person who never realized until recently what a serious crime against the environment it is to use plastic drinking straws. As someone who has sipped far too many after-school cherry Cokes through thin paper straws at Long's Restaurant in the fifties and sixties, I was just happy to finally have a straw that wouldn't disintegrate before I slurped up the last drops of my chocolate milkshake.

We've now come to realize that those convenient plastic straws are killing wildlife and polluting the environment. What's a person to do? The answer is simple; invest in some inexpensive, reusable stainless-steel drinking straws. Stainless steel straws may not be practical for commercial use in restaurants or bars but I did receive a strong, heavy-duty paper straw for my Coke at a restaurant recently and it held up well. Paper is a renewable resource and recyclable, so paper straws also make sense.

Drinking straws are a part of my daily routine which means I've been guilty of tossing a lot of plastic into the garbage. I sip water through a drinking straw throughout the day. When driving, I always have an insulated container of water in the cup holder of my console. I prefer to drink through a straw so I'm not obscuring my vision by tipping a cup up in front of my face while driving. Even when I'm sipping my Timmie's steeped tea in the car I use a straw for the same reason. I do realize eating and drinking are not recommended while operating a vehicle, but water, tea or Diet Coke are my preferred fuel while on the road, particularly on long trips.

When I test-drove my first stainless steel drinking straw in my insulated cup of water, it worked great. Metal is, however, a conductor and the straw will be colder or hotter in your mouth than a plastic one, depending on the beverage you're drinking. In fact, drinking Timmie's tea through a stainless-steel straw is probably safer than risking the possible carcinogenic effects of drinking a hot beverage through plastic.

I purchased a set of eight straws 10.5 inches long to accommodate a variety of beverage container sizes; four of the straws were bent for easier use. They're slightly narrower than most plastic straws but I didn't want to get the really fat smoothie style. The package even contained two long, skinny brushes for cleaning. I ordered them on-line when I couldn't find them in the store and they arrived the next day with my Amazon Prime service. Let's all do our bit to mitigate damage to the environment.

Dinner at my door thanks to a friendly neighbour

One day few years ago, after my husband retired and after consuming several glasses of a lovely Cabernet, he offered to cook dinner twice a week. *"Now that I have time on my hands it's only fair that I help out around the house a bit more,"* he said in a weak moment of benevolence no doubt brought on by the wine. *"How about I cook dinner Tuesday and Saturday nights?"* Not being a huge fan of the kitchen arts, I was thrilled, ecstatic even. The next morning, in the light of day I thought he might a) conveniently forget his offer, or b) try to weasel out of it. He did neither and a culinary star was born, sort of.

The first week was glorious beyond my wildest imaginings. He cracked open one of my dusty, neglected *Barefoot Contessa* cookbooks and delivered a meal worthy of a fine restaurant. During preparation when I asked how he was doing, his response *"I'm just waiting for my sauce reduction"* was not only music to my ears but a phrase I don't recall having ever used personally in my entire life. We then spent a lovely hour enjoying the meal he had lovingly and carefully prepared. He was an eager and enthusiastic novice who shared with me in minute detail his tips and techniques throughout the entire meal. But I'm not complaining.

As time went on, he did not renege on his twice-weekly cooking adventures although conversations with friends were liberally peppered with *"We're available any Tuesday or Saturday if you want to go out to dinner or invite us over."* More recently I noticed however, his culinary creativity is largely determined by what appeals to him at Longo's prepared deli counter. The *Jamie Oliver 5 Ingredients* cookbook he got from Santa is growing metaphorical mold. But I'm still not complaining.

Then, this weekend my lovely neighbour Fauzia rang the doorbell bearing one of those complete meal-in-a-bag kits that are delivered with an ice pack directly to your door. Each kit contains pre-measured fresh ingredients for a complete meal you select from an on-line meal preparation company. This one was for Tuscan sausage linguine made with pork which her family doesn't eat so she kindly offered it to us to try. Coincidently, it was Saturday night, not my night to cook.

While I took a nap on the couch (something I *am* skilled at), honey took over the kitchen, banging pots and pans to assemble the dinner. The commentary about how much cookware was involved was further complicated by the tab breaking off the can of diced tomatoes requiring an assortment of tools to crack it open. Eventually the dinner was ready. It was tasty, cost effective (we'll get two meals out of it), amortizing out to about $6.00 per person per meal, although thanks to Fauzia, we got it free.

It was a worthwhile adventure but he found the preparation more labour intensive than he would have liked, especially compared with picking something ready-made from Longo's deli counter. *"Only the onion was precut!"* I was just thrilled to have a night off. And, as part of our arrangement, the cook also does the cleanup. Sort of. Tomorrow I'll rewash the kitchen floor, rewash the stove top, the counters, the pots and pans and empty the dishwasher. But as Scarlet O'Hara so eloquently stated, tomorrow's another day, and a night off is still a night off. Sort of.

How to hamper those Halloween pantry raids

You know what it's like. Every year we pick up Halloween treats from the grocery store, usually two or three weeks before the big night and for some reason the supply mysteriously evaporates before October 31st even arrives. This strange phenomenon is particularly puzzling when it's something you like. Boxes of Smarties, tiny Mars Bars and potato chips are highly vulnerable while little boxes of raisins usually remain safely stacked in the pantry.

We must be so careful about what we dispense these days. When we were kids, the best treats were the always the home-made ones like sugary maple walnut or chocolate fudge. Taffy and peanut butter cookies were freely passed out in little orange and black paper bags with witches on them. Our closest neighbours used to pack "special" bags for us "special" kids who lived next door and they were always *the best*. Now everything has to be commercially sealed and inspected for tampering before being consumed. It's amazing we survived.

Every year I'm never sure how many kids we'll get at our door but I plan and hope for plenty as I love seeing the little ones stuffed into their costumes stretched over winter parkas and toques. We live at the end of a dead-end courtyard and are very tricky to find, despite leaving all the outside lights and  illuminated pumpkins on. Last year we had only two visitors; one little boy from two doors down and another little three-foot superhero of indeterminate gender.

I'd stocked up on chips and chocolate bars, then at the last minute sent my husband out to buy red licorice just in case there was an unexpected deluge.

The bottom line, to my everlasting shame is that last year I ate **90 little bags of red licorice** during the first few days of November, all by myself. How else was I supposed to get rid of them? Consign them to landfill? Then, at lunch the other day, my friend Deb made an innocent comment which is a brilliant solution to the annual problem of preventing the inevitable evaporation of treats before the big night, and how to dispose of Halloween candy afterward.

JUST BUY WHAT YOU DON'T LIKE!

Genius! Why didn't I think of that?

One of the guys I used to work with was mortified every Halloween when he was a little boy because his dentist father handed out toothbrushes to his trick or treating friends, and their house inevitably got egged. That's one approach.

Or, I could distribute sealed bags of kale chips or packets of hand sanitizers. Even stickers might work but I'm afraid of my home being egged if I gave out something like pencils or pens. *I'd* be happy with that, but kids today are far more affluent, more discriminating and not as happy with any old thing as boomers were when we were kids. And furthermore, I've already stocked up on Smarties and little chocolate bars. Maybe I could eat the Smarties and chocolate immediately (for the sake of the children, of course) and replace this year's handouts of candy with recipe cards. Parents and their little ones could then make their own politically correct, nut-free, non-GMO'd, gluten-free treats. Nah!

Do you ever play the grocery cart shame game?

On my more virtuous days when my grocery cart is full of organic produce, fresh-pressed Green Goddess juice and two kinds of quinoa, I like to cast a critical eye on what's in the cart of the person ahead of me or behind me in the lineup. It's a bitchy and small-minded exercise in me getting all sanctimonious and judgey. When I see a cart overflowing with bags of white Wonder Bread, cases of soft drinks, frozen mac n'cheese, Doritos and heavily sugared breakfast cereals, I get all self-righteous and mentally think, *"No wonder you weigh 300 lbs."*.

Then, there are the days when I'm dropping in for a few less healthy pantry staples like ketchup (Canadian *French's*, of course), mayonnaise, Rocky Road ice-cream and a couple of bags of Ruffles, I'm more than a tad embarrassed. I avert my eyes and hurry my purchases into the bag. Should I explain to those in the lineup ahead of or behind me, that this isn't the sum total of my weekly

Shame, shame, shame. (Didn't Shirley & Company sing about that in 1975?)

shopping? I feel obliged to explain that my normal weekly groceries generally include organic produce, grass-fed cow's milk, fresh fruit, chia seeds, and extra virgin organic olive oil. I buy quality Ace bread (which I only allow myself to eat on weekends. How's that for discipline?), hormone-free, organic meat and as many fresh and non-GMO'd products as I can manage. I feel like *someone* should care. Seeking vindication.

There's another nasty habit I have that I shouldn't share, but it's just you and me here so I will. I also tend to be critical of the food choices by people who claim that eating well and/or eating healthy is expensive. I've seen ten-pound bags of carrots for $5.00. Fresh, in-season beets were only $2.99 for a ten-pound bag the other day. Tomatoes in season are cheaper and easier than trying to grow your own in a pot on your deck or balcony. Zucchinis are so abundant and cheap they're practically free. For the price of a small container of ice-cream (which I'm ashamed to say I can consume in a single session), you can get an entire bag of grapes or a bunch of bananas.

Much better, and not necessarily more expensive.

Ontario apples are ridiculously cheap when purchased by the five-pound or ten-pound bag, particularly in the fall when they're in season. I'm a true believer in *"An apple a day keeps the doctor away"*.

Our twenty-first-century taste buds are so conditioned to needing food that is overloaded with fat, sugar, and salt, that it takes some time to readjust our pallet to appreciate real food at its best. Years ago I stopped taking sugar in my tea and then started reducing it in other areas of my diet as well. It's been a journey. I've also become an enthusiastic label-reader. I'm far from perfect (having a sweet tooth) but I do try.

I'm also extremely concerned about the high percentage of us who are getting unexplainable cancer. Most of us know not just a couple of people suffering from the disease, but far too many. It's rampant and I wonder if there's something in our food chain that Big Agra and the corporate food producers should answer for and are not fully disclosing. I understand the rationale behind all the pesticides and fertilizers used to protect and grow our crops but how much of it is getting into the food we consume daily?

Sometimes, however, science and logic defy the rules. There are people who consume all the foods I look down my nose at, who smoke and drink to excess and amazingly live to a ripe old age. Then, as we've all witnessed, others who live a healthy lifestyle and are careful about everything they eat, yet they're the ones who face a health crisis. It's unfair and illogical. But that does not mean we should just throw caution to the wind and live on junk food.

I did once advise the woman behind me in the lineup to not the buy the dried pigs' ears she had picked up for her dog. I cautioned her against Asian pet food and treats, which she seemed to appreciate and removed them from her cart. (We have a friend whose dog died of kidney failure after eating dried "chicken tenders" from Asia loaded with unknown, unlabeled chemicals so I'm on high alert.) We can eat whatever we choose, but please do not feed helpless animals something that might harm them.

I'll probably never stop mentally critiquing your purchases in the lineup at the grocery store but in order to avoid public violence, I should probably keep my opinions to myself. But, I'm warning you, I'll be watching your shopping cart. Don't make me say something! Unless, of course, there's some Blackjack Cherry ice-cream or Ruffles in my cart, in which case I'll just keep my big mouth shut. Then, it's shame on me.

A little whine about about my little wine problem. The good, the bad and the what happened?

This aging baby boomer has a confession. *I just can't drink like I used to.* Some of us can't. Has it happened to you? Liquor never was my personal cup of tea. I dislike the taste of rye whiskey; I hate gin; scotch burns too much going down, and because you can't taste it, I think vodka is just a waste of money, unless you're drinking it solely for the buzz. But it's the buzz that I've come to be concerned about. In fact, for me, the buzz now feels more like the burrr!

Those were the days, my friend.

Where I once became all swoony and romantic after a couple of glasses of Pinot Grigio, I can barely get through a single glass now without getting an instant mild hangover. Not to mention, there's a distinct possibility that I could fall asleep right before your eyes.

Each of us has our own personal history of drinking. For me, it started in the sixties with the boomer's ubiquitous bubbly of choice, Mateus, a sweet rosé. Those empty, wide-bellied bottles lent themselves beautifully to what we young boomers considered to be sophisticated candle holders in our not-so-sophisticated singles' digs. Friends could always be counted on to bring a bottle to a party; it was cheap and everyone liked it because it was one step up from drinking pop. Our nights in the pub were always accompanied by a table full of draft beer, again because it was cheap and we calculated we were getting more bang for our buck. I certainly swilled my share of whatever was on tap even though I never was a huge fan of beer, except on a really hot day.

Over the years, my tastes have progressed, although I can't actually say they've improved. In my attempts to be one of the cool urbanites, I went through a DuBonnet phase, a Blue Nun phase and a particularly nasty Black Tower phase back in the seventies, the details of which I won't go into. Then, about twenty years ago, I discovered Pinot Grigio and we had a love match. The colder the better. In fact, I prefer it with ice because as a friend pointed out, as the ice melts, it lasts longer. I did learn the hard way, though, never to drink at a business lunch. If I did, the afternoon was a complete write-off. I'd feel discombobulated and in serious need of a nap. Because I worked in the construction industry, boozy lunches weren't uncommon (things were different in the seventies and eighties. Remember Mad Men?) and the men I lunched with didn't seem to be encumbered with my problem of after-effects.

When my husband and I first got together (he's the one who introduced me to Pinot Grigio), we'd enjoy long dinners with lengthy conversations often lasting three or four hours, over multiple bottles of wine and good food. I'm sure you've noticed how multiple glasses of wine enhances conversation! I enjoyed the taste; I enjoyed the buzz and I could handle it without getting too sloppy or stupid. But, all good things must come to an end. I can't pinpoint exactly when the transformation began, but I started to notice I felt terrible, even ill after a few glasses of my favourite PG. Sadly, my ration is now down to about one glass a week, on a Saturday night with a nice meal. But the effects begin before I am even half-way through my glass.

My ability to always be able to handle my alcohol intake has definite upsides. I've never had to worry about whether I drink too much. My liver is probably as good as new and I never have to apologize the next day for bad behaviour, well, at least not as the result of drinking. I could never be an alcoholic although addiction issues are a possibility considering my taste for and lack of resistance to President's Choice (Made in France) chocolate almond bars and Kawartha Dairy's Rocky Road ice-cream. We all have our Achilles' heel.

Getting drunk or getting high has never been something that appeals to me. I prefer to be mostly in control of my faculties at all times but I do love my cold white wine, particularly the first cold, crisp couple of sips. Umm good. But as time goes on, I am being robbed of the pleasure of enjoying anything more than a 6-oz. glass of Santa Margherita and that restriction just pisses me off.

I've tried switching to red wine but that's not where my tastes lie. I do enjoy a few silky sips of Tignanello, an amazing Brunello, but at around $100.00 a bottle, that's never going to occupy a spot on *our* wine rack. No wonder it's (supposedly) Meghan Markle, Duchess of Sussex's favourite. At that price, you need to be a Duchess to afford it, and I will never be in a financial position to find out if I'm able to handle more than a glass. I was first introduced to it when we toured the Antinori Winery in Tuscany, Italy a few years ago. Talk about spoiling you by upselling. As for wine alternatives, I'm reserving the gummy bear option for when my joints (!!) become too painful to manage. Hopefully, not until I'm in 'the home'.

In the meantime, like sailors of old who were issued a tot of rum a day, I'm rationed one small glass of white wine a week. Ugh! Does anyone else have a problem with their wine consumption? Are we doomed to a life of abstinence?

Chapter 7

Current Events

We're fighting our own personal trade war

A favourite pastime of old retired fellers like my husband and his buddies is to spend a day visiting car lots. These 'research' excursions are enormous fun for them especially in Florida where car dealers have thousands of pre-owned, like-new luxury cars with low mileage. These vehicles have never seen winter and are being sold for unbelievably low prices.

Florida is full of geriatrics whose adult kids don't want the big ol' Cadillac when their folks can no longer drive (or worse) so they end up jockeying for attention on used car lots. The guys' excursion usually includes a normally forbidden feast of chocolate-chip pancakes, bacon and sausages at IHOP, all part of an idyllic outing for a bunch of car junkies. Much as they would love to slide into a shiny new Lincoln, BMW or Jaguar SUV, it's more likely we'll stick with our several-years-old Ford Edge or Escape.

There are amazing deals in the United States but bringing that car back to Canada is a nightmare. People with Canadian passports cannot drive a car with American plates into Canada. We know that from experience because we once unknowingly tried it and had to leave the car in New York State until we got the paperwork sorted out. It was prohibitively expensive, and I would never recommend it. Among the expenses was making physical modifications to the car for such things as bumpers to meet Canadian safety standards, which was more trouble than it was worth. And now that we're engaged in a trade war with the United States, there are obvious advantages to buying Canadian-made vehicles.

Florida is a strong Republican state where millions of Canadians winter and vacation every year. We speak the language. We can drink the water without requiring hospitalization (another issue for another time). We understand the currency. We love the weather. Many visiting Canadians often buy lovely pre-owned American automobiles to leave in Florida garages while they return north for the summer. Hell, sometimes we even buy the shoes if they're a deal and not available in Canadaland, but don't tell Donald Trump. We love to escape our crappy winters and our dollars keep the Florida economy afloat. All in all it's a pretty agreeable situation for both sides.

As a result of those tire-kicking excursions with his buddies, my honey has been getting regular follow-up emails from a car salesman at a Lincoln dealership he chatted up last winter in Florida. When another email landed in his in-box this week, we were able to make a political statement that is bound to resonate across all fifty states.

Buy Canadian-made and save yourself a lot of trouble, not to mention saving Canadian jobs.

My guy politely informed the salesman that *the American 25% tariff puts Lincoln MLKs in Florida financially out of reach. No sale.* It's actually cheaper in Canada. Ouch! That is bound to be a major blow to the U.S. economy. We'll show them what their crazy tariffs really mean.

Taking this a step further, many Canadians may find it difficult to visit the United States at all. With Donald Trump treating us as trade enemies and citizens of questionable character, does the United States even deserve to benefit from our tourist dollars. Imagine Florida if the 3.5 million Canadians who spend billions each year in the sunshine state decided to stay home and spend our billions here. The

Republication state of Florida would collapse. Our parents were right. Ignore the bully and play nice. This too shall pass, we hope.

Here's how to win an election

The promises that accompany every election campaign pile up like the proverbial you-know-what. The Liberals promise universal childcare and frighteningly increasing debt/deficit. They're tried desperately to cover up the great smoldering pile of doo-doo they've created over the last few years. NDP'ers promise free drugs and better healthcare (does that mean free facelifts?) for everyone. The Conservatives say they are going to give us the infrastructure of our dreams, but with absolutely no fiscal accountability. Just like Trump promised a wall between the United States and Mexico and to reopen the mines in West Virginia, or the Labour Party in U.K. promised Brexit, the political rhetoric and hollow promises fly free and wild.

One thing is guaranteed about election promises. They're all lies. Bait to lure in gullible voters. Why do politicians keep doing it to us? Worse still, why do we keep falling for it? We're not stupid. Right-wing Americans fell for it big-time, to their everlasting peril. Britons are now questioning their choices. Canadians are  left to cope with the unfortunate shortcomings of Trudeau's hollow election promises and shocking debt/deficits and Ontarians are wondering how in hell we're going to make a decision among three disastrous parties running for election, four if we factor in the impotent Green Party. It baffles me how political parties can be so phenomenally inept at representing the best interests of the people.

The only blessing in this cesspool is that our election campaigns have a time limit of a few weeks, unlike in the United States where the agony never ends. We should be thankful we live in a democracy where we *have* free elections, but the politicians treat voters like idiots and corporate lobbying makes a joke of the laws they enact.

Let's be clear on one thing: politicians are in it for their own personal interests *not* in service to the people. After a mere six years sitting part-time on those comfy seats in parliament, members of parliament get full, pork-barreled pensions for life. Who in real life gets benefits like that? Don't raise your kids to be doctors; being an MP or MPP is the best gig going. And don't even get me started on The Senate.

During an election campaign, personal insults and hollow promises fly like confetti at a wedding. Whoever makes the most outrageous promises in sucking up to voters will probably win. And don't forget, all that cash they keep promising to buy our favour with is *'our'* hard-earned money that we pay through taxes. Government money is not fairy dust; it's debt, mine and yours.

Keeping election promises will inevitably be pushed aside by the winning party with the qualifier *"things were worse than we were led to believe"* or *"the situation has changed so we've had to adjust our position"*. The rhetoric is so predictable. As a concerned citizen I'm frustrated and angry. I always vote because, tempting as it is, a protest vote is useless. I'll make up my mind about which of the incompetents I'll go with but as a proud Canadian and a conscientious citizen I'm not a happy voter. But who cares? After all, we voters just pay the bills!

Should privileged university students be punished for the sins of their parents?

As if there's not already enough bad news in the daily paper to get my blood boiling, the latest scandal about wealthy parents paying bribes to get their offspring into prestige American universities just sent my blood pressure off the Richter scale. Hollywood celebrities Lori Loughlin and Felicity Huffman are just two of dozens of people indicted for paying vast sums for fake credentials to ensure that their under-achieving, entitled millennial lieblings could attend upper-crust universities like Yale, University of Southern California and Georgetown University.

Huffman's husband, actor William Macy recently posted on public media that the college application process was so stressful for their daughter that he felt a year off for her to recuperate would be appropriate!! I imagine it *is* stressful having your parents write those enormous checks and pull multiple strings not available to hard-working not-rich kids who were turned away because they didn't have wealthy parents. And, there are some Canadian parents involved in this scam too. Although so far it seems to involve American universities, perhaps the Canadian system could use some scrutiny as well.

I'm sure you're as appalled as I am that this has gone on for as long as it has without someone blowing the whistle sooner. Rich kids buying term papers and having others sit in for exams is not new. I'm surprised it's been allowed to exist as long as it has. As a baby boomer growing up in the fifties and sixties, most of us did not come from wealth or privilege. A university education

How many students earned their degrees honestly, and how many had parents who bought them?

was not as de rigueur back then as it is now, in part because it was beyond the financial means of most of our generation's parents. I have friends who made up for this by earning degrees over a period of several years, at their own expense, taking night courses and correspondence courses while working full-time jobs and raising families. Others worked after-school and summer jobs and took student loans to finance a hard-earned education. It wasn't easy and should not be easy to be fully appreciated.

Now the real work begins for some students – paying off the debt? Was it worth it?

171

Part of the appeal of attending a prestige university is the opportunities it presents for graduates. Having a degree from Yale or Georgetown on a résumé looks infinitely more attractive to future employers than a local state-funded college degree. But, there's also an ongoing discussion about whether the quality of the education is actually proportional to the money it costs to attend these high-priced institutions. Taking this premise even further and based on recent events, how can employers actually be sure applicants genuinely *earned* that expensive degree through their individual merits rather than pampering parents writing fat cheques.

The fact that these privileged, entitled students have displaced other potential and genuinely deserving hard-working students from a more challenged socio-economic background whose parents couldn't afford and would probably not even consider bribes absolutely galls me. And now the universities are questioning whether the students who were admitted through these false credentials should be entitled to stay and complete their degrees. I say *absolutely not!* They were admitted through fraudulent methods and it is high time they learned that life isn't easy and earned benefits are infinitely more meaningful than hand-outs. They also need to see that what their parents did was horribly wrong, and they should not be entitled to receive an education that they did not honestly work for and earn themselves.

But we don't need to worry about the offspring of the wealthy. They will always have adoring, indulgent parents standing in the background to smooth the way, grease some palms and generally make life easier for them. That's just a sad and unfair fact of life. These young people shouldn't be allowed to stand in the way of deserving students who worked hard at school and achieved on their *own* merits not their parents' fat back accounts and privileged connections. I'm glad no one I know is rich enough to participate in a scam like that; otherwise I'd have to unfriend them. Absolutely.

Why Canada should annex the United States

When Donald Trump expressed interest in buying Greenland, it was suggested that Denmark buy the United States in order to finally provide Americans with decent universal health care and an improved education system. Touché. That got me thinking about how much *more* practical it would be for Canada to take over the United States.

- We're geographically united and they wouldn't have to start a war with us over access to our Arctic shipping routes and resources. Being the benevolent beings that Canadians are, they would then be one of us and free to share in our bounty without bullying.

- Americans would benefit from learning that democratic socialism is not a bad word. It means we take care of each other by spreading the cost of social services equally among the population. It is overall more economically viable and just the right thing to do.

- Unlike Americans, most Canadians do not worship, need or possess guns. We acknowledge that the bad guys are still a problem but we're working on that and we recognize that possessing guns to protect our families is an unnecessary and counter-productive approach to solving the problem.

- If Americans became Canadian, security at airports would be vastly different. We do not carry guns. See above.

- They would benefit from having a Tim Horton's on every corner. It's a place to meet and understand new people while waiting in the endless lineups. And some of us even "pay it forward" by buying coffee for the person behind us. We're nice like that.

- While Canada is not free of racism, we have embraced multi-culturalism as a benefit to be enjoyed by every race welcomed to our country. Having a country populated by so many different cultures and ethnicities has enriched our society immeasurably.

- That Electoral College thingie absolutely must go. Where is the equality in having a state with 40 million people represented by the same number of senators as a state with one million people? They would be better off with our parliamentary system and more than two parties.

- No walls required. I remember the time when we could enter the United States from Canada without a passport. Our word that we are Canadian and live in Toronto was good enough. The border guards used to ask us to recite the phone number for Pizza Pizza (967-11-11) to confirm our national identity.

And the list goes on. There are so many reasons why Americans would be better off being Canadian. Contrary to what Americans are constantly told, they are *not* living in the best country in the world. Many, many surveys, polls and studies have determined that **Canada** is currently the best country in the world to live in, but most Americans aren't exposed to international news on their regular networks so how would they know that. Last year it was Denmark with the United States consistently much further down the list.

That's not to say we don't love our American cousins and friends. We do, very much. If you've ever doubted this, go see **COME FROM AWAY** at the theatre (which we just did) and you'll be forever reassured. It's the true story of 7,000 airline passengers being forced to land in Gander, Newfoundland in the wake of 911, doubling their population in a few hours. In fact, take your President to

The theatre production of COME FROM AWAY is a proud example of the Canadian way of life.

show him that generosity and kindness are far more effective in building relationships than tariffs. Although it might be tempting to annex the United States and show them the light, I think we'll just remain very modestly Canadian and keep our heads down, our eyes on the road and our sticks on the ice. It's our wonderful little secret . . . and it's not our nature to brag.

Chapter 8

In the year 2020

Pandemic reveals the secret side of first-world problems

Bald guys are laughing their asses off. Who cares that barbers, hairdressers and nail salons are closed until further notice? Not someone who does their hair with a razor every morning in the shower. However, there's a ginormous portion of our population that depends on the regular services of hairdressers  and nail technicians to keep us presentable enough to be seen in public. Baby boomer women have come to depend on these services as much as our mothers' generation counted on being on good terms with the local butcher, the milkman or the payday once-a-week wash and set at the hairdressers.

If you see someone who looks like Keith Richards self-isolating on my front porch, don't be alarmed. It's only me. Before the sky started to fall, I kept postponing my bi-monthly trip to the hairdressers. Then, I came down with a bad cold and had to cancel an appointment booked two weeks in advance. Now I'm screwed. I'm a month past my best-before date for a trim and my highlights haven't been touched up since November so my roots are nearly three inches long.

By comparison, I'm lucky. For some strange reason, I have little to no gray hair so I can live with my boring natural colour without looking like a complete freak. I guess my lack of grey hair is minor compensation for the fact I'm going bald. For those of us who need 4-6-week root touchups, though, you have my deepest sympathy. Not only can we not get to our hairdresser, but so many supply stores are closing, *Miss Clairol* or *Nice n'Easy* could be the next in-demand product harder to source than toilet paper and hand sanitizer.

Those of us with Maye Musk or Helen Mirren-type aspirations of going grey naturally, now's the time. We could be in for a terrible shock. Or not. Grey hair is becoming increasingly more fashionable and before long, an entire generation of boomer broads will be sporting the look, whether we like it or not.

How hard can it be to do it yourself?

Then, there's the issue of our nails. Once again, I'm lucky. I don't have acrylic or gel nails requiring regular professional fillers and servicing. I can't grow a decent head of hair, but my fingernails are turbo-charged and grow at an alarming rate. Without regular clipping and filing, I'd resemble Howard Hughes in a couple of weeks. And, I'm quite capable of doing my own manicures from the vast stash of products I already have in my bathroom. We can always take care of our own pedicures. And if you're unable to reach your toenails for clipping, isn't that what grandchildren are for? We're going to be witnessing some pretty weird finger appendages very soon which should not be confused with fungus or neurofibromatosis (Elephant Man's disease). Be aware.

Fortunately, dating is strongly discouraged these days which is a good thing because trips to the esthetician for personal and *extremely* personal waxing are now verboten. Eyebrows, nose and chin hairs can be managed at home in the privacy of our own bathrooms with the help of 10X magnifying mirrors and tweezers. We're in for all kinds of horrific surprises though on the follicular front. And make sure you take your heart and blood pressure meds before sneaking a peek at that 10X mirror. Lordy, lordy.

Many of us have also lost the services of our dog groomers. Once again, I'm lucky. With a three-and-a-half-pound Yorkie, I can dunk her in the kitchen sink and pretty much handle the rest myself with a pair of scissors. I am concerned about doggie toenails, however, and hope this Armageddon ends before she's tripping over her tiny feet.

We're going to discover all kinds of everyday services that we previously took for granted are no longer available. When this is all over, we owe it to our service providers to be better tippers. Or, perhaps we'll become more resourceful and start doing things for ourselves.

Our parents' generation lived through The Great Depression and World War II making sacrifices and making do with a lot less than we're coping with today. It could be a valuable lesson for humanity to re-evaluate and re-engineer our lives to be smarter, kinder and more sensitive to our environment. Mother nature is definitely trying to get our attention and we'd be wise to listen and learn.

These shoes were made for . . . social distancing? I don't think so.

Another first-world problem has emerged during the current health crisis. I know it's frivolous but at times like this, we have to lighten up or we'll go crazy. This past winter I bought some new shoes. In truth, I bought more than one pair of new shoes (the actual number will remain our secret in case my husband reads this). Is

there anything in the world that makes a woman feel more glorious than a new pair of shoes? And spring is the perfect time to crack open the box and wear them outside. But, because of COVID-19 and the restrictions of physical isolation, I can't go anywhere. We are confined to quarters wearing our slippers.

Who remembers when we were little girls in the fifties, the first time each spring when we trotted out in our street shoes, unencumbered by clunky winter boots and snow pants? We felt light as a feather and

Shopping for new shoes in the fifties was a rare treat.

177

literally skipped down the street with our leather soles clicking on the finally dry pavement.

Easter Sunday was often the big reveal when we would finally put on our shiny Mary-Janes with fresh white socks, our spring coat, and no mitts. Back then, shoe stores still smelled like leather and it was such a treat when my mother took me to the Bata store in our small town to buy a new pair of "good shoes" for Easter Sunday.

Spring 2020 is finally here and my shiny new shoes have nowhere to go. I suppose I could wear them around the house but I've discovered it's too much trouble to take them off and put them back on every time I lie down on the couch or recline in my LaZgirl to read a book. So, they languish in the front hall closet. My busy schedule of reading, snoozing and making tea precludes the requirement for shoes. It is highly possible they could even be out of style before I get to wear them in public.

By the time boomer gals reach the age we're at now, we've pretty much nailed down the brands of shoes we prefer and know our size in each brand. That makes it easy to shoe-shop online and I've had great success doing this. There is definitely an upside to being stuck in front of my computer screen. Stilettos and heels are distant memories replaced by industrial-strength arch supports and soft soles. I trawl *ShopStyle* and *Amazon* for sales and I've scored amazing deals on my faves.

For years now, I've been a devoted fan of *FitFlops*, the *brand* (not flipflops the style). Designed by a British foot doctor, they have thick rubber soles and

Mama has new shoes and nowhere to go.

decent arch supports. I have more pairs of their sandals than I care to admit and have recently purchased a few pairs of their slip-on loafers.

Many boomer gals prefer Birkies but I find they're not soft enough and they're a bit too flat. This winter, I discovered *Vionic* shoes that have amazing arch supports and certain styles of *Ecco* that also have substantial arch supports. I have high arches, one of which is collapsing, and twice I've been downed by plantar fasciitis for extended periods of time, so support is essential.

Prior to the current crisis, I'd been test-driving my new Vionics and Ecco shoes to see which ones would earn the privilege of accompanying me on the writers' retreat in Paris I'd booked in June 2020. I had plenty of walking planned during that trip. Well, it looks like the trip is off, or at least postponed for who-knows-how-long. I'm sure the shoes are almost as disappointed as I am and we can only hope they will see the light of day and tread the streets of Paris or at least a local mall before they go out of style.

Self-isolation and quarantine reveal my true colours

There's a proliferation of news articles and online information these days about how to fill our days while confined to quarters with the ones we love. Suggested activities include yoga and exercise videos, online singalongs and games, Words With Friends, Scrabble, Tik Tok videos, closet purging, basement cleaning, homeschooling tips, art classes, guided meditation, the list is endless. No one has any excuse for not being active and productive during these trying times. So, please tell me why I am not active and definitely not productive?

The answer is simple. I am obviously extremely lazy. My friend Terry is baking up a storm. She even posted a picture of yummy, fresh egg bread she'd made from scratch and she's mastered difficult sourdough. Maryse is working her way through *"The Artist's Way"*, an excellent workbook by Julia Cameron designed to inspire and develop our creativity. I read it a few years ago and while it's an amazing book, I lasted two days on her program. Other friends are working their way through their cheap Canadian wine collection, while my friend Perry is creating amazing art.

How I'm coping and turning idle time into productive time
We're now several months into quarantine and here's what I've accomplished so far:

- I suggested to my honey that he start getting rid of crap in our basement. He informed me his stuff isn't crap and perhaps I should start work on my own larger and more plentiful assortment of crap. We've reached an impasse.
- I made an enormous chicken pot pie, enough to feed us both for six (6) evening meals, eliminating the need to cook supper for six nights. That cleared a lot of time to do . . . nothing.
- I took the dog for an outside walk *once* in order to go to the mailbox. We were back ten minutes later. She's still sulking and refusing to cuddle.
- I had plans to groom the dog but she's not speaking to me. See item above.
- A cheque arrived in the mail a week ago and I put it on my *To-Do* list to use my phone app (that I recently learned how to use) to photograph it and deposit it in the bank before it's stale-dated. Still on my *To-Do* list.

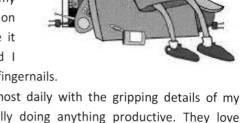

- I've finished reading several books. Stay tuned for book reviews to follow, as soon as I get them written.
- Yesterday I removed my old chipped nail polish and trimmed and filed my fingernails. Why bother putting on new polish when no one will see it except me and my husband and I don't think he even realizes I have fingernails.
- I've been emailing my friends almost daily with the gripping details of my isolation in order to avoid actually doing anything productive. They love hearing from me and marvel at my lifestyle.
- This morning I noticed a couple of new chin hairs so I took care of them. A woman's work is never done.
- I made a mental note to spare some time to read the backlog of helpful, instructional blogs I follow about how to be a better blogger. Must get at that. Add to *To-Do* list.
- Each morning I hop on the scales and lament the rising number. Must do something about that too.

- Lest we starve to death, I visited the PC Express, Instacart, and Grocery Gateway websites to investigate ordering groceries online. Home delivery will not be available until sometime in 2023 in our area and even pickup has a closed waiting list, so I abandoned that idea. Must email my friends to try and keep on their good side so they'll fetch food for us. They'll be thrilled to hear from me.
- I have taken advantage of the reduced rates at Ontario Hydro (or whatever they call themselves these days) to do laundry during the day instead of restricting myself to those middle-of-the-night off-peak hours. Damn proud of myself. Must put that basket of ironing on my *To-Do* list but in view of the fact I hardly ever get dressed up and go anywhere, why bother.
- I once read that getting plenty of sleep is a guaranteed remedy for improving aging skin and losing weight, so I've conscientiously devoted more than the average amount of time during the day to preventing wrinkles and keeping fit. Good girl. You probably won't recognize me when this pandemic ends; I'll be gorgeous.
- I've been very diligent about pointing things out to my husband that need to be done around the house. He has accomplished quite a few little jobs that otherwise would have been overlooked. I am confident he's very grateful for my gentle reminders and I'm feeling quite chuffed about his productivity.

I expect you're also struggling with keeping as busy as I am during this time of self-isolation. I'm expanding my mind and body by spending great gobs of time watching movies and television shows that I would never have considered under normal circumstances. That helps me sleep (see above item about good skin and weight loss), which is always a good thing.

I wonder what this tired, old world is going to look like when we resume our normal, pre-COVID-19 lives if we are fortunate enough to survive. Personally, I look forward to resuming my weekly mall haunts and sushi in the food court, going to Five Guys for an order of fresh chips with a pound of salt and a splash of vinegar, accompanied by a bottomless serving of fountain Diet Coke. I might even return to going to the movies unless I figure out in the meantime how to maximize the use of my Amazon FireStick. Another item for my *To-Do* list.

There is definitely an upside to the pandemic

The current isolation has afforded me time for serious introspection and soul-searching. Despite my guilt-inducing lapses in motivation, I've discovered I am actually very good at certain things.

- I am a champion creator of *To-Do* lists. That's probably because I'm a Virgo, the perfectionist and being organized is one of our hallmarks.
- Stress is no longer part of my vocabulary. My stress-free state is obviously a natural biproduct of my superior time management skills.
- Based on the numerous little household chores that have been completed by my honey in the last couple of weeks, I obviously possess strong executive and leadership skills.
- As an avid observer of the human condition and current television programs, it seems obvious to me that cable and network executives should consult me first before airing certain programs. At the risk of sounding a bit Trump-ish, I have genius-like abilities to assess good and bad TV programs and movies. My friends absolutely rely on my recommendations.
- On the subject of taste, I can think of several television programs that could definitely benefit from my input on their fashion choices. Just sayin'.
- I'm a procrastinator of Olympian proportions. If you're feeling overwhelmed, run your *To-Do* list by me and I'll get your life in order *tout suite*.
- I finally learned how to use the *UberEats* app. My honey and I were craving a Harvey's burger the other day at lunch and when I called Harvey's they told me they do not take orders directly. I would have to call *UberEats* or *Skip The Dishes*. Fortunately, our son-in-law installed the app over the winter and it was just sitting there waiting to be tried out. It only took the combined efforts

of the two of us slightly more than two hours to figure out how to use the app and we placed our order. Next week, after we've recovered from the mental strain of learning the new app, we're going to try ordering Chinese food.

You too can learn so much about yourself

To my credit, I learned all these things about myself, by myself, without resorting to online meditation videos or watching tiresome *Be The Best You Can Be* podcasts. These insights just flowed naturally from personal introspection gathered in a horizontal position during my isolation. There are endless benefits to having a lot of time on your hands. You can do it too if you adopt my daily routine of reading, napping, neglecting chores, avoiding cooking, and especially, avoiding watching CNN.

These are strange times indeed. There are just so many everyday routines and rituals we've had to abandon in order to stay alive and keep those around us alive. It doesn't hurt to remember how our parents and grandparents experienced far worse deprivation during the war. We still have heat and electricity, the internet, television, Netflix, an abundance of food, and our homes and communities are not being bombed.

The environment is also seeing the benefits of fewer cars on the road and reduced air travel resulting in less air pollution and more opportunities for nature to thrive. I may be lazy, but I'm also definitely and profoundly grateful. This pandemic too shall pass and then I can go back to being lazy in a normal world. Have you been as productive as I am?

There's a glint of silver lining behind that COVID-19 thundercloud

The COVID-19 (coronavirus) pandemic is without a doubt a grave and horrifying situation. We've been watching the news and reading the papers, talking to friends and family about what to do and generally pulling together while keeping our distance. We keep hearing *"We don't know"* from the experts while we muddle through washing our hands fifty times a day while singing *Happy Birthday To Me* and avoiding crowds. Worrying about it stresses our immune systems which further increases our risk. What's a person to do?

I've kept myself somewhat isolated in the interests of personal safety and I must confess I've rather enjoyed my alone time. My bliss will no doubt not last forever, but it has served to remind me that there's an upside to every downside. Yin and yang. The Merriam-Webster dictionary defines it as *being or comprising opposite and especially complementary elements.* There *is* an off-setting counterbalance and now's the time to investigate the possibilities.

At times like this, the world has a way of presenting new perspectives and ultimately providing learning opportunities on how we live our lives. Look at how the simple *Keep Calm and Carry On* served the people of Britain during World War II. We've created a bit of a mess in this old world and perhaps this crisis will give us the time and means we need to reassess and redesign our lifestyles.

As seniors (baby boomers), my husband and I are in the high-risk category. Therefore, I feel it's particularly important to be sensible without panicking. We're taking it one day at a time but our current approach is to lie low and take advantage of the restrictions on our lifestyle. I'm not thrilled that I might not be able to attend the writers' retreat I was soooo looking forward to in Paris in June of this year. Perhaps it will be rescheduled and postponed to a date when travel is safer. C'est la vie!

From the glass-half-full perspective, there are many ways, however, of approaching this situation that could have a positive outcome and improve our lives:

- My decision to avoid shopping malls will have a markedly positive effect on my credit card balance and clothing inventory, despite the obvious hit to the economy resulting from my absence.

- I am currently on the waiting list for eleven E-books at the library with varying wait-times. That should take me well into fall and my mind will be so enriched by then no one will be able to stand being around me. I'll be an expert on everything.

- My pantry is well-stocked thanks to the suggestions of all those daytime women's television shows I've PVR'd over the years. I have many cans of diced tomatoes, boxes of pasta, cartons of chicken broth, lots of frozen vegetables, enough frozen meat that I won't be protein-starved, and enough boxes of Red Rose tea to take me into the next millennium. I'd already made a run to Costco before this virus let loose so I have plenty of soap, tissues, paper towels, toilet paper, and fish oil. I'm prepared for a nuclear disaster.

- Remember how lost we were the last time our power/electricity went out at night? And that was only for an hour or two. I was OK with my books on a backlit iPad but my husband was totally bereft without television and sports channels. I'll be fine during this crisis but I may have to get a new husband. Or I could teach him to expand his cooking skills. That would improve my life enormously.

- Thankfully, we still have electricity. Until Putin messes with our grid, we can still watch television, listen to the radio, do laundry, enjoy our music, torment Alexa, and generally live relatively normal lives.

- We are going to be spending a lot more quality time with our loved ones for a while. Young people, in particular, might take advantage of the opportunity to learn the forgotten art of in-person conversation. Parents could reconnect with their offspring. Husbands and wives could reconnect with each other.

- **We're being forced to slow down and I'm convinced this can only be a good thing**. Let's use this timeout to sit on our porch or patio and simply watch the world go by. It's a scientific fact that new ideas, creativity, and inspiration come from idle minds wandering. We've been driving in the fast lane too long and we're killing ourselves. This may be the most important benefit of all.

So, enjoy your time off. We're in it together. I'm already feeling lighter about reading the day away without guilt. My husband's experimenting in the kitchen, and cleaning issues aside, that's a good thing. Catch up on sleep; Skype the grandkids; try new recipes; play board and card games; exercise or do yoga;

cuddle with your sweetie; purge your closets and basement; dig out those art supplies and put them to use. This may be a once-in-a-lifetime opportunity to do some of the things we claim we never have time for.

Imagine the new ideas, music, art, and literature that could blossom from this time of self-contemplation. Maybe we'll get lucky and a cure for cancer will finally emerge from all the scientific research and experimentation that's taking place now.

Whether we're already self-isolating or social distancing, let's consider the advantages of our enforced downtime. There are positive ways of coping with the impact of this pandemic. The world will go on and with patience and cooperation, we will emerge safely on the other side. We'll learn from this experience and hopefully grow on a personal level as well. We need to be patient, cautious and sensible. We're all in this together and we'll come out stronger for the experience. Even though it's tempting to run around in a panic because the sky is falling, slow down and enjoy your time-out. And be thankful for the amazing people in the health-care sector who are taking care of us.

We have no idea how long the current situation will prevail but when it is finally over, hairdressers, nail salons and shopping malls will be stampeded. Boomers with sad, DIY haircuts and long grey roots will storm the Bastille wearing bold animal print shoes, bright pinks, and citrus greens, sporting every accessory we own. We'll be dancing in the streets, just like they did on VE Day in 1945 but in gorgeous new shoes. It's important to have something to look forward to. Right?

I miss murders, robberies and car accidents

In the old B.C. world (before COVID-19), I avoided television news and was somewhat discriminating about what I read in the daily newspaper. You can only take so much negative news about crime, inept politicians, consumer scams, opioid death statistics, and rising taxes before you're reaching for the nearest kitchen knife to slit your wrists. It's all too depressing. Then, the sky fell—for real. Tragic as the world situation is, it is impossible to watch television or read a newspaper on a continuous drip of gloom and dread and still hoist your aging boomer backside out of bed in the morning. So, let's try and lighten things up a bit.

Haven't you wondered lately:

- Where are Prince Harry and Meghan living this week? Kelowna? Moose Jaw? Jane and Finch?
- Is Jennifer Anniston is still trying to have a baby with newly single baby-dad Brad?
- What's the price of gas—not that we can go anywhere?
- Does drinking kale juice cause cancer?
- Will my RRSPs last as long as I will?
- What on earth is going on in the world of bad fashion? Now that sweats and gray roots are back in style, are there some "Don'ts" I am missing and should know about?

There are just so many important issues that have been upstaged by COVID-19. The newspapers are wall-to-wall filled with nothing but rising numbers of fatalities, political mishandling, tragedy, and despair. Television news is similarly focused on that one topic. Other things must surely be happening in the world, but we will have to wait a few months to find out.

So, I thought you could use a bit of levity during the current Armageddon. I came across one of my old blog postings the other day from a couple of years ago when we could still go to the mall, which I hope puts a smile on your isolated, makeup-free face.

I've been conducting a few COVID-19 scientific domestic experiments of my own

The world's greatest scientists aren't the only ones conducting experiments related to the current pandemic. Having been housebound for several months now with the man I love (surprisingly, I still do!) and my little dog (whom, surprisingly, I have not yet eaten), I've been carrying out a few highly scientific experiments of my own.

While my friend Terry has discovered it takes two to three days and extensive knowledge of physics and chemistry to bake a single loaf of sourdough bread, my friend Margaret concluded you could artificially inseminate and deliver a baby in less time than that. So, Margaret and I will continue to buy our bread at the store, whenever flour once again becomes available here in Canada. Someone should investigate how the country with the world's largest wheatfields has run out of flour, my friend Terry's baking blitz notwithstanding?

With plenty of time for navel-gazing and while still contemplating the secret to cold fusion, I've been researching a number of other issues all by my uneducated, unscientific self during our incarceration:

I'm not sure even Einstein had the skill level required to accomplish sourdough from scratch.

1. Does leg hair have a finite growth period or if I leave it unattended for a long enough period of time, will I be so hirsute that I no longer require pants when I finally go out in public?
2. What is the total number of days or months required for my pink pedicure to completely grow out and disappear on its own, assuming I clip the ends from time to time?
3. Will my skin finally clear up and wrinkles disappear now that I'm no longer putting anything on it to irritate, cleanse, moisturize, tone or manipulate it in any way other than rinse with water during my morning shower?
4. Will my hair grow thicker and healthier if I never wash it?
5. Are my strange moods in any way related to the utter lack of fresh air and sunshine while confined indoors?
6. How long will it take before my car resembles the one owned by Little Edie on the front lawn at Grey Gardens? Should I maintain it or let it go au natural and self-destruct like the Titanic?
7. Exactly how long can I expect to live without renewing the prescription for my mood meds?

8. Will my friends still recognize me if and when we finally meet in the distant future with my long hair and an extra eighty-five pounds around my middle? Will they still love me? Will I still recognize them? Will we live that long?
9. What is the average drying-out time frame required to break a TV addiction?
10. Do people still hug? Ever? Where?
11. How many hours can I sleep in a 24-hour period before I am officially and legally declared dead?
12. What is sex?
13. Is there still a Dairy Queen (in case this ever ends)?
14. How many days can a human being endure indoors without sunlight, while getting even longer in the tooth, and sprouting excessive facial and body hair before qualifying as a werewolf?
15. If you ignore dust and household mess long enough will it eventually disappear from your field of vision? (I am discovering the answer is joyfully, *yes!*).
16. Are daily showers absolutely necessary when never actually meeting fellow human beings in person?

Oh, the list could go on. There are just too many computations and complications to contemplate. Some of these questions are self-solving while others are still being field-tested. I've learned a lot, however, during my confinement. For example, and this is statistically proven, the size of my Visa bill is directly proportional to the number of trips to the mall I make, or in the current world, do not make.

It is also actually possible to live on my fixed income if I only spend money on groceries and utilities. Fortunately, wine is considered 'groceries' and taxes are under negotiation (or should I say deferment) at the present time so, in the words of Scarlett O'Hara, *"Tomorrow is another day"*. We're managing, despite our savings and investments being depleted by about 75%.

On a more anthropological level, I've learned marriages *can* survive isolation with your spouse. Compatibility is accomplished by having separate televisions, even though there are no longer 24/7 sports programs being aired. You each make your own lunch to spread out the workload, and avoid CNN, in fact, most news programs for that matter to spare your sanity.

I can also confirm that emailing friends or talking on the phone from time to time comes nowhere close to getting together for late afternoon drinkies, dinner parties, morning coffee, or ladies' lunches. Society will suffer permanent and irreversible damage if the current situation persists and restaurants and retail stores go broke.

We've also learned that some of our elected politicians truly do care about their constituents while others are absolutely and utterly useless, perhaps even dangerous during a pandemic. Not mentioning names but you know who I'm talking about. The newfound avalanche of government money (which is actually being slyly added to our future Visa/tax bill) is welcome but I'm thankful I'm old so I won't live long enough to be the one stuck with paying it off. I wonder where this money was hidden when it was needed to provide clean drinking water, housing, jobs, and medical services for our First Nations' people.

I'm learning a lot about personal money management too. I could save at least $2,000.00/month if we got rid of both vehicles (that includes capital costs, insurance, maintenance, gas, etc.) which are currently collecting dust in the garage. I've learned we can survive on an infinite array of local and exotic foreign food like pizza and fried rice delivered from *Uber Eats*. Shoppers Drug Mart also delivers prescriptions, and if we get really sick, I'll just call an ambulance for a ten-minute run to the hospital where thanks to socialized medicine we have free room and board.

We're learning to do DIY haircuts and colour. We have more clothes than we'll wear out before the next millennium, and our bills are on autopay at the bank so we don't need cash. We'll never need new shoes again because we never go anywhere and as long as the bank keeps deducting our utility costs we can just stay in and binge-watch Netflix all winter, or forever, for that matter. No need for coats or boots. I'd say we're pretty self-sufficient.

This pandemic has been quite an education in so many ways. While I've been conducting these complicated experiments, I'm sure you've been equally productive. I may produce a scientific paper on my findings to benefit humankind or I might just roll over and go back to sleep (researching Item 11 above).

Being a scientist is an enormous responsibility and I want to make sure my data input is reliable, my field tests are air-tight and my conclusions worthy of a Nobel prize. Mr. Thompson, my high school science teacher would be shocked and impressed at the output of his worst-ever student. Sometimes, the slow ones fool 'ya, eh Mr. T? If I'm never seen again in public, at least my work will live on. Isn't that what we all want ultimately? Immortality.

I'm not an accredited scientist but I wouldn't say no to a Nobel Prize for my findings.

Our entire home is under attack by a virus

Can houses get COVID-19? They must because our home is collapsing around us. Well, not the house per se, but all the gadgets and equipment that keep us functioning. Everything we own is contracting a virus at a rate that would have Dr. Fauci retreat to his 'safe room' and never come out. Our recent dryer fiasco was just one in a prolonged series of equipment failures that are driving us batty.

Viruses are everywhere.

The first thing to go was the faucet in the shower. We barely noticed its slow death over the years until the effort required to turn the lever on without hearing major crunching and grinding became too alarming. Something was obviously wrong so we broke down and called in a plumber who effortlessly replaced a simple cartridge in the faucet, handed us a huge bill, and twenty minutes later he was gone. Now, every time I turn on the shower, I burst into giggles, delighted with the silky-smooth efficiency of our shower lever. Wow! It doesn't take much to make this old boomer happy.

Next, on one of the hottest days of the summer so far, our air conditioning system died. I spent more than an hour on the line waiting my turn for someone to take our call and inform us that it would be a week before they could get a technician out to our house. I need to qualify this issue by stating that last year we purchased a very expensive ($66.00 per month) supplementary service and repair contract with Enercare that we hoped would result in premium service. Hah! No such luck. After a week of me and my honey sweating it out, the technician finally arrived and solved the problem.

A couple of weeks later, I received an email from Enercare reminding us that it was time for our (off-season) furnace service call. Thinking summer would be the perfect time to get our furnace serviced as those guys definitely would not be too busy at this time of year, I made an appointment for a week later. The day before the appointment, I received another email from Enercare advising us that our appointment would have to be deferred because they were so busy with priority air conditioning  calls. We sure as hell weren't a priority when our system was down a couple of weeks earlier. You can't win.

Then, the strange virus struck again. Hubby lost one of his hearing aids. He figures it flew off when he was removing his face mask and we've never been able to find it. We once had a former dog eat one of my hearing aids, but that's another story. The device was gone and at a cost of several thousand dollars for a replacement, this was not a frivolous loss. Ever in denial about his hearing issues, he decided to soldier on with only one hearing aid, which this week also succumbed to COVID-19. Two new hearing aids. Kiss several thousand more dollars goodbye.

It's not over yet!

These issues pale, however, compared to our ongoing problems with our Bell television and internet service. Ever since we've lived in this house (ten years now) we've had ongoing issues with the street cable delivering a weak signal to our house. Apparently, there's a fault in the outside line somewhere and at least once a year the signal diminishes from half-signal to zero. It usually takes numerous calls to the call centre and multiple visits by various technicians with different skill sets to stick a Band-Aid on the problem and restore our service.

Because of lockdown restrictions, we've been confined to quarters and television is the lifeblood of my husband's life. We endured four days of no television and intermittent internet service so we were both going a bit squirrely. Hubby was bored and cranky and not terribly receptive to my gentle suggestions that he read a book. It works for me. As a result, though, our lawn and gardens are now one hundred percent weed-free and we can boast not a single blade of crabgrass.

Unfortunately, he missed four days of up-to-the-minute updates about Trump's screwups which we count on to keep his heart rate up. Withdrawal can be painful. We had a big celebration when the nice Bell guy finally got us back in service after two technicians worked all afternoon at various terminals on the street.

In fairness to the virus, I should probably discount an earlier technical issue with my television which I'm embarrassed to even tell you about, but we're all friends here. My honey and I watch separate televisions (for obvious reasons, i.e. *sports*) with headphones so we don't hear the other's programs. One day my headphones died and refused to be resuscitated, despite all efforts. I ordered a new set, and with a little help from son and grandson, got them installed.

A problem arose, however, as soon as they departed, when I discovered I could not control the volume or turn the television on or off with the TV remote. I had to do it manually on the side of the TV. That's odd, isn't it? I put up with the inconvenience for a month or so because I was so fed up with malfunctioning electronics I couldn't emotionally deal with trying to rectify the problem. When I finally gave up and sought professional help from the Geek Squad, it turned out I'd placed the receiver in front of the sensor on the front of the TV and that was why the remote control wasn't receiving On/Off or Volume signals. My stupid. Not the fault of the virus.

Now that COVID has infected most of our household appliances and gadgets, I'm wondering what could possibly be next. Our roof should be good for another ten years, *but* I wouldn't be surprised to look up one day while I'm reading the morning paper and see drips from our kitchen light fixtures. Nothing is safe. How much longer will it be before my laptop screen turns irretrievably black except for a strange FU message. We rarely get into our vehicles to go anywhere these days or they too would probably be flashing *"Urgent Service Needed"* on the electronic dashboard.

The message here, *mès amis*, is you don't have to worry and wonder about whether COVID-19 is transmitted through air particles, touch, or via family pets. I can personally confirm its insidious tentacles penetrate every molecule of our lives including household appliances and gadgets. If my iPad mini dies, I might just have to pack it in too. Being able to download library books has been my lifeline. I've been mainlining fiction, murder mysteries, non-fiction, and biographies for so long I don't think I could carry on if I couldn't read. Thank goodness my optometrist is once again open for business in case my reading glasses mysteriously self-destruct. Plumbing, washer, dryer, air conditioner, television, internet, electronic toys—no object, device, or service is safe from the pandemic. Trust me. I've lived it and so far I've survived. Be safe out there my friends.

Queen's Park: We have a problem

Dear Premier Doug Ford:

I'm truly embarrassed to approach you in the midst of a worldwide pandemic with such a frivolous, first-world problem. I know you're pretty busy sorting out issues with under-staffed, under-funded nursing homes and the shortages of supplies in hospitals, but we boomer women have a teeny little problem which can quickly be taken care of by answering *one simple little question* that will only take twenty seconds of your time. The thing is, I need more information about your proposed phased rollout for relaxing COVID-19 restrictions

Specifically, I need to know exactly when hair salons will be reopened so we can get our hair issues attended to? Will it be a month? Two months? *Six months?* An entire generation of formerly blonde baby boomer women is struggling with how to conceal our grey roots and manage our overdue trims. If you could just be specific about this one simple question, I promise I'll never bother you again, I'm pretty sure.

It's been five months now since I had my highlights done. The last time was in November 2019 and my next appointment which was scheduled for early March was canceled because I had a cough and bad cold. My hairdresser has a little girl and I didn't want to take a chance on passing along my germs so I canceled the appointment. It turned out to be the right move. Then, the sky fell and everything slammed shut faster than my neighbour's door when the Jehovah's Witnesses come calling.

Hair grows on average at the rate of half an inch per month which (even though I'm hopeless with math) means my roots are currently at least three inches long and my overdue trim is proportionately past due. Fortunately, my own roots are dirt-coloured with no grey, so the results are just very unpleasant, not downright scary. But many of my boomer friends are sporting truly horrifying roots in varying shades of white, grey, salt and pepper, and dirty snow.

Do I or Don't I?

I've reached a crossroads, a dilemma of significant proportions for a retired old lady who's way past her best-before date. Unless I have a date I can reasonably count on to be there waiting in the eighteen-mile-long lineup outside my regular hair salon on opening day, I'm faced with a dilemma, a looming fork in the road. Should I attempt to cut my hair myself or continue to tough it out, au natural? And,

Will I end up with a mullet?

speaking of au natural, my legs have been hidden in sweats for several weeks now and will probably need a threshing machine to make myself presentable when legs are once again allowed to go bare in public. But, that's my problem, not yours. Sorry.

I could probably manage to trim the sides and top of my hair OK. I've been trimming my own bangs for years so that doesn't intimidate me but I'm very, very concerned about how I'm going to do the back. You see, I don't have a nice easy bob that I can get hubby to cut in a straight line (assuming he could, and I assume he can't). It's a precisely layered and textured short cut that cannot be easily handled even with an assortment of hand mirrors and limited dexterity. Do I risk ending up with a (gulp!) *mullet?*

Do you touch-up your blonde buzzcut yourself on occasion? Otherwise, you must have a barber living under your roof because you look exceptionally tidy and presentable at your daily press conferences, unlike us common folk. Does Mrs. Ford do the job for you? *Or, are you getting contraband trims not available to the rest of us?* That would make it hard for you to understand our angst.

The time factor is critical. If you could please provide me with a date when hair salons will reopen (obviously with strict guidelines for personal protection in place), otherwise, I'll have to haul out my hazmat suit, mask, and gloves and head to Shoppers' Drug Mart for a *Clairol Frost n' Tip* kit? It's been forty years since I've used that plastic cap to do the job myself but I'm pretty sure I could still manage it. We don't all have gorgeous natural white hair like Maye Musk, Catherine Gildiner, or my artist friend Perry McEwen whose colour doesn't require professional intervention.

"Hair-acy" by artist Perry McEwen illustrates boomers' rapidly escalating hair issues with gray roots and bad DIY trims.

It's not just the cut and colour I miss. I also miss the hug my stylist gives me when I arrive and depart, the mini scalp massage she delivers so deliciously when she shampoos my hair.

I miss eavesdropping on the gossip and personal problems being shared by other clients. I miss watching the other stylists and their clients for their before and after looks, and I miss the little shopping spree and foodcourt lunch I enjoy after I'm finished. Most of all, I miss looking like the finest version of myself I can be when I walk out the door of the salon and face the public. I walk a little lighter and I smile more readily.

I know you don't have a crystal ball and this crisis is so unpredictable, but if you could just slip me the tidbit of vital information about when hair salons are going to reopen, I won't tell a soul . . . well, other than all my old boomer gal pals and my millions (you never know!) of *BoomerBroadcast* followers. We stick together in a sisterhood of mutual support since the rest of the world tends to ignore us.

I suppose I should admit I voted for you in the last election, but under duress, because I truly hated what the Liberals had done to this province with their various financial and other mishandlings. Thank you for temporarily eliminating the prime-time rate assessments, but my hydro bills still give me palpitations. So, if you could help me out here, you can be assured I will cast my vote for Doug Ford in the next election with a smile of confidence on my face.

Neither the federal* nor provincial governments have done anything to ease the plight of tax-paying seniors (including baby boomers) during this crisis. Now's your chance. Please feel free to reply anonymously in the comments section below or on your fancy embossed official Premier of the best province (Ontario) in the best country (Canada) in the world stationery that I can show around to my friends. I've reached a crossroads and I need to make plans.

Your friend and generous tax contributor,

*c.c. Prime Minister Justin Trudeau, Ottawa**

Are you getting as antsy about self-isolation as I am?

Few people enjoy alone-time as much as I do. I can spend an entire morning alone in my sunny little office working on my blog. I'll have a quick lunch while I catch up on FaceBook and then retreat to a shady spot in the back yard for an afternoon of reading. After forty years in the corporate world with stressful deadlines timed right down to the minute, combined with the aggravation of daily commutes, and little to no control over my own time, I'm loving being the sole arbiter of how I now fill my days. It's an elastic resource that I can now stretch or contract however I wish. So, for the most part, I've not really minded the restrictions of self-isolation. But I must admit it's starting to negatively affect me and I'm getting impatient. Thank heavens I don't live in an extended care facility.

Every time I'm tempted to complain or rebel against the constraints of COVID house arrest, I remind myself how lucky I am compared to people like the family of Anne Frank and other Jewish families or individuals who were confined in small rooms for *years* without adequate food and provisions during the Nazi occupation of Europe. They also had to endure a nocturnal existence and were unable to access any fresh air or sunshine for the entire duration of their time in hiding. We're so fortunate by comparison.

But that does not diminish the fact that we're all going a bit crazy being restricted from living our lives the way normal human beings were designed to live. We're social creatures by nature (at least, most of us are) and we depend on each other for meeting our basic needs. Working, shopping, attending to ailing friends or relatives, socializing in large or small groups, expanding the scope of our everyday world, and hugging those we love are natural and necessary human behaviours. How can we ever forget those horrifying Harry Harlow experiments on rhesus monkeys in the last century. When baby monkeys in the lab were deprived of touch, they died.

It's a waste of time to even smile at someone on the street or in the grocery store these days as they can't see me smiling at them under my mask. I miss those little

I certainly don't plan to do this again any time soon.

personal interactions. While I can keep myself busy reading, writing, doing a little bit of housework (as little as possible), preparing and eating meals, and making the odd phone call to a friend, I'm starting to feel *starved of life.* My husband has returned to golf, under strict physical distancing rules and is happy to be working again in his garden, but there are so many simple everyday experiences that we can no longer enjoy.

Some people may not regard shopping as a joy per se, but it has its advantages. I always enjoyed going to the mall for a hair appointment (another deprivation), then browsing the stores and treating myself to a nice lunch in the food court or restaurant, perhaps meeting a friend to join me so we can catch up on the latest news. I have always been comfortable chatting up fellow shoppers in a store or in the food court which is another social interaction we can no longer enjoy.

Last week, I made my first and probably last trip for a while to Costco to stock up on a few necessities. I had to line up outside the store according to pathways delineated by wooden pallets before I gained admittance to the store. Behind me in line was a couple in their mid-thirties with their two children, probably aged six and eight, none of whom were distancing or wearing masks. I felt my rage welling up as I wondered why it takes four of them, the entire family, to make a Costco run for toilet paper. Could the mum or dad individually not have handled the chore by themselves?

Masks were mandatory inside the store, so the family of four was issued masks upon entry but I noticed them not wearing them as I raced through doing my shopping. As everyone knows, it's uncomfortable wearing a mask, especially if you wear glasses that keep fogging up and hearing aids that tend to pop out when you remove the elastics from behind your ears. Everything is a chore these days. But that's nothing compared to what health care professionals have to wear and endure for entire shifts of eight to twelve hours every day. They're trussed up in hot hazmat suits, face shields, caps, and various other items of safety gear designed to keep us all disease-free. Bless 'em all!

The stress of my Costco expedition demanded a treat. I know, in a perfect world I should never eat hot dogs. All the nitrates, chemicals, and questionable animal parts they contain will kill me, but Costco's hot dogs are literally to die for, and for a mere $1.50 I get a juicy dog and a bucket of Diet pop. Somehow that always makes me feel like I've "beat the man". Eating a hot dog in Costco is now verboten but I did manage to

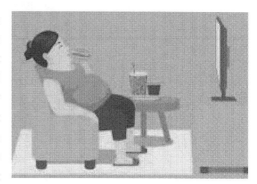

If one thing won't kill you something else will. Sometimes you just gotta have a hot dog.

buy one for take-out and stuff it into my purse for later consumption, adding my own toppings at home.

Fortunately, the Costco staff were fast and efficient at getting us checked out and out of there. As soon as I got into the car, I slipped my mask off, drank some of my ice-cold water from the stainless steel refillable cup I keep in the console, and breathed a sigh of relief that I don't have to do that again for a while. Whew!

Grocery shopping is similarly fraught with inconvenience, a lack of inventory, a few careless and thoughtless fellow shoppers without masks, and the threat of contamination. We are all trying to reduce the number of trips we have to make to the store and we're stockpiling basics to help us cope. When I'm confronted with the lack of flour on the shelf or the absence of my favourite dish detergent, I'm once again reminded to think of the deprivation in third-world countries or Russians lining up in freezing temperatures at dawn for a loaf of bread in the fifties, which often they could not obtain. That assuages my frustration somewhat.

Is there a Plan B or even an A-?

Now that we're into several months of this pandemic and the entire world is locked down, I'm beginning to wonder if our political leaders have a plan for the possibility this could go on for an indefinite length of time. The death toll and numbers of people infected continue to rise in most places around the world. I'm not advocating we line up like those idiot American rednecks in camo gear bearing sidearms and AK47s on the steps of the legislature demanding freedom, but **pretty soon we are going to need a clear Plan B** before we all go crazy. We could use some creative leadership here.

If only it were that simple!

Most of us are obeying the rules: Minimal outside excursions, wearing a mask, constantly washing and sanitizing, and physical distancing. Our politicians line up in front of the television cameras at the same time every day and give us the same old line. I'm sure it's difficult for their speech writers to rearrange the same words in a different way every day. I realize their job isn't easy but there must be some positive information they can share that will help us get through this.

At least in World War II they offered suggestions beyond the obvious to help people cope. I bought a tea towel once at The British War Museum in London with recipes for mock goose and fake cake to help citizens cope with basic food shortages. **Shouldn't some of those highly educated science nerds be advising us on how to build up and strengthen our natural immune systems?** Sure, we're eating a lot more meals at home, but are they healthy or are too many people opting for processed, prepared foods with little nutritional value thereby increasing their chances of infection?

I'm also concerned that all this sanitizing will weaken our natural immune systems. Now, more than ever, we need to pay attention to what we eat and put into our bodies to make sure we're as strong and germ resistant as we can be. Prevention involves more than masks and hand sanitizer. We can't spend the rest of our lives obsessively avoiding germs. Human beings need exposure to certain good bacteria and some germs to build up immunity. That's why young children born into homes with pets develop fewer allergies than children whose parents are constantly sterilizing and avoiding germs.

After several months of lockdown now, there is still no clear message from the scientists about the specific, confirmed transmission properties of COVID-19. We're relying a lot on hearsay. Can it be transmitted on surfaces? Yes or no? Exactly how long can it live in the air? An hour? A day? We'd like some absolutely reliable facts on these issues to help us cope in our everyday lives. We're still a little short on scientific facts. They must have learned *something* by now.

I know the beginning of the end starts with the much-anticipated vaccine and hopefully, that will happen before the end of the year. But I can't help wondering how we're going to cope with the next few months of isolation without a sign of relief. We're doing all the right things, being good citizens. We're self-isolating, physical distancing, dutifully performing all the recommendations we keep hearing updates from our leaders, but we don't seem to be making a dent in the pandemic. The numbers keep going up, every day. I have spent far too much time on the couch wondering how and when this is all going to end.

Remember when?

I miss the olden days of shopping in person for lipstick, shoes, and other girlie things.

In the olden days, B.C. (before CORONA-19), whenever I felt like I needed a little pick-me-up, a new nail polish or lipstick always did the trick. I could pick up a snazzy new nail colour at the drug store or grocery store but shopping for a new lipstick required a trip to Sephora, Nordstrom or Hudson's Bay. The purchase required a carefully executed comparative analysis of colours, texture, depth of pigment, and an assessment of how much it would bleed. Their vast selection allowed me to test dozens of colours on the back of my hand, before choosing a final one to be sterilized by the sales associate and tested on my lips. Such a fun pursuit is no longer available to us.

I've been so desperate I've even contemplated ordering a lipstick online to see if it'll give me the same high I get when I purchase one in the store, but I doubt it. There's something special about selecting the final colour in person, admiring its glitzy case and popping it into my purse for later. Little luxuries like shopping for a new lipstick are no longer an option for alleviating our boredom and elevating our mood. Will playing with testers be a thing of the past when we return to living a normal life?

Then, yesterday as I was wallowing in self-pity on the couch, our air conditioning crapped out—a first world problem for sure. I spent more than an hour on hold waiting in the queue for the Enercare call centre to even take my call, only to be informed that I have to wait a further week for a service technician to come out and fix the problem—as if I wasn't cranky enough already. But there is an upside. At least I get to see another human being.

We've given up our daily lives, routines and families to fight this pandemic. Many have given up so much more—their jobs, the ability to attend graduations, weddings, births and funerals, the ability to support their families. *What more can we possibly do?* Much as I enjoy my own company, I'm wondering if you're going as COVID-crazy as I am?

And . . . she's out of the gate!

After months in lockdown, my credit card was begging, gasping for air. So, when Nordstrom emailed me to announce they had reopened their Sherway Gardens store in Toronto's west end after three months in COVID darkness, plans for my coming-out began. They missed me! What

Clear the track!

to wear? What time of day is best to go? Will their café be open for lunch? Will they be displaying piles of old winter stock for sale or will it be fresh new spring and summer merchandise? Will I be able to try out the testers in cosmetics if they're sterilized first? After all, I'd been planning on buying a new lipstick, and as any boomer gal knows it's impossible to make a selection without trying on. Should I maybe get a new cream blush too?

It's been a horrible spring. On top of the shitty weather, we're all suffering from being house-bound with nowhere to wear our new spring tops and shoes and now it's summer already. We've almost forgotten how to properly accessorize. Will I have to relearn how to apply eyeliner? Then, there's the bigger issue—will my white jeans still fit? I'd love to wear them with the new animal print sneakers I bought over the winter that have been collecting dust in the front hall closet. And, will they let me in the door with *this hair?* I look pretty scary after months without a visit to the salon.

This venture out is nothing like grocery shopping where I can get away with yoga pants, a loose top, and face mask. Mall shopping is *real* shopping. It involves checking out and judging fellow shoppers' fashion choices. It means browsing the merchandise and pretending I can afford to drop the equivalent cost of a month's groceries on that silk *Equipment* blouse (I cannot). I must remember to employ my old protocols; scope out every single item in the store before making a purchase. In fact, if I can go home and think about it first, I might not make the purchase at all and spend the money on wine instead. The prospects are dizzying.

When I mentioned to my husband that I planned to hit the newly opened Nordstrom store for a browse, he made a sideways comment about me needing another white blouse. (As any gal knows and as evidenced by my own closet, you can never have too many.) And this from a guy who has seventy-two golf shirts. It's a much more complicated issue than needing a new lipstick, white blouse, or pair of shoes. It's about freedom—finally. At least a degree of it. I can finally put on normal clothes, makeup, jewelry, and proper girly shoes. I'm me again. Except for lipstick and blusher as they rub off on face masks and no one can see you smile anyway.

Masked, sanitized, and armed with credit card, I'm out of the gate.

Start the car! Start the car!

Nordstrom is in fact my favourite retail store and I certainly wouldn't want to be responsible if they went bankrupt so it's important to do my bit to keep them afloat. I was there shortly after the doors opened at 11:00 a.m. and was greeted by a friendly mask-wearing employee overseeing a hand sanitizing station. As I took careful steps into the vast cavern of retail delights I felt like Dorothy entering the world of Oz. But, there were noticeable changes along the yellow brick road:

- Many of the display cases were empty. Nordstrom always has a lovely assortment of costume jewelry and there were many pieces available on display tables but the cases of watches and fine jewelry were noticeably empty of inventory.

- The shoe and purse departments were similarly 'lean'. Aisle tables featured the latest merchandise including a display of high-end Valentino rock stud shoes but the wall shelves were almost bare.
- I inquired about a Charlotte Tilbury lipstick I had my eye on B.C. (Before COVID) but not being able to touch and sample the product meant I'll postpone purchasing until the world returns to normal. It's not like I don't have any other lipsticks! The sales associate was incredibly helpful and knowledgeable about the product even though she came over from another counter.
- Riding the escalator to the second-floor fashion department (without touching handrails, of course), I eagerly anticipated having sales associates falling all over me to show off their wares. Nordstrom is known for having lots of great sales personnel to help (unlike Hudson's Bay Co.) and they were in evidence dusting displays and moving things around to look busy. There were a few shoppers, not quite as many as normal, but still a good showing.
- The fashion floor was a sale-seeker's dream. Nearly every single item was on sale, some at drastic reductions. They were obviously clearing out winter merchandise and tempting us with a few spring and summer items, but pickings were not what they would normally be at this time of year.
- Fashion merchandise resembled a giant clearance sale. Entire sections of the store were empty and contained empty display racks. It looked like they were going out of business.

I did see a nice Alice + Olivia blouse I liked that was on sale, but who in the world can actually fit into an XS? Not this old boomer. I photographed it so I could check online when I got home. Sadly, their café was not open. I'd been hoping I could enjoy a nice lunch there but it was not to be.

When I walked back to my car I noticed quite a few cars outside Saks so I figured they might be open too. And, they were. It was a similar situation to my experience in Nordstrom. The atmosphere was quiet and a bit desperate. On the second-floor fashion section, the sales were amazing. There were a lot of beautiful winter things they were flogging at 70% off but not too much to choose from in the spring and summer line. I expect they probably canceled a lot of orders to manufacturers but it was, once again, a picker's dream. I actually managed to score the Alice + Olivia blouse marked down 75%—in my size. Joy to the world.

Even further discounts were sometimes offered at checkout.

Pusateri's food department on the lower level was strictly cordoned off in sections with no seating for customers to have lunch or a cup of tea but grocery shopping was allowed so I picked up some sushi to bring home for lunch. I was tempted to buy some Mary Macleod's shortbread which is the best ever, but I restrained myself when I thought about the numbers appearing on my bathroom scale every morning. I'm usually not so disciplined.

When I returned from my little retail reconnaissance mission, I didn't have the usual feeling of satisfaction I get when I've spent the better part of a day browsing various stores and enjoying a lunch out. It was great to do something we haven't been able to do for nearly three months now, but doing it encumbered by a mask and constantly sanitizing my hands definitely diminishes the enjoyment.

The sales associates were exceptionally friendly. I'm sure they were happy to be back to work and having personal exchanges with people other than those they live with. But, my shopping experience was like a chocolate sundae without the Spanish peanuts on top. I didn't get quite the buzz I normally do. With all the restrictions and the clearinghouse atmosphere, it was not entirely as pleasurable as it could have been. I even missed being able to smile at other shoppers and perhaps exchange a word or two.

I sympathize with retailers trying to survive this pandemic. It'll be a miracle for those who survive. My excursion served to reinforce my commitment to online shopping for comparative pricing and selection. Another blow for brick and mortar stores. But, nothing beats trying things on, getting inspired by new and colourful fashion, experimenting with new makeup in the cosmetics department, and, of course, meeting a friend afterward for lunch. My little excursion did satisfy that itch. I really do miss the world as it was though. Have you ventured out beyond the grocery store lately? What did you see?

Pssst . . . wanna place a sure bet on NHL, NFL, NBA and major league baseball during the pandemic?

Hockey was great in 1967, especially when the Leafs played the Habs on Saturday night.

Three mornings a week I send my husband off to the golf course with a cheery, *"Score lots of goals, honey"*. That's what good wives do. Lord knows I do try to be a good wife. That also gives you an idea of how much I know about sports. Practically zero. Well, I do understand hockey. What Canadian boomer kid can possibly grow up without watching Hockey Night in Canada on our old black and white televisions coached by an enthusiastic father or brother?

Back then, it was a lot more exciting with only six teams and the Leafs versus the Habs on a Saturday night was the pinnacle of excitement with Foster Hewitt or Danny Gallivan calling the plays. Remember Howie Meeker hyperventilating, *"It's a real barn burner"*? The French-Canadian players with their endearing accents, the toothless, sweaty between-period interviews with Jacques Plante or Davie Keon were great fun.

Will Bobby Hull's blond toupé stay put? Will Frank Mahavolich get a hat-trick? No sissy body armor, helmets and face masks back then. The players wore their scars with pride. And, they played *real* hockey, the skillful kind with minimal fighting, not like the cage games we see today.

My own career in sports includes playing softball in a girls' league as a teenager but I was never a star player. In fact, I was barely even a player, out there in left field with my dad's glove worn sideways on my right hand so I could chase grounders and throw with my left hand. If I'd ever learned to pitch as a leftie . . . well, who knows what glory I could have achieved . . . with my wrong-handed glove. Despite winning a tie for first place for girls one year in field day at our public school as a nine-year-old, I'm pretty much a writeoff in the realm of sports.

My husband, however, is a sports enthusiast. I'm confident that if he'd known how minuscule my knowledge of sports is he probably would never have married me. I guess he was so smitten with my beauty and brains he missed that failing in his new bride—or chose to overlook it thinking I'd come round. He tried. When we first got married I promised I'd learn how to golf when I retired. So, he bought me a set of golf clubs and six lessons. Having scored in the low 300s at our company golf tournament I had a lot to learn.

I dutifully showed up for that first lesson in the spring. The instructor placed the seven-iron on the ground at an angle to guide me through the various complicated swing stances and club-holding techniques. She was patient and instructive, and I couldn't wait for the lesson to be over. My brain was muddled, and my patience was stretched to the breaking point. It rained the day of my second lesson and I never went back. It was all too complicated and I figured I had about eight hundred other things I'd rather be doing with four hours of my time. If you see a lost seven-iron that I left lying on the green somewhere out there at Horseshoe Valley, take it. I don't need it.

Golf wasn't my game. In fact, neither is tennis, pickleball, or any of the other sports I've tried that my generation seems to favour. Pity my poor husband who really deserves to be married to someone who at least understands the basics of football. In my opinion, it's a game of *nothing-ever-happens.* Each play lasts about twelve seconds while a bunch of big fat guys run three yards, then all fall down—a

Will they get by with a little (ahem) help from their friends?

boring waste of time. Obviously, I don't get it. But my husband *loves* the game and could watch it 24/7. In fact, he loves all sports. He even listens to sports radio wearing earbuds in bed. Last night he woke me up to inform me that the Raptors had a sixteen-point lead on the Lakers. Bless his heart.

Get to the point!

Which brings me to the point of this piece. As little as I know about sports, I do know one thing for sure. Professional athletes are considered celebrities in our society. They're over-paid jocks with overblown egos and hordes of over-enthusiastic fans. Shockingly, a large percentage of these fans are women and there's a sub-category of women who have special ways of showing their love for professional athletes. Groupies follow their teams and dispense their favours according to who's in town. Professional athletes are known to have active (understatement?) sex lives and they have the prescription bills to prove it. To be fair, some players are probably devoted, monogamous family men, but let's face it, there are a lot of Wilt Chamberlains out there scoring big numbers. Just ask Tiger Woods' ex-wife about groupies.

My husband has an endearing habit of relaying sports updates by yelling the latest developments at me from the other room where he watches TV with headphones so I can't hear. He can't help himself. He actually thinks I care. He's been keeping me up to date on the various leagues' plans for playing in empty stadiums and rinks during the pandemic. According to his play-by-play updates, hockey players are going to be quarantined in a hotel for two and a half months, traveling to and from practices and games without coming in contact with the outside world.

If you believe that these professional athletes are going to go for two and a half months without getting laid, then I have some swampland in Florida I'd like to sell you. The question is not whether the players will be safe from contracting and spreading COVID-19 but more to the point, how on earth will they be able to go without sex. The crotch-grabbing baseball players will no doubt have to get creative to get them through this crisis. I'm willing to bet it's impossible for them to keep it zipped, in the dugout, or on the bench for the required time needed to get them to the playoffs.

How long do you think the players will be able to play without scoring? Maybe they're being subjected to scientific tests to confirm the old myths about withholding carnal relations before the big game in order to conserve testosterone. Is it true that if players are denied . . . um, certain pregame pleasures, they'll have all that testosterone in reserve for the big push on the home stretch? Is 'saving themselves' fact or fiction?

Personally, I think they'd sooner risk a COVID-19 exposure rather than being condemned to celibacy. That's going to be the biggest challenge for these professional athletes, not who wins the game. It will be interesting to watch the sports tower of Babel come tumbling down simply because the boys can't behave for the time required, no matter how many millions they're paid. Don't say I didn't warn you in advance, in case you have any bets on who will make it to the so-called playoffs. I'm betting on testosterone overruling brains and shuttin' 'er down for good. I may not know a lot about sports but I'd put big dollars on that one!

Chapter 9

Business

He turned my cellphone lemon into lemonade

Hello. You've reached Lynda. She doesn't know how to use her new cellphone so please call her landline.

You may find this shocking and impossible to believe, but I rarely use my cell phone. I have no burning desire to be in constant contact with the people in my life every minute of the day. Nor am I interested in posting pictures on FaceBook or Instagram of what I had for lunch, or the colour of my latest pedicure.

Therefore, it came as a shock to me one day when I picked up my handy dandy flip-phone to call my honey and discovered it was dead—not resting, not asleep, and definitely not on a time-out. When I called my phone provider, I was informed that my equipment was so old and outdated, they no longer supported it.

My former phone plan that I paid a mere $18.31 per month for, including tax, suited my requirements just fine, so I made a call to Zoomer Wireless to see what kind of a deal we could do for a new phone. We came to a mutually agreeable arrangement that resulted in them sending me a new phone to catapult me into the twenty-first century. A couple of days later, my shiny new Samsung phone arrived with some pamphlets and basic instructions.

That's when my problems started. You see, tech suppliers probably assume everyone is as savvy about this stuff as they are. They take for granted we old-timers know the basics about their equipment. After sitting down and looking at all the scary bits and pieces sitting on my coffee table for a few days, I decided to dive in and see if I could set it up, according to the instructions provided. I'm not very good at linear thinking or following instructions, but one simple but critical instruction was missing. And that critical bit of information left me with a useless phone and a serious case of embarrassment.

I have never once in my life changed a SIM card. Zoomer Wireless naturally assumed I probably had (hasn't everybody?) but they were wrong. If there's a chance it can be done incorrectly, I'll do it—and, naturally, I did. I managed to extract the little tray on the side of the phone where the SIM card should go but I swear to God I did not know that the little SIM card I punched out of the credit-card-sized thingie that came in the package was supposed to fit onto that tray before being inserted back into the phone, *together*.

After I inserted just the tiny piece of plain white cardboard (the actual SIM card) I separated from the larger card into the slot on the side of the phone, I thought I was done. Then, I thought *"It seems odd that I still have this little black bracket left over."* And my phone would not turn on. I then tried to jam the little tray into the slot too but it wouldn't go.

You see, it seems the SIM card fits into the little black tray; it does not function independently. You probably already knew that but I did not and naturally I screwed it up. The nice guy at Zoomer Wireless suggested I wrap a piece of tape, sticky side out, around the corner of something thin and see if I could fish the SIM card out of the slot that way. It didn't work. I tried a safety pin, tweezers, even tiny forceps. The little card is buried so deep in that slot it's never going to come out.

All of this happened pre-COVID-19 when we could still go out to stores. The next step was to visit the young-uns who work at one of the cell phone kiosks in the mall and see if they had any suggestions. They told me my phone was ruined and I needed to buy a new one because the new phones are all sealed and they couldn't open it. Naturally. Further calls to my provider had the same message.

Then, my husband, who knows even less than I do about technical thingies (he doesn't even know how to use the PVR on the TV and I have to show him *every single time* he wants to watch something). He suggested I try going to the Telus Mobility store since they carry Samsung. Lo and behold, when I went there, they referred me to a tiny little independent storefront place that is licensed for Samsung, Google, and other brand names. It has a funny name like *"You Break It, We Fix It"*, or something obvious like that for people *just like me.*

The young guy there glanced at my phone while I told him my long, pitiful story. He took it into the back room and returned a couple of minutes later with my problem solved and my phone set up and ready to. And the best part is . . . he said, *"No charge"*. Can you friggin' believe it?

After I left I felt I should have given him something as he'd just saved me the cost of a new phone. Greatly relieved, I took my new phone home, set it back on the coffee table, marveled at its untapped capabilities, and there it sits to this day. I'm afraid to use it. I guess you could say I'm afraid to drink the Kool-Aid a.k.a. lemonade. Can you blame me?

The moral of this story is . . . well, there is no moral, but I do know for sure my phone's smarter than its owner. I need to get with the

Maybe she could show me how to use it.

times and keep up with technology or I'll be unable to call for help when I get a flat tire or need to share a picture of what I had for lunch. I suppose I should upgrade from dialup and Eudora while I'm at it (just kidding!!). While the world is racing toward disaster, I'm in the slow lane. But at my age, that's not a bad place to be.

Timmie, come home. We miss you and we need you

We knew it would happen didn't we? It was a predictable outcome when American/Brazilian-owned Restaurant Brands International (who also owns Burger King) bought Canadian icon Tim Hortons in 2015. When the Canadian-themed commercials disappeared from our televisions, so did the level of service and quality of the products. It's now strictly a numbers game for coffee bean counters at the big foreign business that now owns Timmies.

I may be going out on a limb here but **I'm pretty sure Canadians wouldn't mind paying a few pennies more** for their daily double-double and maple glazed donut to have them freshly made in-house and promptly served by happy people who receive benefits. We don't ask much. After all, we're Canadian. But the natives are restless and unless Tim Hortons takes drastic steps to improve the service and quality of their products without penalizing their employees' benefit plans, we could be screwed by foreign owners. Oh, that it should come to this.

What can we do?

We hate to say *"We told you so"* but . . . customers are unhappy; franchisees are unhappy; employees are unhappy. Stock prices are going cold. Under American leadership, Timmies has lost its basic Canadian flavour, its *essence*. Being a good corporate citizen is about more than the bottom line and we are sure that bottom line would bounce back up if they treated their customers, employees and franchisees with more respect. Taking care of each other is the Canadian way.

Should we pass the toque and buy back what should still be ours? We could have bake sales (ironic!), get the Leafs to play a charity fund-raiser game (after all, do they really deserve to get paid for what they do?), or get little kids in red mittens with donation boxes around their necks to stand in their skates outside Beer Stores. Should we ask Justin and the missus to put on their Indian costumes and pray?

There has to be a way we can bring Tim Hortons home again. It's our heritage, our right and should still be *our* Timmies. The CEOs in charge in 2015 should have never sold out and now all Canadians are paying the price. Get out the old handbook, the one that spells honour and flavour with a "U" and films its commercials in places like Grande Prairie and Chicoutimi before the Yanks messed with our special formula, our secret recipe. We're dyin' here. **We need to buy back our Timmies.**

Here's what I wrote in www.BoomerBroadcast.net in 2015 when Restaurant Brands International took over Tim Hortons:

Is Timmies still a Canadian cultural icon?

For better or worse? No longer Canadian.

Canadian Baby Boomers remember the *real* Tim Horton, the handsome young hockey player who helped the Toronto Maple Leafs win *four* Stanley Cups back in the sixties. Tim Horton was killed in a tragic car crash in 1974 shortly after one of his entrepreneurial endeavours had just started up. *Tim Hortons* was originally just a system of franchised donut/coffee shops in Ontario and grew to become a national icon, representing everything Canadian. In fact, I think they should change their corporate colours to red and white.

Is there a Canadian alive who hasn't at least once walked down the street with the iconic brown cup in hand? Over the years, customers have supplied the material for Timmie's feel-good commercials showing young kids and parents getting into the car on  freezing winter mornings to drive to the hockey rink; our soldiers enjoying Tim's in faraway desert postings, and seniors meeting over a newspaper for an early morning assessment of the world situation at their local Tim Hortons.

When American-owned Restaurant Brands International (owner of Burger King) purchased Tim Hortons, Canadians were collectively horrified, nervous and skeptical that our national identity would continue being treated with the respect it had earned over several decades.

They offer menu items that are fast and affordable, with seasonal promotional treats. I am concerned, however, that they might diversify too much into fast food menu choices which are bound to affect the culture.

What I have noticed, however, is that the always-slow lineups are growing longer and slower. Where there previously would generally be eight or ten people ahead of me, there are now eighteen or twenty. I recently waited so long in a line at Tim Hortons on Mavis Road in Mississauga that my roots need retouching. If there's a lineup of cars extending down the street waiting for the drive-thru, I often opt to park the car and line up inside only to find that the drive-thru is *still* moving faster.

I do miss those feel-good Canucky commercials though. Please tell me they're not using an American ad agency now too. Where are the scenes of red maple leaf mittens hugging a hot chocolate, the maple donuts, all the pedestrians cradling a cup of Tim Hortons as they make their way through daily life?

While I am politely (like any good, true Canadian) waiting in the Timmies lineup for the seasons to change or my Canada Savings Bonds to mature, it gives me time to look around and appreciate the common denominator that brings every ethnicity together under that ubiquitous brown and cream-coloured logo every day. It's a reminder to be thankful I'm living in  the best country in the world where we don't have to clutch our precious children and flee down railroad tracks, over mountains or cross seas in leaky boats to simply be safe while drinking our morning coffee or steeped tea. We are fortunate that we are not living in refugee camps because our lives were at risk in the place we once called home.

Every single one of us now living in Canada is the product of an immigrant. The next time I'm tempted to become impatient with the lineups at Tim Hortons, I'll stop and think about those millions of people lining up to flee terrorism in their own homelands who would give anything to be in my place. The fact that many

Tim Hortons are owned, staffed and frequented by immigrants is a testament to our tradition of welcoming newcomers to our country. We can only hope that the world leaders will soon get their act together and come up with a solution that will allow these families to rebuild their lives in safe, new countries such as Canada, or better still, to live safely in their home country.

Maybe we should export Tim Hortons to the Middle East, invite opposing sides to sit down and talk over a steeped tea or dark roast with some Timbits, and perhaps they would see that we're not so different after all. We can all get along. Under that iconic logo we're polite to each other; no one's packing a gun; we're not ducking mortar shells, and we're sharing warmth and friendliness in a place we all love. You can't get more Canadian than that, unless we bring the Stanley cup back to Toronto. We can only hope.

Are you guilty of smuggling shoes into Canada?

Comments made by Donald Trump about scuffy contraband shoes being smuggled into Canada is just too delicious for this Canadian serial shoe wearer to ignore. In one of his latest unhinged rants Trump attempted to horrify patriotic Americans into vilifying Canada and mistakenly defend protectionism. By informing them that Canadians were so desperate for shoes and to avoid Canadian duties (or tariffs as he called them, which are not the same thing) he announced that we make covert trips to the United States to purchase and smuggle their prized and precious footwear back into Canada. Then, in order to deceive those pesky Canadian border security agents, we toss our old straw clogs at the border in Buffalo, scuff

up our new made-in-America Reeboks and trip across the border undetected, fooling those filthy Canadian revenuers. What more proof do Americans need that Canada is a terrible place?

I have a confession. In fact, any Canadian who has ever visited the United States would probably admit to being guilty of the same thing. *I have purchased shoes in the United States and brought them back to Canada.* But I'm confused. I didn't realize what I was doing was wrong, immoral or

Psst. Mr. Trump. Wanna buy some protection? Good Canadian style.

unpatriotic. And I certainly didn't break any laws so there was no need to scuff up my shiny new shoes to fool border security because I'm legally allowed to bring back up to $900.00 in merchandise *duty-free* after an absence of a particular number of days from Canada. If I exceed the legal spending limits, then I'm prepared to pay duty to Revenue Canada for the chance to pick up something different from what I might find at home. And what sane woman in her right mind would ever scuff up her new shoes anyway?

So how is this hurting anyone? I supported American business. I kept border security agents employed by checking my passport and sitting in their little booth to ask me a few simple questions to ensure I'm not packing heat or smuggling drugs. And the banks rejoiced at the service charges and exchange costs they levied when I converted my Canadian dollars to American. If I hurt anyone, it's probably China, the mother lode of cheap shoes. And, of course, this whole exercise is moot if you're a man; everyone knows that men only own two pairs of shoes, one brown and one black, unless they're under thirty, in which case they may also own a pair of runners. Cross-border shopping is a non-issue for men.

HIS shoe closet.

HER shoe closet.

The ironic thing about this whole fiasco is that if Donald Trump actually cross-border shopped like real people, he'd realize that we have far better quality shoes in Canada than they have in the United States. Many of our shoes are Italian

220

imports thanks to our large Italian immigrant population who have created businesses here. See, Donald, immigration is a good thing. The quality and styles we can get here are far superior to what most American stores offer and our prices are competitive.

No one in the world manufactures better winter boots and coats than Canadians and thanks to our global business practices we have access to imported as well as locally manufactured merchandise that is far better than south of the border. Just ask Meghan Markle, Duchess of Sussex who regularly sports Canadian-made brands.

Sorry Mr. Trump. You got some fake news there. You've somehow taken the issue of non-existent Canadian protectionism and twisted it into something you hope will justify American protectionism, but you've shot yourself in the foot. And unless you were wearing genuine Canadian-made steel-toed Kodiaks, Timberlands, Royer, Canada West, Caterpillar or other superior brands made in Canada, you could be missing a few lower digits. You're certainly missing something, and that's not fake news.

A retailer who actually listens to customers. Glory hallelujah!

Holt Renfrew (for my non-Canadian readers, it's our answer to Neiman-Marcus) wanted to improve business so they did something I've been suggesting to The Hudson's Bay Company in letters, emails and blog posts for years, which they've categorically ignored. Holt Renfrew (are you sitting down?) **asked their customers what they could do better.** Remember us? The often-ignored customer is retail's entire raison d'être but few retailers recognize that obvious fact.

Holt Renfrew President Mario Grauso is either a regular follower of **boomerbroadcast.net** (yeah! right!) or he's as smart as I am!! He invited real, live customers of Holt Renfrew to a meeting and listened to their suggestions on how to improve business. And, to his horror and enlightenment, they told him. Here are just some of the things Holt's customers wanted but were not getting:

- more sizes that address a wider range of real-life bodies, including half sizes in shoes.
- greater personal assistance in interpreting trends and styling.

- better editing of merchandise so the shopping experience is not so overwhelming.
- improved on-line shopping

Well. Blow me down. Aren't these exactly the same things I've been ranting about for years? Grauso fired about half of Holt's top executives and corporate staff, and eliminated many brands including Clinique and Michael Kors as well as their HR2 off-price locations that weren't producing. Grauso is reinventing and repositioning Holt Renfrew to better serve (hold your breath) yes, it's true . . . their **customers**. Who knows better than we do what we want to lay out our hard-earned cash or credit card to buy? It would seem obvious to most consumers of retail goods but not to The Hudson's Bay Company and countless other retailers.

The transition for Holt Renfrew will not happen overnight and probably will not be without some pain involved, but I think we'll all be the ultimate beneficiaries, not to mention the owners of the privately-held business, the already-wealthy Weston family. Ironically, I'm not a prime Holt Renfrew customer (now that I'm retired) as their price points are somewhat beyond my budget, but I admire and heartily endorse their initiative. And I love to browse their stores, holding up lovely items to admire myself in the mirror in futile attempts at my quest for a new and improved me.

A patriot's guide to shopping during a Canada-U.S. trade war

Macleans magazine's Tom Yun once published a summary of products we Canadians can purchase to offset the idiotic trade war launched by Donald Trump. While we may feel helpless in fighting back, we're not. Here's a summary of choices we can make to  preserve Canadian business, excerpted from the article:

- Buy **French's Ketchup** manufactured in Leamington, Ontario, not American Heinz.

222

- Buy **J.P. Wiser's Deluxe Rye** distilled in Windsor, Ontario, not American bourbon from Mitch McConnell's home state of Kentucky.
- Buy **Minute Maid** orange juice from Peterborough, Ontario (even though parent Coca-Cola is a U.S. company).
- Buy Canadian-made sweets and candies like **Coffee Crisp, KitKat** and **Smarties** made in Toronto and **Mars Maltesers, Milky Way, Three Musketeers** and **Mars Bars** made in Newmarket, Ontario, **Ferrero Rocher, Tic Tacs**, and **Kinder Surprise** from Brantford, Ontario instead of Hersheys' from Pennsylvania.
- Buy **Cascades** toilet paper manufactured in Quebec and Ontario instead of Kimberley-Clark products from Pennsylvania.
- **Canadian Dairy** products are always available and preferable to heavily government-subsidized American products from Paul Ryan's state of Wisconsin. And ours are hormone-free.
- **Fresh produce** from Canadian producers is now readily available across Canada. Read your labels to avoid American producers. Mexico is still acceptable.
- Buy **President's Choice soy sauce** brewed and packaged in Canada instead of Kikkoman from the U.S.
- Buy **Canadian-made maple syrup** instead of imported syrup from Maine or Vermont.
- Buy Canadian-made automobiles and SUVs such as **Honda CR-V and Civic** made in Alliston, Ontario, **Dodge Grand Caravan** and **Chrysler Pacifica** manufactured in Windsor, Ontario, **Ford Edge, Flex and Lincoln MKT and Nautilus** are Canadian-made. General Motors makes **Cadillac STS, Chevrolet Impala, Chevrolet Silverado, and Sierra** pickup trucks are made in Oshawa. **Toyota Corolla and Lexus RX** are made in Cambridge, Ontario and the **RAV4** is made in Woodstock, Ontario.
- Choose **Godin or Michael Heiden guitars** crafted in La Patrie, Quebec and Vancouver, **Sabian Cymbals** from Meductic, New Brunswick.
- **CCM, Sher-Wood and Colt** hockey sticks are still made in Canada
- **Sam Bats** for wooden baseball bats manufactured in Carleton Place, Ontario

We can do it. Read labels. For a full transcript of the Macleans article by Tom Yun, here's the link:

https://www.macleans.ca/news/canada/a-patriots-guide-to-shopping-during-a-canada-u-s-trade-war/

The irony of drug marketing

Last night I watched a series of programs about the late Anthony Bourdain on Gusto TV. During one episode, he spoke honestly about his entry into the world of drug abuse, heroin in particular. He sat with a group of recovering addicts in Greenwood, a small town in Massachusetts plagued with the problems associated with opioid abuse. A local doctor explained how doctors freely prescribed Oxycontin and other painkillers for everyday problems like sports injuries, getting wisdom teeth removed and back pain because the drug companies assured the doctors the meds were not addictive. When patients can no longer get legal painkillers, they resort to street drugs and heroin. It's a problem no longer limited to big city slums. Small towns are now victims of big-city drug abuse problems.

Nearly very commercial aired during this hour-long show was by a major pharmaceutical company promoting an assortment of remedies for real or imagined ailments. *'Just ask your doctor',* followed by an exhaustive list of qualifiers. If you've ever watched television *in* the United States (not U.S. stations in Canada with substituted Canadian commercials) you'll know what I'm talking about. I've counted up to thirteen drug ads in a commercial break of fifteen commercials on American television. Just an observation. Be very, very careful.

What do you want to be when you grow up?

When young people graduate, they are officially launched and become full-blown adults. Hopefully these two milestones occur simultaneously. But I keep reading about the stresses faced by young people in choosing their college or university career path. They demand greater support from mental health services to help them cope with the stress.

How on earth is a teenager qualified to determine what he or she wants to do with the rest of their lives when they're still coping with acne, learning the ins and outs of the opposite sex and micro-managing their social media profiles?

Even today, at the age of seventy-plus and with more than forty years of work experience behind me when I retired, if someone asked me what I would like to do with my life I'd be hard-pressed to come up with a satisfactory answer. Sure, I'd like to edit a leading-edge women's magazine or write best-sellers that would make me rich. But how realistic are those goals? Expecting a young person who is barely beyond puberty to know the answer to that question can be challenging. Pick a course of study that is too restrictive and you're denied flexibility. Pick the flexibility of an arts degree and what are you trained for? Not an easy choice.

What complicates this decision, in my opinion, is the misguided direction to *"do what you love"*. I think that misleads many young people into thinking that is the singular key to success. It creates false hope because it's not always possible to earn a living and support a family when all you really enjoy is playing video games, making music or taking selfies (the Kardashians being the exception to the rule).

It is not always practical or possible to earn a living doing what you love. Aptitude may be lacking. A favourite activity may not lend itself to a sound business case. Loving writing does not mean you're going to be a self-supporting successful author. In fact, few authors are able to support themselves with their writing. The same applies to acting, art, music and even technology. Although individuals with strong technological skills have a better chance, particularly if they know how to write code. Sometimes doing what you love must be relegated to a side hustle or a hobby, not the full-time job.

When baby boomers were finishing high school in the late sixties and early seventies, there was not as much emphasis on post-secondary education as there is today. Most of us were never asked *"What do you want to be?"*. We simply left home, moved to the big city and got a job with the telephone company or an insurance company. If we were career oriented, our options as females were teacher, nurse or secretary. Boomer guys could work for Ontario Hydro (which in retrospect would have been the best career choice if you consider their overblown benefits and pension), become a mechanic or get a job at General Motors.

Once that was accomplished, we started assembling the components of what eventually became our lives. There was no great discourse, no years of scholastic preparation, no months of consultation with parents and guidance counselors and no particular stress involved. And since most of us did not go to university, no crushing student debt.

I also worry that extensive post-secondary education may lead some individuals to naively believe that high-paying employment automatically follows. There are many people with several degrees and tens of thousands of dollars in student loans who are unemployable. Women's Studies and Psychology are wonderful subjects to study but a tough fit in the world of business.

There are alternatives

While all this pressure on young people to pursue multiple degrees continues, there's a serious shortage of electricians, plumbers and tradespeople. Not everyone is well-served by attending university and there should be greater encouragement for those who opt for alternative careers. We must remember that educational institutions are still businesses that need customers so further education accompanied by its attendant debt is encouraged. These businesses need to be fed regular infusions of cash.

When I was still in the corporate world and in a position to hire young people, I never looked at the marks applicants got in school. Other qualities such as interpersonal skills, creativity, motivation, energy and resourcefulness were more valuable in the world of business. Most of what we needed to function in the working world (with the exception of doctors, nurses, teachers and other trained professionals) we learned on the job or developed through supplementary training throughout our working lives.

In a way, baby boomers were lucky. We escaped the *"What do you want to be"* pressure. We were happy to just have a job and we personified the **"Bloom where you're planted"** philosphy. Most often, we were happy to break free of the restrictions of living at home and get out on our own. We worked as receptionists, bank tellers, manual labourers, secretaries or salespeople when we finished school. From there, we ran with whatever we were dealt and many of us did very well despite our lack of education and degrees. I'm glad I'm not young anymore. I don't think I could take the stress of deciding what I want to be. I'm so glad I'm old.

Twice . . . we found a prize inside

If it is true things happen in threes, then I hope our lottery tickets are the next big win. Twice this week we've been the recipients of unexpected prizes, or more accurately *surprises* inside something we brought home. The first could require some 'splainin' by my husband but I'll give him the benefit of the doubt about how this gift came about.

He took his car in to get some work done. The shop needed to keep it for a few days so he was sent to Enterprise to pick up a rental. Coming home with a navy-blue Hyundai Santa Fe, he was less than impressed with the rental compared with how much he loves his Ford Edge, but c'est la vie. It's only temporary.

The disappointment was mitigated, however, by the little bonus he found in the vehicle. With a giant smile on his face, he came in the front door waving a little green package that you can appreciate has enormous value to a pair of old boomers (a.k.a. seniors) like us. The previous users of the rental Hyundai left behind a pair of bedroom slippers under the front seat

We scored part of a soft-drink machine (foreground) and a free pregnancy test (in front of cup).

and *a pregnancy test kit* in the glove compartment. At least that's the story he told me. You can imagine the "mileage" we're getting out of that one.

Our second big score was hidden in the lunch he picked up (one of the reasons I love him) at Five Guys on his way home from golf. When I finished eating and slurping the last dregs of my fountain Diet Coke, I popped the top off the cup to pour the ice that was still rattling around in the cup down the drain. With a clunk, out fell a plastic nozzle that probably came off the pop dispenser. I'm now debating how to pursue recourse for that one. Am I entitled to a free drink? A free lunch? A year of free lunches? Or will they charge me with shoplifting?

It's been a bountiful week and we're obviously on a winning streak. Much as I'm tempted to start making lists of all the lovely goodies I'm going to buy with my lottery winnings I'd better play it safe and wait until the money is in the bank. As the previous occupant of that Hyundai rental recognized, *better safe than sorry.* In remembrance of our *Paradise By The Dashboard Light* days, maybe we should just leave some condoms in the glove compartment of the rental car when we return it, call it a day and walk home.

Is there a future for lifers in business today?

Who spends their entire working life with one company anymore? Does the end of careers spent with a single employer mean the end of alumni associations and their attendant lunches/get-togethers, long-term service awards and even retirement dinners? Most baby boomers probably had more than one job during the course of our decades-long working lives, although there are some who may have spent the majority of their career at one company.

When I started working for Bell Canada (then called The Bell Telephone Company of Canada in 1965), it was common for people to spend their entire lives working for one large corporation like Bell, General Motors, an insurance company or Ontario Hydro. Those companies attracted new hires with such incentives as paid on-the-job training, benefits and pensions, even though those perks were the last things on our young minds way back then. Now that we realize the importance of company pensions, it's too late and most companies no longer offer them.

Job security and guaranteed pensions have become an anachronism.

228

Perhaps we intended to stay with a single employer when we started work. After all, our parents grew up in The Depression and just *having* a job was something to be revered and appreciated. But as time went on, perhaps we got restless, wanted a change of scenery or were offered a better position at another company. Consequently, most of us had half a dozen jobs or so over the span

of our working lives. I did spend a major portion of my working life with EllisDon Corporation (builder of Rogers Centre, formerly SkyDome, and other multi-million-dollar projects) but I did have enough other jobs to qualify as being well-rounded career-wise.

I was honoured recently to be asked to speak on **The Joy of Retirement** at an alumni lunch for retired and former Toronto area employees of **Coca-Cola Canada**. With my baby boomer-targeted blog and a new book **BOOMER BEAT,** they thought my message would resonate and inspire. In discussions with attendees and fellow speakers prior to the luncheon, it soon became obvious that while we have so many common denominators, we're not like earlier generations of retired people. We're healthier; we live longer; we're working from a different playbook in planning and living out our retirement.

We're also a vanishing breed in a world of young people with short interest spans who change jobs every couple of years. This means the day will soon come when there will be no alumni associations because workers will no longer identify with a single employer. Any friendships we develop with co-workers are most often maintained by the individuals themselves as corporations lend very little support to the alumni ethos. The old days of "Bell Pioneers" and other groups of retirees supported and respected by their former employers may be numbered.

One of the lessons I learned during four decades in the corporate world is that there's no reward for loyalty in business. Those all-nighters we pulled to meet a deadline, the weekends spent working instead of being with family, the stress associated with our jobs will not be noted on our tombstones, nor would we want it to be. It is most certainly not noted by our former employers. Having watched

229

their parents or grandparents sacrificing so much for their jobs, millennials have rejected this mindset by insisting on more balance with their personal lives and much as it irks me at times, I cannot fault them.

So, as we pay out of our own pockets for those alumni lunches, let us enjoy the company of our former coworkers as long as we can. Those people understand what we've been through together and they share our joy in being retired, as no one else can. Those lunches are just another one of those dinosaurs going the way of long-term service awards and company pension plans . . . and baby boomers.

One ringy dingy lights up my world

Remember when Lily Tomlin's character Ernestine ran the entire phone company single-handedly? From her little PBX switchboard, she efficiently dispatched installers and repairmen while simultaneously providing harried customer service, challenging delinquent bill payers and dispensing unsolicited advice to business and world leaders. I worked for the phone company in those days and understood her loyalty and determination, not to mention her romantic crush on Vito, her favourite repairman. Back then, I too had a favourite repairman. In fact, I married him. But that's another story.

Then, along came new technology, a.k.a. cell phones. I am not a complete Luddite; I bought one of the early ones, the size of a brick, in the nineties. Over the years I have tried to keep up as new ones came along but I'm rapidly losing ground. In fact, I'm ready to revert, and I don't think I'm alone. It requires far too much time and effort (not to mention money) to keep on top of all the newest features and apps, and still have time to pluck my chin hairs.

Jake Howell of The Globe and Mail is on my side. His article *Dumb, but happy* perfectly summed up my position when he confessed to giving up his iPhone 5C in favour of one of the old no-frills, basic phones. When he found his addictive use of the smart phone *"akin to a glorified fidget spinner"*, he went cool turkey, not completely cold, but severely curtailed.

When Candice Bergen produced a 'flip phone' on the first episode of the new Murphy Brown recently, it was the source of much laughter and derision, but Jake Howell and I empathized. We know a good thing when we see it.

Maybe it's because I don't have kids in school or a cheating husband whose emails and browsing history I need to monitor but give me that old-time phone service any day. I've gone entire weeks without using my cell phone. I never have to worry about exceeding my data plan. I'm baffled when I see groups of people sitting together having lunch or dinner

Sadly, the world as we know it.

and everyone's looking down thumbing their phones. Young people are going to entirely miss out on the art and joy of unencumbered personal conversation.

I've had a smartphone for a while now but I'm seriously thinking about tossing it and digging out the simple old flip-phone that I bought at Walmart for $14.99 back in the aughts. I'm never sure if my so-called smartphone is on or off and just last week I couldn't figure out how to turn it off in the dark at the movie theatre. Maybe it wasn't even on; I can never tell.

And I can never figure out how to access WiFi in public places (*my* problem, not the phone's). I haven't set up the voice mail because the phone is never turned on and frankly I don't know how to do it. I keep the phone only for emergencies. Imagine that! My monthly cell phone bill from CARP (Canadian Association for Retired People) costs me a whopping $18.31 including taxes.

Many people have ditched their landlines in favour of cell service only. That's fine if you want to carry it around in your hip pocket 24/7 (which it seems most people actually *prefer*), take it to bed with you, into the shower, into the hospital labour room, and while having sex. I just do not get it.

I expect smartphones will soon be implanted as a microchip into our wrists. Until then, if you need to reach me, you'll probably get no answer. Whether or not I respond immediately is not crucial to world survival. I'm probably on my lunch break splitting a six-pack with Ernestine. And if this is the party to whom I am speaking, then I will get back to you when I'm good and ready, after our break.

What's the real price of economic progress?

It's all so complicated . . . and expensive.

When I reviewed my recent 'bundled' telecom bill (for telephone, internet and Fibe TV) this week, the total nearly knocked me on my old lady ass. It was about the same as the mortgage payments on our first house in the seventies. How did this happen? I've tried unsuccessfully to cancel some channels only to reinstate them again because my honey *needs* three thousand sports and movie channels, the car channel and every news channel from  the Outer Hebrides to Inner Mongolia. I'm no better with my HGTV, HBO, various History channels and BBC that I'm convinced I couldn't live without.

That prompted me to think about all the services that *baby boomers did not grow up with* that we cannot imagine surviving without today. Tally up what these luxuries add to our monthly budget expenditures and we get an understanding of why we always feel so broke. Here's a sampling:

- I remember when a basic phone line cost $15.00 a month, plus long-distance charges, which we were very careful to minimize by calling only on weekends and for short periods of time. We received three television stations through an antenna on the roof. Compare that with **$350.00** a month today for hundreds of stations but we still have trouble finding something we like.

- Speaking of phones, tally up what your family's cell phones cost every month. Another **$300.00**? Or more? More importantly, we managed to survive *without* cell phones not that long ago.
- Mani-pedi's are de rigueur for most women today to the tune of about **$50.00** a month. Many of our mothers never even had a professional mani-pedi and back in the sixties and seventies we always did them ourselves. We also coloured and cut our own hair to save money.
- Modern washers and dryers are now capable of doing everything but our income taxes. Growing up, we reused wash water for several loads and hung clothes outside to dry. A clothes dryer alone is a huge energy-eater to the tune of another **$60.00** per month and that's if we schedule laundry for the middle of the night or weekends when hydro is cheapest.
- Growing up in the fifties and sixties, families were privileged to own a car. Now, vehicles for every member of the family are lined up in driveways like a used car lot. Factor in the monthly payments for the vehicle, gas, maintenance and insurance and we're looking at an additional **$1,000.00** per month **per car** and many families have at least two cars.
- Home security anyone? We never even locked our doors half the time when we were growing up and our family lived across the road from a high school. **$50.00** per month?

These few items alone total about $2,000.00 per month **($24,000.00 per year in after tax income)** and I haven't even touched on our astronomical hydro bills, bank fees and interest charges on credit cards for merchandise we've ordered on line but really didn't need and probably threw out a few weeks later. Then, there's the cost of keeping up with the latest fashions, maintenance costs related to skin care, makeup and gym memberships. Nor have I discussed restaurant meals (which were rare for our parents' generation), entertainment, overseas vacations or expensive hobbies like golf or skiing.

As teenagers, when our pocket money ran out, we were broke until next allowance day or payday at the drive-in burger joint where we worked on weekends. Now, parents shell out continually and without regard for limits. Seeing high school students with expensive designer purses, jeans or sneakers, leather jackets and even their own cars is mind-boggling for those who lived through The Depression.

It's natural (or at least it used to be) that subsequent generations do better than those who went before. But there's still a lot of fat that can be trimmed from our monthly budgets that would go a long way to ensuring a financially secure retirement. Just a few decades ago, most young people did not go to university. That was a huge cost-saving but now a university education is considered essential. When I look at the shortages in skilled trades, service jobs and other occupations, I question the validity of this line of thinking.

Being able to afford a house requires discipline. There's a lot of room for trimming the fat from monthly budgets to build up that down-payment. And your first home does not have to include granite countertops and be located close to work. Certain accommodations and sacrifices must be made to get a foot in the market. On one hand I sympathize with the challenges faced by young people trying to get into the market, while at the same time I sometimes think their expectations are too high.

It wasn't easy for baby boomers when we bought our first place (especially when you consider that mortgage rates were upwards of 20 percent in the seventies), and just as hard for our parents. My parents sold their used car and went without a vehicle for a couple of years to help scrape together the down payment on their first house, and they already had two kids.

We've all grown fat and lazy on the improved standard of living for average North Americans. So many goods and services that were considered luxuries by our parents are now part of our everyday lexicon. Amid all this affluence, boomers are also trying to downsize. We're hauling truckloads of valuable furniture, clothing and other possessions to charity stores and consignment shops. Have  we become too smart too late? I've started turning off lights to save power, refraining from buying more clothing and shoes I don't need and generally thinking twice instead of laying down that credit card for an impulse purchase.

It's always been my belief that earned money is more meaningful than handouts. Spoiled children grow up to be entitled adults. There's something surreal about swiping our so-called Smart phones or credit cards that has inured us to the real value of earned money. It's like we're playing with Monopoly money and sometimes we forget how hard the hard stuff is to come by. A quick stop at Starbucks could cost us the equivalent of fifteen minutes working in our employers' cubicle.

As the gap between the rich and poor widens, we're going to have to become more aware of our spending habits and face the reality that we're jeopardizing our future security. We could learn a lot by remembering how our parents handled money. Is the cashless society a good thing or a scam and a deceit that will be our ultimate downfall?

Our oceans are full of plastic waste; the polar ice cap is melting; certain species of wildlife are disappearing; thousands of hectares are being stripped of valuable trees, and our natural resources won't last forever. It sounds like a depressing prospect but it's not too late to change our ways. I don't envy the Gen Xer's, Y's and millennials who'll be left to clean up the mess.

I certainly don't advocate abandoning technology but maybe there's some justice in the standard of living pendulum swinging the other way for a few years. Let's hope this old earth survives long enough to rejuvenate itself. Our standard of living may be better than it was for our parents but is *life* truly better? What started with me questioning my telecom bill now has me reevaluating my entire life. Boy, do I need a glass of wine. Time to chill out.

The solution to problems at General Motors and Condé Nast

The media has been very unkind to General Motors recently, and rightfully so. They marked the American holiday of Thanksgiving by closing plants and laying off thousands of workers. While I sympathize with those negatively affected, I'm also pragmatic. I've been downsized; my husband's been downsized; nearly everyone I know, at some point has been the victim of reorganization, restructuring or whatever euphemism you wish to employ. Jobs-for-life and careers with one company are a thing of the past, gone the way of company pensions, rotary phones and carbon paper. We should not be surprised.

What does strike me, however, is the pattern of arrogance in major corporations that results in these drastic measures. Something has been ignored and it's called (sit down; this is a biggie) *"Listen to your customers".*

Large corporations like General Motors and so many others like them have long regarded themselves as invincible, even *omnipotent.* Sears, American Motors and Blackberry are prime examples of big business paying the price for not paying attention to who actually pays their bills. *Not* the company, the **customer.** General Motors was too slow off the blocks in recognizing that their customers now prefer SUVs and pickup trucks with their improved safety and fuel efficiency over conventional sedan cars. Sears' executives kept flogging the same old haberdashery while they were falling apart at the seams. Tragically, their

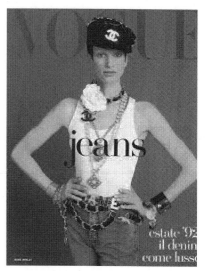

No longer relevant.

senior executives got big bonuses and golden parachutes while they raped the pension plans of their minimum wage hourly workers.

According to The New York Times, Condé Nast, the giant media organization and publisher of such magazines as Vogue and Glamour is also now trying to mitigate the effects of bad management. They've fired Chief Executive Robert A. Sandberg Jr. and shuffled various editors.

Some publications like Glamour are going to digital only, ignoring old ladies like me who like to rip pages out of magazines for my inspiration file.

Which brings us to the core of the problem. There's little to no inspiration in fashion magazines these days. Vogue is particularly irrelevant and my commitment to my subscription is hanging by a thread. *Have they ever considered asking what their readers would like to read?* I've been a subscriber for years and no one ever checks with me. It seems pretty obvious but not to those occupying the exalted thrones at the top of corporations. Now, I'll move on to the auto industry.

General Motors: Here's your lifeline

The solution to the problem at General Motors is surprisingly simple. *Go into competition with Bombardier.* They seem to have more business than they can handle, extraordinarily little competition, a guaranteed source of financial handouts from various levels of gullible government (taxpayers) and no particular business or management skills. Anyone could do better than that with a little business savvy, some creative thinking and an already available source of skilled workers. The recent news that Bombardier is laying off 7,500 workers worldwide including 2,000 in Canada prompted me to revisit a piece I wrote earlier.

During my lifetime, I've watched automotive manufacturing plants grow and expand to meet new technologies, then retreat and ultimately close. I worked for the construction company that built a major portion of those Ontario plants. To see Oshawa's General Motors operation go from almost thirty thousand employees to zero is heartbreaking. Ford has also closed facilities in southwestern Ontario.

As we know, Bombardier, the manufacturer of subway cars and streetcars is a perpetual sinking Titanic-sized case study in bad management. Taxpayers keep futilely bailing out the chronically mismanaged privately owned corporation like it's a giant money pit. Despite this, Bombardier continues to be awarded new contracts for transit vehicles which they are guaranteed to not deliver on time. They're years behind on delivery of stock for Toronto and other major cities.

The workers and the plants are in place. Do the work.

Obviously there's not enough competition in the business of manufacturing transit vehicles.

The answer is simple. **Retool the automotive plants to produce subway cars and transit vehicles.**

Put the workers in Oshawa and southwestern Ontario back to work and let them show Bombardier how it's done. Small fortunes were spent updating auto manufacturing plants in Ontario and they're now sitting empty waiting for weed growers to lease the space and sell the equipment for scrap metal. The problem of trucks encountering insurmountable traffic problems moving stock across Toronto's choked highways would be eliminated. At the risk of sounding immodest (!!), I think my solution is brilliant. Does anyone have any influence with GM President Mary Barra or the Unifor? Put in a word. Better still, put the kettle on and sit down at the kitchen table and make this idea work.

It is a perfect storm and has all the ingredients needed to launch a successful business enterprise. There is a strong market demand for both present and future products, skilled, available workforce, existing manufacturing plants available for retooling, tested financial metrics and business case, and an obvious shortage of reliable manufacturers. All that is needed is a smart team to pull it together and

Imagine the jobs that could be created in Oshawa, Windsor, Talbotville, St. Thomas and other Ontario towns. Let's talk.

we are in business.

Bombardier is a train wreck of back-ordered stock on a track to disaster. For years we have been enduring the ongoing saga of mismanagement, government bailouts, law suits and failure to deliver. They are being sued for failure to deliver public transit vehicles on schedule. Toronto Transit Commission is at their wits' end trying to get delivery of long overdue streetcars and could face similar difficulties with future transit vehicle deliveries. Yet Bombardier keeps accepting new orders because buyers seem to have nowhere else to turn.

Well, dear readers, I have the solution. We did it during World War II and it could work again. Re-open the General Motors and Ford plants throughout southern Ontario that closed when manufacturing jobs went south, and tool them up to build streetcars, trains and other heavy industrial mass-transit vehicles. Get Oshawa, Windsor, Talbotville, St. Thomas and other automotive plants making streetcars and trains. If Bombardier cannot do the job, then give the work to those who can.

I am sick to death of hearing about the incompetency of Bombardier and failure to meet their obligations when half of Oshawa is collecting employment insurance benefits and would love to be back to work. **If automotive plants could switch to making tanks and fighter planes during the Second World War, I am confident Canadian ingenuity could make it happen again for trains and streetcars.**

Set up a conference call or better still, a meeting at Tim Hortons somewhere along Highway 401, between the automotive execs, the unions, the Quebec and Ontario Government Ministers of Economic Development and Bombardier. Let's get this show on the road. I will buy the Tim-Bits if it helps sweeten the pot. Time is being wasted and jobs are waiting. Let's put the kettle on.

Should we allow Patriots' owner Robert Kraft to get off with a time-out?

When I saw the picture in The New York Times of the "Day Spa" where Patriots' football team owner Robert Kraft met his Waterloo recently, I was amazed at how innocuous the storefront appeared. Situated in a nondescript suburban strip plaza, the spa advertised waxing and facial treatments as well as the more nebulous services of massage therapy and body treatments. Yikes! I could have easily entered such a place to get my eyebrows waxed without knowing it was fronting a "rub n' tug". Life's full of risks.

In case you're not familiar with the story, Kraft was arrested getting his hot rocks off at such an establishment. Not only did he get a penalty for holding but the shakedown unleashed an entire snake pit of charges including human trafficking. While I do not deny these places often harbour any number of illegal activities, the darker side of these establishments is not what I would like to address today.

As a 77-year-old billionaire widower, Kraft could be a bit more discriminating about where he sources his time-outs. There are endless women who would have come to his home and offered discreet services in return for a gold Rolex or perhaps season tickets to Patriot games. Hell, he probably even has a Superbowl ring or two he wouldn't miss if he gifted it to someone special. Pee Wee Herman was similarly demonized and blackballed for enjoying himself a bit too much in a theatre. And boomer women forgave Hugh Grant for his famous indiscretion years ago. We only wish he'd picked one of us for some quality time. We'll never understand why these men of means do such stupid things. Perhaps it really does have something to do with the location of their brains.

Readers of **BoomerBroadcast.net** know I am no fan of football but sometimes when you're scrambling in the end zone and no one is blocking, you're entitled to a late-in-the-game touchdown. I've been known to beeline it pretty quickly to the nearest Dairy Queen when I'm feeling that irresistable urge for a Blizzard, so how is this any different? I think he deserves credit for still having an interest in scoring long after his best season is behind him. Let him enjoy the game while his contract still stands.

Or maybe Mr. Kraft really *was* just trying to get his eyebrows waxed and his nostrils trimmed. When I think of how I could have just as easily been in that place at that time waiting my turn for a therapeutic mini massage with a happy ending, well, it's just plain scary. Next time I go for a facial perhaps I should check out the activity in the other treatment rooms before I lay my money down. Let's give the guy a break. A time-out is more than enough. And be careful out there ladies.

What do you do when your dryer is condemned to landfill?

LG Appliances has some 'splainin' to do. I can overlook the fact that the ice dispenser on my LG fridge always jams and the door to the ice storage bin tends to pop open at will and bangs around until I manage to slam the faulty closure until it holds. Those issues are mere annoyances compared to my latest major appliance complaint. When we moved into our current home ten years ago, we purchased new appliances with the assumption they would last us until we go to the *'home'*.

Then, last month my clothes dryer refused to produce the necessary heat to dry a load of clothing. The vent wasn't plugged or twisted and no matter what setting I used, the machine refused to heat up. It's easy to suggest that after ten years, it might be due for a service call but the fact is I'm a devoted user of outside clotheslines. That means our dryer is used for perhaps two loads a week for only half the year, so in a way, it's only five years old. Compare that to a family with children who does laundry every day. In terms of mileage, my dryer is practically new.

A call to the appliance repair company resulted in a service call that suggested a new heater unit was needed. Wrong diagnosis. Then, it was suggested the problem was the electronic control panel which could cost upwards of $600.00+ to replace—*if* they could get the part, which they weren't sure about. After checking with LG, the repairman was informed that the part is no longer available and they don't know if it ever will be. Well, isn't that lovely? Apparently, after a mere seven years, the dryer is considered obsolete and not only are parts no longer available, LG doesn't even recommend servicing it.

The lifespan for built-in obsolescence on appliances has shrunk considerably in recent years. When my dad moved out of his house into assisted living a couple of years ago, he still had the original McClary refrigerator that he and my mother purchased in 1953. It was their first electric fridge; it was still plugged in and running in their basement and it was pristine, more than sixty-five years later. I was six years old when they bought it and the new fridge meant I could no longer enjoy the chunks of ice the iceman chipped off on the sidewalk for neighbourhood kids when we restocked our old icebox twice a week.

They just don't make 'em like they used to.

So, I was left with a giant, shiny appliance in my laundry room that is virtually and literally useless. After years of trying to save hydro costs and the environment by hanging my laundry outside, I now owned a mammoth door stop. How complicated can dryer parts be that they are rendered obsolete so quickly? Having to purchase a new dryer filled me with rage at the indifference to environmental concerns displayed by LG. And I'm sure the other appliance manufacturers are just as guilty. They've forced me to add to landfill and subtract from my bank account when both should be unnecessary.

I refused to say goodbye

The first repair diagnosis required two separate visits by the repairman for a total of two hundred dollars and after ordering a couple of new parts that didn't fix the problem, the final recommendation was to buy a new dryer. *I refused to accept that my dryer was dead.* So, I visited Google and YouTube to check out various solutions undertaken by other consumers, only to learn that dismantling the dryer, removing the drum, checking various sensors and connections with electrical thingies, the job was beyond DIY, and definitely beyond the capability and patience of me or my honey.

After contemplating my dilemma for a few days, and checking the price of new dryers online, I decided to seek a second opinion. So, I called another local appliance repair shop and they dispatched a technician to my home a couple of hours later. So far, so good. When the gloved, masked man arrived at my door, he was shown into the laundry room via the garage where he dismantled the machine and again informed me I probably needed a new control panel, which, miraculously, they had in stock. This could cost almost as much as a new dryer. We thought it was worth the investment, so he ordered the part and the next day made another service call to replace it. It was not the control panel.

Further tests by the second repairman on what was our fourth service visit (now totalling more than four hundred dollars excluding parts and labour) finally detected the problem. *The electrical outlet was only getting 110 volts, not the required 220 volts. A quick trip to Home Depot for a six-dollar replacement outlet solved the problem. Jeeeeezzz!*

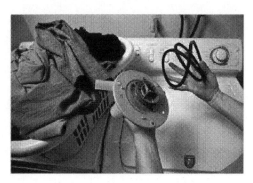

If the so-called experts can't figure out the problem, what chance do the rest of us stand?

What's a person to do? It happens all the time, with cars, electronics, and household appliances. We're totally at the mercy of the so-called experts. But 'expert' is a highly subjective term. During the first service call, the repairman alluded to an electrical problem but failed to detect it. After four separate visits, being without a dryer for a month, and an outlay of nearly $500.00, we're finally back in business. No dryer went to landfill. LG was unable to upsell us. And if something like this happens again, the first thing we'll check is the electrical connection—well, after we've checked the venting. It's enough to make me want to go back to a low-tech washboard and clothesline. Not really, but you get my point.

So, I guess I owe LG a wee apology. In view of the litany of curse words, insults, and expletives I hurled at them in the last month, they deserve a bit of a reprieve, but only a small one. While my dryer problem turned out to be electrical and not exactly the fault of LG, they're still guilty of making products that can be reduced to landfill in as little as seven years and that's just shameful.

If you run into problems with a major appliance, trust your instincts. I recommend taking the chance and spending money on a second opinion. Better still, encourage a grandchild to become an electrician or plumber. They'll have guaranteed employment for life and make a fortune. Maybe they can even help you pay for that private room in the 'home' where someone else will do your laundry, for a fee.

Next, I'm going to tackle my television issues—or maybe I'll just watch CBC for the rest of my life. I'm still recovering.

Will you miss Victoria's Secret?

The announcement recently that Victoria's Secret was one of several American retailers closing stores in Canada came as no surprise to me. The United States will take the brunt of the downsizing with fifty-three store closings and three in Canada. While I'll miss their bright pink window displays in suburban malls and mourn the loss of jobs for hundreds of staff, I'm afraid I

Pretty but not practical.

must accept part of the blame for their closing That is because . . . I. Never. Shop. There. That's what happens when they target only skinny teens.

The first time I bought something from Victoria's Secret was nearly forty years ago, before the brand was available in Canada. They had a great mail order catalogue (in the days before on-line shopping) which a friend brought back from a skiing weekend in Ellicottville, N.Y. I fell in love with a moderately priced sweatshirt and leggings combo which I immediately ordered by phone. It took a couple of weeks to arrive and when it did, I was shocked at how much the items ultimately cost me in Canadian dollars. Added to the catalogue price was the conversion from American to Canadian dollars (around 35% at the time), import duties, shipping costs for out-of-country and, of course, local sales taxes in Canada, ultimately more than doubling the original cost. That was pretty much my first and last experience with Victoria's Secret.

Then, a few years later, to our great amazement and delight, it was announced that Victoria's Secret was opening retail stores in Canada. My excitement turned to disappointment when it became evident that the stores featured mainly brothel-wear and dorm-wear, with none of the lovely leisurewear I had grown to love in their mail order catalogues.

Nothing in the stores appealed to this boomer broad although I regularly perused their stock foraging for something I might like. No luck. The quality was dubious, the lace embellishments were itch-inducing and the sizes inconsistent and unreliable. Compounding the lack of appeal in their merchandise was their total disregard for anyone who wasn't stick thin and pubescent.

Maybe if you're surgically enhanced and haven't eaten since 1992.

It seems to me they totally opted for form over function, eliminating a huge margin of consumers. Their pretty pink window displays were seductive and price points manageable but overall they offered nothing that appealed to me and my demographic. Trying to fit their Barbie doll lingerie on this boomer body would have involved extensive and expensive surgical intervention.

Boomer gals were probably the first generation that sported sexy, feminine lingerie daily that wasn't constructed of sturdy white cotton that our mothers wore in the fifties. We embraced demi-bras, bikini panties and all the colours, lace trimmings, see-through fabrics and modern styles generated by the sexual revolution. Back then we had cute, tight little bottoms, firm boobs located where they originally sprouted and flat stomachs. Cellulite was still in the far-distant future. For a brief period in our lives when we were young and compact we could wear the tiny little shreds of lace Victoria's Secret marketed.

Sadly, no lingerie retailer has followed aging boomer preferences since which has left a serious gap in the supply market. The consumer market is not made up entirely of millennials. I'm constantly bemoaning the lack of feminine, sexy nightgowns for our age group. We're forced to choose between frumpy granny gowns with white cotton eyelet trim in bunny or teddy bear prints or strappy little wisps of nylon that do nothing to flatter our boomer waistlines and saggy knees. What's a boomer gal to do?

There is one retailer in the United States called _Soma_, affiliated with the Chico's and White House Black Market brand, that has wonderful lingerie and loungewear that's comfortable and appropriate for baby boomer women. Hopefully, they too will join their partners in opening Canadian retail outlets.

Whenever I'm in the States, I load up but even Soma rarely has the kind of nightgowns I like. I'm just not a pyjama person. I keep emailing their customer service people and answering on-line customer surveys but feminine, attractive nightgowns that flatter our body shapes and still allow those hot flashes to vent are

Not in Canada . . . yet. If you go to the U.S., load up. They also give you $10.00 trade-in on your old bras.

harder to find than good calorie-free wine. Boomers will also remember a couple of decades ago when Britain's Marks & Spencer still had retail stores in Canada. They had the best knickers and bras *ever* and we do miss them.

Finding comfortable, feminine lingerie is a tricky business. The Hudson's Bay Company stores have extensive lingerie departments that offer an excellent choice but sizes and individual preferences require a lot of sleuthing to find exactly what works for each of us. It's like shopping for jeans. We have to try on and test drive dozens of pairs before we find something that works. Then, our loyalty remains firm.

The lesson for retailers here is: **IGNORE US AT YOUR PERIL**. The GAP is closing. Sears bit the dust. If you don't carry what me and my boomer gal pals would buy, you have no future, plain and simple. When are retailers going to get the message? Victoria's Secret never worked for me. What about you? What brands do you like and where do you prefer to shop for lingerie?

Thoughts on a trip to the mall

It's a rare occurrence when I visit one of the local shopping malls that I come home empty-handed. In fact, when I do leave without purchasing anything, I feel rather virtuous and self-satisfied having once again narrowly escaped the sirens' call. Giant, shiny shopping malls that sprang up in the suburbs across the country in the last few decades are modern cathedrals, a holy gathering place where humble worshipers go to deify the goddesses of consumerism. The bright window displays of the latest fashions draw us in and tempt us to lay down our souls and over-loaded credit cards in the name of instant gratification. How many times have we gone out to purchase a single needed item like a new pair of winter boots only to leave with multiple bags of not needed and not appreciated extra items of clothing, jewelry or skin care products?

The curse of consumerism hasn't escaped me. If I'd purchased fewer pairs of shoes and purses during my working years and been less concerned about strutting out in the latest disposable fashions, I'd have a lot more money in my RRSP to draw from now. But that's all past history. The important thing is I learned something, and that lesson affects my behaviour today. If I could give young people a word of advice it would be: *Financial freedom = Overall freedom.* Save for the future. You will never be totally free until you are financially independent.

A lot of my boomer friends reached a plateau around mid-life. Many of us had been at jobs that were unsatisfying or highly stressful and wanted to consider other ways to spend the rest of our days. We wanted *options.* That's not possible when you're broke, have crushing mortgage payments or onerous consumer debt. By middle-age things should be getting easier but because of profligate spending in our glory years we were chained to our weekly paycheque.

Now that I'm retired, I'm free to do what I please. Doing what we like doesn't have to be expensive. It can mean having the time to ride our bikes on a beautiful day, visit friends during the week for a cup of tea and a chat, even during the day which is so lovely. There are so many little benefits that come with retirement but let's face it, retirement is that much more fun and satisfying when we can scrape together enough toonies and loonies every year to indulge our hobbies, take a vacation or splurge on a golf or tennis club membership. If we're creative types, we need money to purchase canvases, paints, craft supplies, or a little fishing boat or RV if we're outdoorsy. During our retirement years the one thing we all have is common is we have to watch our spending habits. Some may continue doing part-time or volunteer work after retirement. The beauty of it all is now we *have options.*

Seniors have made a science out of pinching pennies although now that Canada has discontinued the use of pennies, I guess I should say pinching loonies. Not only does it give us an intellectual challenge, it helps ensure we're going to be able to finance a comfortable lifestyle for as many years as possible. There is no way in the world I need another pair of shoes. I have more than enough of everything but going to the mall to get my hair done on a quiet Tuesday morning still requires a hefty dose of discipline to not pick up that cute pair I saw on sale in Ron White's window.

The best way I've found to keep myself in check is to not visit the mall unless absolutely necessary. When I see a gorgeous white blouse at Hudson's Bay on sale, I remind myself I already have too many white blouses hanging in my closet that are barely worn. Although I admit, I feel somewhat vindicated when I think about a mother I saw interviewed on Oprah once who confessed to owning ninety-three (93) pairs of jeans and her five children didn't have health insurance. I'm not that bad!

Then there's the online shopping issue and it's not to be underestimated. And, as we get older and less inclined to get out and drive to the mall or local store, we'll be increasing our use of online shopping. It is convenient and allows us to price shop from our livingroom LaZgirl. But we have to watch those sneaky advertisers. Once we purchase an item online, we'll be forever bombarded with ads for the same or similar items available from different retailers making it sometimes too easy to click "Purchase".

I have more success with staying away from the mall altogether and constant vigilance is necessary. Who isn't a sucker for a good sale, especially when it's a brand we favour? They're always trying to outsmart us. Many large retailers are closing bricks and mortar stores in favour of fewer outlets and expanding the online experience. I wonder what shopping will look like in a couple of decades. Considering all the changes that have taken place in the last few years, it's hard to imagine what things will look like when drone delivery and digital technology amps up further.

Even the grocery store can be seductive these days with their Joe Fresh clothing line and too many tempting edible treats that should never land in my grocery cart but somehow do. But the biggest culprit is still THE MALL. Breathing that hallowed air with sunshine streaming in through strategically placed skylights, wearing my most comfortable and stylish 'shopping' shoes, it's far too easy to succumb to temptation. Just like losing that last 10 or 15 lbs., it's all up hill and takes a lot of discipline. Sometimes it helps to remind myself how lucky I am to have such first world problems and nothing exemplifies this better than a trip to the mall.

Kudos to Chatelaine and Dove soap for recognizing that all women are beautiful

When I received the June/July 2019 issue of Chatelaine magazine in my mailbox I was a little taken aback at first. Featured on the cover of the annual swimsuit issue is a full-bodied woman of indeterminate age wearing a coral-coloured swimsuit, a straw sunhat, and a huge smile. The more I thought about it and went through its pages, the bigger the smile grew on my own face. *It takes courage for a major magazine to turn the tables on the media's narrow definition of beauty.*

Canada's own Chatelaine magazine and Dove soap have joined forces to recognize that even though we are not all six feet tall, blonde, blue-eyed and weigh less than a single maple leaf, we're still beautiful. Dove has been running this campaign for many years. They've earned kudos for their marketing and women appreciate their efforts, but this is the first time I've seen a national magazine take it a step further.

Just as I was considering canceling my decades-long subscription to Chatelaine, they've totally redeemed themselves. I still prefer most of my mags in print version so I can rip pages out to save recipes or inspirational fashion pics.

The spread on pages 20-22 is a summary of book recommendations for summer which is always appreciated, especially when it includes Canadian authors. I like the way they're categorized: *Best Character, Best Dystopian Thriller, Best History Lesson* and so on.

They included their *Drugstore Hall of Fame* picks for makeup, skin, body and hair care products. It's always fun and somewhat reassuring to read what others are using and prefer, especially when we are assured we don't have to lay out $400.00 for an eye cream. There are the usual fashion items, sensible advice on health issues and a *Winners' Spotlight* on everyday household products preferred by Canadians. I haven't had a chance yet to read the extensive piece about Chrystia Freeland written by Leah McLaren but it's on my to-do list.

There's plenty more great material in this issue but I don't want to spoil all the fun for you. Do yourself and print publications a favour. Please pick up a newsstand copy of the June/July edition of Chatelaine. The cover appearing at your newsstand or grocery store may not be the same as mine as Chatelaine has published its June/July issue with a series of different covers featuring pictures real women can identify with and relate to. Imagine that! Show your support for their brave editorial step. It's also a vote for a more diverse definition of beauty, something long overdue in media. Put the June/July 2019 issue of Chatelaine on your grocery list and pick up a copy while it's still available.

Glory hallelujah! It's road construction season again. Help wanted

There must be a better way.

It's a common saying here in Canada. We have only two seasons, **winter** and **road construction**. As I drive around the city and surrounding countryside, I'm experiencing my annual surge of anger and frustration with the state of our transportation system. Once the snow melts, roads and highways are cordoned off, lanes are reduced and then nothing happens. *If* there is any activity on the site, two bored-looking workers are wandering around with a shovel in their hands but most often there's *nothing* going on. I realize road and highway maintenance and improvements are necessary and we need the end result. I just wish some actual work would take place and more quickly. How much can two lowly workers achieve by themselves, even with a backhoe?

The answer to the problem is simple. I learned it from watching home construction in Florida. **Blitz the job with workers and get it over with.** In Florida, I've watched the concrete trucks arrive early in the morning, pour the slab for a new home, then the (Mexican) workers finish it and leave at the end of the day. The next day another crew of a couple of dozen workers arrives, erects the block structure followed the next day by different crews who frame the entire house inside and out, and then they go home at the end of the day. Finally, a roofing crew arrives. Well, you get the picture.

We once had our entire property including, sod, trees, and shrubs landscaped in a day. There were probably twenty workers on the job. Everything was planned out in advance and the work fell into place like clockwork. The secret is careful planning and scheduling and maximizing the use of labour. Why can't road and highway construction be done the same way? The same amount of labour is expended and the cost is the same; it's just compressed into a much tighter time frame. **Bring in crews of dozens of workers and git 'er done.**

This could take a while. And, this is definitely not what I meant by blitzing the job with workers. (Looks like an Ontario Hydro job, doesn't it?)

Does it take a genius to properly plan a construction project far enough ahead to maximize resources in the shortest possible time period? Having worked in the construction industry for most of my forty-year career, I witnessed fifty-storey office buildings go up and be occupied in less time than it takes to reconstruct an intersection. If major hospital construction can proceed concurrently with the performance of health care and surgeries without closing services, why can't altering a street or road? Part of the reason for this is the total absence of actual work happening on road construction sites most of the time. Maybe our grandchildren can make it better.

Here's how your grandchild can make good money and have job security?

The problem of slow road construction is a positive argument for immigration. In the 1950s, thousands of Italians immigrated to Canada and were the heart and soul of the construction industry building major cities like Toronto and Montreal. They worked hard, contributed to the community and raised a generation of equally hard-working offspring who went to college and university. Now the industry is suffering from a serious shortage of tradespeople. Construction unions and employers have been waving the red flag about worker shortages for years. Our blue-collar workforce is shrinking and young people are being encouraged to ignore high-paying trade jobs in favour of going to university for degrees in dubious careers like psychology, kinesiology or women's studies. **Not everyone is well-served by going to university.**

The construction industry is always looking for people.

While I'm on the subject, it's not just hands-on tradespeople who are needed in construction. The industry is crying out for estimators, schedulers, software developers, project managers, field engineers, superintendents, health and safety professionals, mechanical and electrical coordinators, project accountants, proposal writers, draftspeople, and on and on and on.

253

So, what are we to do while we negotiate around blocked off streets and construction bottlenecks? Maybe we should be sending those illegal immigrants who are sneaking across rural borders down to the union hall and putting them to work instead of providing free winter parkas and housing. Those people fleeing political terror in Central America who are being rejected at the Mexican border would be welcome in Canada, if they're willing to work to help rebuild our infrastructure and go through proper legal channels.

I realize my rant will change nothing. Until I'm in charge of running the world, I'll have to put up with all of life's frustrations and inconveniences. I'll avoid my usual Walmart because Dundas Street has been a sewer construction nightmare for two years. Thank the heavens above that I no longer live near Kipling subway station at Dundas and Bloor Streets. A long-overdue rework on that intersection (Six Points) will be a local traffic disaster for who-knows-how-long.

I'll also steer clear of the 427 and QEW interchange because heaven knows how long that project will last. And we won't even discuss the 401 across the top of Toronto; it's beyond words. I had to change my doctors from North York to Mississauga because traffic getting to their offices was such a nightmare. Just getting across the city and back took the better part of a day. Imagine all the unreported lost productivity incurred by businesses when their people are sitting in traffic jams.

It's a shame Toronto and the provincial government were so short-sighted in keeping our subway system and transportation networks robust and up to date over the last few decades. Highway 407 is great, but, *dang,* it costs a fortune to drive it, unless you can expense the costs, which only adds to the net cost of doing business. As retired seniors on a budget, we avoid it.

As boomers age and lose our drivers' licenses, we're going to increasingly rely on public transportation that probably won't be adequate to meet our needs in our lifetime. Hopefully, our children and grandchildren will get it figured out and fix the mess. In the meantime, encourage them to have lots of babies because the construction industry needs workers. And hopefully one of them will be smart enough to reinvent and re-engineer the approach to road and highway construction. Unfortunately for us boomers, by then it'll be too late. We'll be dead. The upside is that my rants will be silenced.

The solution to the problem with the Toronto Maple Leafs is so obvious

Even an ignorant non-sports enthusiast like me can see the solution to the problem with the Toronto Maple Leafs. They tanked, blew it, and generally lived up to their dismal reputation in the psuedo run-up to the Stanley Cup finals again this year. Ho-hum. Tim Horton, Johnny Bower, George  Armstrong, and their teammates must be absolutely horrified as they look down from the big gondola in heaven.

One thing can be said for the Leafs though; they are consistent—consistent losers. By the way, I didn't watch any of the games. Why bother? We all knew they weren't going anywhere. And any time they shockingly scored a goal, my husband would shout the miracle to me from the other room.

They've tried switching coaches, managers, and players, updated their uniforms with a newer, sexier logo, jacked-up salaries for so-called star players and nothing has worked. In my opinion, the solution is obvious. With more than seven decades of life under my elastic waistband, it has been my experience that no one has a greater incentive to work harder or produce more than those who are a bit 'hungry'.

Those twenty-something young guys with multi-million-dollar contracts have no incentive to go for the cup because they already have everything they need—in fact, far *more* than what they need. They're making bazillions of dollars already, whether they make the playoffs or not. *Why try harder?* They can already afford to drive Teslas, rent expensive condos downtown, and pay for a round of beers after the game without worrying about their card being rejected. Their wives and girlfriends reap the secondary benefits with more than enough money to maintain those expensive blonde highlights and extensions, lip injections, and designer handbags. Why bother working above minimum requirements when those big dollar numbers will land in the bank account whether they score goals or not.

Remember when the Leafs of the sixties made around $10K a year? That was considered a lot of money at the time but nothing compared to the proportionately stratospheric salaries earned by the players today. Back then the

This team of Stanley-Cup-winning Toronto Maple Leafs earned $10K a year and had to get summer jobs to make ends meet.

players used to spend their summers attending university or working other jobs to pay the mortgage. And those players from the original six-team league had to launch a monumental years-long legal battle to get any kind of pension. Gordie Howe resorted to selling autographed hockey sticks in his old age to make ends meet.

My solution is quite simple. Pay each player a good living wage, say, $150,000.00 a year, which is still even more than the rest of us receive. Ever heard of piece work? Factories used to employ this method of compensation to encourage workers to produce more work pants, sew more tongues in shoes, or bolt more bolts. What about paying players a bonus for each assist or goal they score? Defensemen and goalies could get bonuses for the saves they make. Penalties that leave the team short-handed and fighting would result in personal fines. Obviously there are still a few details to be ironed out but that's a good starting point. If they make it to the semi-finals, they would get a modest bonus with the really big bonus coming if they make it to the finals. Of course, winning the Stanley Cup is the pot of gold.

It doesn't take a genius to see the problem with professional sports salaries today. **There's no incentive to work harder or do better.** Keep 'em a bit hungry, throw in some incentives, and they'll suddenly start scoring goals and winning games. Boomers learned early on that we wouldn't get raises or promotions unless we earned them. Even then, we were never 'spoiled' by obscenely huge salaries so we always had to work hard and keep striving to make our car payments or pay off the thirty-year mortgage at fourteen percent.

If Leafs' management would like to contact me, my advice is free and available at any time. If I don't answer the phone, it's because I'm busy watching Masterpiece Theatre. It's more rewarding than the hockey game. Whatcha' think? Leave a message at the beep.

NO! I definitely do NOT need my ducts cleaned.

Those annoying telemarketers give the entire industry a bad reputation.

Does anyone know how to stop those infernal, annoying, never-ending calls from telemarketers trying to sell me duct-cleaning services? It's been going on for years and they nail me anywhere at any time. I was sitting in the hairdressers yesterday and *ring...ring...ring*. I rarely use my cellphone so when it rings it's always my husband.

Not this time. After fumbling in my purse, digging out my phone from the bottom layer of purse detritus and trying to figure out how to turn it on to take an incoming call, only to hear . . . *"This is XYZ Duct-Cleaning Services calling . . . "*

The other day I was pickling beets in the kitchen. Just as the sticky mixture of cider vinegar and sugar came to a boil on the stove, the phone rang, and once again it was duct cleaners. They interrupted me just long enough for the sugary vinegar mixture to boil over on the stove . . . and there aren't words to describe the mess it created, not to mention the stream of bad-swears uttered in anger and frustration. For the record, a boiling mixture of cider vinegar and sugar turns hard as titanium when it erupts like a volcano from the pan and hits a flat surface. Or a vertical surface like the front of the stove. Or the floor. You get the picture.

Is it still illegal to put out a contract on telemarketers?

Even though I'm on a Do-Not-Call list for telemarketers (which obviously is not effective), I have a variety of responses when they do call. It ranges from a simple hang-up to screaming at them, informing them I have radiators, not ducts (a lie), yelling at them to never call me again, and ordering them to take me off their call list. Nothing works. They're as persistent as . . . well, telemarketers selling duct-cleaning services. Our neighbour told me that when she informed them she didn't have ducts, they *insisted she did*! What's a girl to do?

They interrupt meals; they interrupt my favourite television shows; they interrupt my entire life. I can't imagine these calls generate enough sales to even pay the minimum-wage earners who place the calls, with a little robo-help, of course. I've considered recording the number they're calling from and blocking it, but the number isn't always the same. Sometimes it's a 289 area code; sometimes it's 416; other times it's 905 or 647, or the ubiquitous 800 or 866. I don't know who's calling until I pick it up and hear that familiar, dreaded pause before the spiel.

It seems self-defeating and counter-productive to have to disconnect my home phone and cell just to avoid the telemarketers but extreme circumstances call for extreme measures. Too bad there wasn't some kind of tear gas that we could release through the telephone lines to temporarily disable them. If you have any suggestions, send them my way. I'm desperate. Even illegal measures will be seriously considered. The greater question that now remains is who should I call when I actually *do* need my ducts cleaned?

Listen up people! Concrete and cement are not interchangeable words

Every time there's a reference in the news or in general conversation to *cement* steps, *cement* porch, curbs or building components, my husband has a nuclear meltdown. We both spent our careers in construction and every time we hear the word *cement* used when the word they should be using is *concrete*, it hits our ears like chalk grating on a blackboard, or, worse, Yoko Ono singing. This mistake occurs frequently including several times on CTV television and their writers should know better. It's one of those petty annoyances like people using 'irregardless' for 'regardless'. Just . . . DON'T do it.

Here's the scoop. **Cement is one ingredient in the recipe for concrete.** Concrete is made up of five basic ingredients:

1. Sand
2. Aggregates (crushed stone)
3. Water
4. Air
5. Cement (powder)

Sometimes, other materials or chemicals may be used as well to modify the strength, density or weight of the finished product but basically, that's what it includes. Interchanging 'concrete' and 'cement' is like making a cake and calling it flour. Cement is a dry ingredient that is just one of the components of concrete.

Step 1: Cement is a dry ingredient.

Step 2: Add water, sand, aggregates and air, mix, finish and cure..

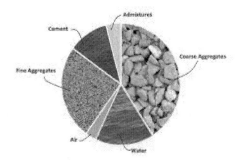

Step 3: The finished product is called CONCRETE not cement.

Various additives and chemicals can also be added to a concrete mixture to make it lighter, stronger or more weather resistant..

Mix Design Content	M20	M25	M30	M35	M40	M45
Cement	300	340	370	400	430	460
Water	144	156	163	164	163	161
20 mm Aggregate	720	700	680	660	650	620
10 mm Aggregate	610	590	565	550	540	525
River Sand	750	770	722	711	708	706
Water : Cement	0.48	0.46	0.44	0.41	0.38	0.35
20 mm : 10 mm	55:45	54:46	55:45	58:42	55:45	54:46
Coarse : Fine	36:64	37:63	37:63	39:61	37:63	38:62

The recipes for mixing concrete can be varied, depending on performance requirements.

Creating concete is much like making a cake. You would never call a cake "flour". That's just one of the ingredients in the final product.

Step 2: Depending on the specific recipe, we add, eggs, butter, spices, nuts and other ingredients.

Step 1: Flour, just like cement (sort of) is a prime ingredient in making a cake. It holds it all together

Step 3: *After assembling and baking all the ingredients, you have a finished cake, hopefully my favourite, German chocolate. And, if you've done it correctly, it should taste nothing like concrete.*

So, do we all now understand? **The words concrete and cement are not interchangeable.** That sidewalk, wall or those steps Rocky Balboa climbed to get in shape are *concrete*, not *cement*. I don't want to ever hear you call them cement again.

Is the war on plastics win-able?

Plastic does not biodegrade so where does it all go?

Every piece of plastic that has ever been created *still exists*. Think about that. I certainly do as I cast my eyes across all the plastic shampoo and other bottles in the shower every morning, as I look at all the plastic containers in my pantry and fridge, when I toss plastics into recycling, never sure if they will actually be recycled. Our world is built on plastic and will die from plastic overload. Each of us is trying her best to be environmentally conscientious but the odds are stacked against us. No matter how hard we try to eliminate plastics from our lives, it's an uphill battle. Third world countries are still dumping it into the streets which flow into the drainage systems, which drain into creeks and rivers, that drain into oceans and collect until a green-minded environmentalist tries to collect it with a net, to be deposited . . . where?

Plastic drinking straws are small in size but huge in the overall impact of pollution on our planet. The banning of plastic drinking straws and other single-use plastics is a controversial and growing problem. It's horrifying to see pictures of creatures in the wild starving because there's a plastic packaging ring wrapped around their mouths making it impossible to feed. Autopsied whales have revealed huge amounts of plastic waste in their stomachs, giving them the sensation of having eaten while gaining zero nutrition.

The most gratifying part of my Mothers' Day surprise lunch from Harvey's was not the food itself but the fat orange paper straw in the (waxed) paper cup full of Diet Pepsi. The Harvey's orange straw wasn't like the ones we sipped our cherry Cokes through in the 50s and 60s that disintegrated before you were finished. This one had heft. It's a small step but a long overdue and much-appreciated option to single-use plastic straws. Paper is recyclable and a replaceable resource.

I'm trying to be conscientious about reducing pollution but I feel it's not working. Today when I rolled those giant bins out to the curb and took a last peek inside, I was shocked to see that my recyclables were twice the amount of my regular garbage. While recycling should be a good thing, viewing my own garbage only demonstrates what a wasteful society we are. All those plastics that are being manufactured and distributed every day are only bloating our planet's wastes. I diligently tear paper labels off cans and bottles before rinsing and disposing of them into the appropriate recycling bin. And I discreetly take things my honey has inadvertently dropped into the trash bin and move them into recycling. But, it's discouraging to learn that much of what we put in our recyclable bins still goes to landfill.

We managed just fine in the fifties and sixties (my boomer frame of reference) without plastic grocery bags, plastic straws, plastic bottles and all the other items we use so ubiquitously today. That got me thinking about what substitutions could easily be made without too much disruption in function. Many plastic items could easily be replaced by paper or wood products which could be sourced from Canada's vast renewable lumber industry:

- Plastic grocery bags – Paper or reusable cloth bags
- Styrofoam takeout food and drink containers – Paper

- Plastic straws – paper or reusable stainless steel
- Plastic cutlery – wooden or bamboo utensils
- Plastic produce bags – cotton net bags much like the ones we use for laundry delicates
- Single-use bottles of water – refill stainless steel containers from the tap

And the list goes on. Every time I drop something into the garbage, I'm plagued with guilt. It's hard to avoid when most of our everyday consumer goods are wrapped in or made of plastic. I have a giant thirty-ounce stainless steel thermal cup and stainless-steel straw I use to tote my daily supply of water around in the car. I use the same kind of cup for my refills at Timmie's. It's gratifying to see some plastic items being replaced with paper but we have a long way to go.

I am restricting my consumption of discretional consumer goods like clothing and tchotchkes. We already have more than we need and I'm getting too old for all the work involved in staging a yard sale. I've donated boxes and bags of goods to various charities but our house is still chock-a-block with *stuff,* plastic and otherwise. I'm not really prepared to go full-on Marie Kondo yet but I

Don't forget to take your reusable bags into the store with you.

know we could live a lot more simply than we do. Do I contribute more to landfill or let it continue to fill my home?

Remember in the fifties when we used to take fish and chips home from the chip shop wrapped in newspaper? Groceries were packed in large paper bags that our mothers reused for garbage disposal. We owned one car per family if we owned a car at all. We had one television, one telephone on the kitchen wall, one winter coat, one pair of good shoes for Sunday and special occasions and another pair for every day, one white purse for summer and a black or brown one for winter.

We could learn so much from adopting many of the methods our parents (The Greatest Generation) used to reduce and save waste. Most boomers probably remember our fathers resoling their work shoes rather than tossing them and buying a new pair. We're shameless consumers with more shoes, jeans, tops, coats, purses, and toys than we need or even use. We need bigger houses with bigger closets and kitchens to store all the crap we've accumulated over the years. As boomers, it's scary to even think of the work involved in downsizing. It's tempting to just dodge our responsibility and leave everything for our kids to dispose of after we die. Imagine how thrilled they'll be to inherit all our old china, out-of-date furniture, worn-out linens, and mismatched crystal glassware.

I'm not suggesting we turn back the clock but affluence has come at a terrible cost to our planet. Third world countries are sending back our garbage. I didn't even realize we were shipping it overseas until China and Malaysia went public with the news they were no longer accepting it.

Baby boomers are a generation of serious polluters who begat generations of even greater polluters. We've realized the error of our ways and most of us are trying to make amends, but the problems seem insurmountable. I'm actually in favour of tough laws at a federal or provincial level that force us to reduce consumption and pollution. We need a strong and united political front to lead the charge. Outlawing plastic bags and straws seems like a tough and perhaps unworkable measure, but that's what we need to consider doing.

I'm willing to pay more for products in glass reusable bottles that require a refundable deposit. Collecting and returning scavenged glass pop bottles as a kid guaranteed I had a steady income stream for Dubble Bubble and red licorice. We became very resourceful at scrounging dirty old pop bottles from ditches and roadways. That system could work again. I'm trying to reduce my own personal consumption. We must keep trying. And we must vote for politicians who will make the difficult decisions needed to get the ball rolling. I'm not sure we'll be able to make much of a difference in our lifetimes, but it's imperative that we convince the upcoming generations of the seriousness of the situation and trust them to do the right thing. Can we? Will they? It's a scary prospect and I hope someone steps up to the plate before it's too late. If it's not already.

Are self-checkouts a good thing or a bad thing?

There was an item on the news this week that demonstrated the future of in-store grocery shopping. Sobey's is test-driving new shopping carts that allow you to scan your items as soon as you pull them off the shelf. Each cart is equipped with a product scanner and sensors so you can scan your purchases immediately and drop them into your (recyclable) shopping bags sitting open in the cart. Easy peasy. No checkout clerk required. And special sensors in the cart alert you if you "forget" to scan something, preventing unscrupulous shoppers from circumventing the honour system.

Although I like the idea of getting in and out of the grocery store in as little time as possible, I have mixed feelings about this new innovation. It would be wonderful to avoid checkout lineups and the process of unloading your purchases from your cart onto a conveyor belt, then having to reload them again into your bags to go to the car. It would also prevent being subjected to clerks trying to sell me the deodorant special of the week, and the lure of gossipy magazines I tend to pick up while killing time in the lineup.

Checking out directly on your cart definitely has its advantages.

My biggest concern with self-checkouts, however, is the loss of service jobs that provide essential employment for so many semi-skilled and unskilled workers. It's no small matter. Those service jobs are disappearing everywhere at a time when we need them. McDonald's is using computerized graphic boards so customers can customize and place their own orders, once again by-passing the human clerk. To their credit, they have compensated for the employment issue by using staff/team members to deliver trays of food to the table in many outlets,a nice little bonus.

Shoppers Drug Mart is now introducing self-checkout as well and I always opt for using a real live person to make my purchases, again because of the jobs issue. Self-serve bank machines and gas pumps were early examples of machines replacing people. Somehow, we were easily tricked into doing the service providers' work ourselves with no apparent benefit. We now must wash our own windshields and even pay service fees to the banks for using our own money.

The voice of customer service is not the same as the face of customer service.

With so many commercial transactions now being conducted online, businesses are increasingly using their customers to do the work of what we used to call 'Customer Service'. Even customer service has now come to mean an anonymous voice in a remote call-centre, an impersonal job often staffed by people in third-world countries who speak English as a second language. Despite their scripted words, "*I understand*", they rarely do.

Sobey's executives have tried to assure customers that jobs will not be lost and they insist the people who were formerly checkout clerks will be working elsewhere in the store. I'm skeptical about this even though I would love to have personnel on the floor who could quickly and correctly direct me to where the maraschino cherries are located.

When boomers were growing up in the fifties and sixties, large supermarkets were just starting to take off. Many of our mothers still did their grocery shopping in small local family-owned stores. They bought meat from a butcher shop, produce from the greengrocer or perhaps all the weekly groceries at a small local general store. Bread and milk were delivered to our door by nice, uniformed men in trucks. If you're a particularly mature boomer like me, you may even remember the iceman bringing blocks of ice a couple of times a week. He'd usually break off some small chunks onto the sidewalk for us kids to chew on and cool off on a hot day. And we didn't die or even get sick from eating ice off the sidewalk. We loved it.

My father grew up in a rural community, even smaller than the one I grew up in. The local village was basically a few buildings at the intersection of two country roads. A weekly trip to the general store was a big deal. Dad told me that his father would dress up in his suit and tie for the weekly trip "into town" and sit on the front porch of the store catching up on the news with the other local men while their wives did the weekly shopping. And there's a lot to be said for having a store clerk who knows your Aunt Mildred had her gall bladder out and asks how she's doing. Catching up on who just had a baby or whose combine broke down was an early version of Facebook but conducted in person.

Human beings need personal, real-life interaction with other human beings. It's a fundamental part of our makeup and conducive to good health. We hear a lot about the plague of loneliness among the elderly but I suspect it's not just older people who feel starved of human connection. It's tragic to see a table full of young people in a restaurant or coffee

Seriously? What is happening to living in and enjoying the moment of one-on-one conversation with in-the-flesh friends

shop each focused on their smartphones, communicating with others at a distance who are obviously more important in their lives than whoever they're sitting with. We risk losing the art of meaningful conversation. It won't be long before even wait staff in restaurants will be replaced by smart devices on each table that allow us to place our order. Then, we'll even be deprived of the opportunity to say *"Yes. Everything's fine, thank you"* to a real human being.

I'm torn on the self-checkout issue. Are they a good thing or a bad thing? On one hand, I like the idea of avoiding the lineup at the cashier's counter. But that cashier probably needs the job and I enjoy exchanging a few words with him or her. I usually try to make their day a little less boring by telling them I like their hair or asking them if they have special plans for the weekend. We all need that human connection. As to whether self-checkouts are a good thing or a bad thing, one thing we know for sure, self-checkouts are an inevitable thing, whether we like it or not. I plan to avoid them as much as possible. What about you?

Footnote: Two weeks later I went into my Shoppers' Drug Mart and the self-checkout machines had disappeared, replaced by a conventional checkout with a real-life human being. Victory for our side and one small step for humankind.

My sympathies go out to McDonald's Steve Easterbrook

Steve Easterbrook, C.E.O. of McDonald's Corp. recently resigned his position because he had a consensual affair with a fellow employee of the firm. Yikes!! I have to say I feel sorry for him because I met both my first and second husbands through work, so I'm speaking from a position of experience. And many of my friends also met their spouses and partners through work. In fact, I'm inclined to think that with today's busy lifestyles and the long hours demanded by career-building, I don't know a better way to meet someone. When you've sat in meetings together, attended business functions and witnessed the behaviours of your fellow employees at the office Christmas party, you learn a lot about a person.

We spend so many hours each week with our coworkers that it's natural they become like family, with some relationships growing closer than others. We see our coworkers at their worst while under stress, at their magnanimous best when being rewarded for superior performance and we soon learn who is kind, who is ethical, who is lazy and who is honest. The hours we spend with our coworkers under stressful conditions offers the most comprehensive insights into their true character.

Now, don't get me wrong. I don't condone bullying or pressure by office predators in order to gain leverage. Heavens, no. We've all walked this earth long enough to know that scum bags exist but that's not what we're talking about here. This is about genuine consensual romantic relationships developing between coworkers, apart from #metoo.

Oh dear! No more free happy meals for Steve Easterbrook, but I am confident his separation package will compensate.

Having worked most of my career in the construction industry which is heavily weighted with male employees, the pickings were pretty good. There were many young engineers, tradespeople, technicians and other staff who mingled often with office staff. In the early years, most supervisory and management positions were male dominated but as women entered more non-traditional fields, their numbers increased. We often joked about the ensuing relationships that inevitably developed and we were tempted sometimes to sit down and make a list of the marriages that sprang from work-related relationships in our company alone. There were dozens and perhaps even into the hundreds that resulted in people getting together at my place of work, my own marriage being one of them.

I don't know the specifics of Steve Easterbrook's relationship. Perhaps he was married. Perhaps his partner was a subordinate. There are so many variables that may have been unsavory but it's not our place to moralize. Love happens. Apparently, McDonald's has a company policy that forbids consensual relationships with fellow employees. Their rationale is that they're a company with strong family values and their executives and employees at all levels have to respect that dictum. Politicians are often subjected to the same moral scrutiny but as evidenced by today's American President, it really doesn't hold much water these days. The moral right makes the rules and they are allowed to break them.

When relationships develop between females and a male with a higher position in the corporate hierarchy, there could be serious fallout if the relationship falls apart. It's difficult to work with someone you've broken up with and women are often dealt the losing hand in these circumstances. Her male superior may want her out-of-sight, out-of-mind and find it easier to terminate her. That's the price women have unfortunately paid for failed workplace relationships since the beginning of time unless you're England's Queen Elizabeth I or Catherine the Great of Russia. When there's an imbalance of power, the power exerts itself. I'm no longer in the workforce having retired a few years ago, but I hope the imbalance of power has eased up with the #metoo movement and allowed women to continue working in the same environment if they wish to do so.

My husband and I worked together for nearly thirty years before we became "an item" and we have now been together for twenty years. He was certainly above me in the management structure, but I did not directly report to him. We've had many discussions recently about how our relationship would or could have been handled under current circumstances. Fortunately, the firm we worked for did not have a *"No Fraternization"* policy and as a result, many happy marriages resulted from employees working together. In fact, some of the offspring of those marriages are now second-generation employees. That is a good thing for everyone. Just ask Bill and Melinda Gates or Barrack and Michelle Obama. Michelle was Barrack Obama's boss at the law firm where they both worked and I'd say that turned out to be a rather productive relationship.

I think the American military has similar policies to McDonald's and as a result, a very senior military advisor was recently forced to retire early when it was disclosed he'd had an affair with another officer. The military may have specific reasons for their policy, but I don't think any corporation has the right to dictate to its workers that they cannot become romantically involved. It has no business in the bedrooms of its employees, but I do think discretion on the part of coworkers is essential.

As long they are doing their job and their relationship is not negatively impacting their performance, then the employer should have no say in the matter. If I'd worked for companies with such outdated policies I'd probably be an old maid today instead of enjoying my life with someone I love and share a similar value system with. I feel for ya' Steve Easterbrook. I hope your next employer is more open-minded.

Tim Hortons . . . I told them so and they listened!

As mentioned in Chapter 2, when Tim Hortons was taken over by the American/Brazilian financial conglomerate Restaurant Brands International (RBI), I was afraid their new marketing strategy would dilute our unique Timmie's Canadian brand. And it did. Big time. One of my biggest fears was that they would start selling burgers, a food item so typically American and so far from Timmie's culture of Canadian red mittens and road hockey commercials that it was bound to alienate and offend Canadians. Then, they did it; they added meatless hamburgers to their menu. But the wheels fell off. Don't say I didn't warn you it wouldn't work. Now, they've stopped selling burgers.

Ever since Canadians gave up control of Tim Hortons it's been a rough hockey game without the Canadians captaining the team. I've written numerous posts over the last few years telling Timmie's to keep their stick on the ice and their eye on the game. They've lost sight of the puck and are playing too fast and loose with our culture, which has seriously eroded their fan base.

The long line-ups both inside their restaurants and outside at the Drive-Thru would lead one to think business is booming and they're raking in the dough!! But the food industry is a low-margin proposition at best and we Timmies' customers can be pretty fickle in our loyalties. Don't tempt us with second-rate hamburgers and don't treat us like bottom line accounting statistics. When Ron Joyce stepped aside and let the Yanks and Brazilians take over, things inevitably shifted to an American sensibility. We're not American and we're infinitely more sensible.

Canadians like plain warm and fuzzy with their double/double, not song and dance teams promoting meat-free burgers.

I first joined Timmie's club many cold Canadian winters ago when they started offering steeped tea that appealed to tea aficionados like me. Tea is something else Americans don't understand. I'm not a coffee drinker and I always felt left out walking around minus that iconic brown cup bearing a hot beverage in my hand. With our strong ties to our British and French heritage, Canadians understand a good cup of tea. We don't like a sloppy bag of inferior quality tea floating in the cup with all the tannins scumming on the surface. Steeped tea eliminates that problem.

Tim Hortons is a Canadian cultural icon and the more they mess with its Canadian-ness the more they risk losing our business. And the sooner they start listening to me the better off they'll be. If they want to expand their menu with something we Canucks would actually like and can identify with, what about quality butter tarts? But not the ones with heavy pastry that tastes like a hockey puck and the heft of shoe leather. No siree. Nice light, flaky pastry with deep, gooey filling and perhaps a few pecans, walnuts or raisins tossed in.

While I'm on a rant here, I'm not entirely sold on their new brown lids for cups. They're easier to pop open and the flaps don't slam back down and wack your nose like the old ones, but it is a little tricky sipping my steeped tea minus my bottom lip on the rim of the cup without getting tea up my nose. Is it possible to revisit the design of your new lids? Praise be, I'm not a complainer (??) but I do think those new lids need a tad more tinkering to get it right. And make sure those new lids are designed and clearly marked as *recyclable*.

As evidence that the big pooh-bahs at Tim Horton's follow my blog, not only did they discontinue burgers, they've launched a new commercial featuring a little boy from my hometown, Campbellford, Ontario (pop. 3500). Eight-year-old Gordie Gilders was selected from among hundreds of hopefuls to play a young Wayne Gretsky when he and his dad Walter visited Tim Horton's in Brantford to get a personal autograph from the real Horton, Tim himself. I really like this new, warm and fuzzy, uniquely Canadian commercial and hope to see more of the good old-style image Timmie was built on.

Has Tim Hortons fired their American marketing people? Is it possible they now rely solely on my BOOMERBROADCAST blog postings to develop future business policy? And, since they're probably reading this, perhaps they could also eliminate the waxy coating from their cups that excludes them from the recycling bin? The entire country and our environment would be eternally grateful. Keep innovating but direct your efforts at worthy goals.

I dumped my stock in Tim Hortons some time ago following the RBI takeover. But I really do want Tim Hortons to do well so I can buy back in again. I'm always available to answer questions on how to run the business Canadian style. Call me. Any time. In the meantime, I'll have a large double-double, a large steeped tea with milk, in a mug, and since you don't have butter tarts, I'll have a peanut butter cookie. Please. For here. Yumm!

Chapter 10

Final thoughts

In my experience, "Follow your passion" may not be the best career advice

I've never bought into the advice given to young people today to just *follow your passion* and the money will follow. If only life were that simple and formulaic. For so many reasons I've instinctively found this philosophy to be flawed, misleading, and even dangerous. Most of us lack the talent to make a living at what we love to do. It's that simple.

First of all, young people rarely have the depth of life experience and knowledge necessary to even properly identify what their passion is without any significant life experience to draw on. I'm now in my seventies with more than forty years in the corporate world and several years of retirement behind me and it's only been recently I've been able to comfortably identify what I most love doing. But I enjoyed a very successful career at a job I would never have envisioned when I finished school. And after seven years of writing a blog, it's painfully evident I could never earn a living at blogging. I do it because I love doing it. Many passionate artists have the same practical perspective on their art.

Baby boomers did not go to university and college in the same numbers that today's young people do. Some of us did have a career goal in mind, such as teaching, nursing, or a profession that required post-secondary education, but most of us just "got a job" as soon as we finished high school, ran with it, and fared pretty well. There was no great career plan when we started our working lives and we certainly didn't expect to turn our passion for The Beatles or playing hockey into a means of earning a living. We recognized our hobbies as just that—hobbies —something to enjoy on the side while working at something else to keep the wolf away.

Imagine telling a young person who is passionate about baseball or hockey to ignore the barriers and set their sights unblinkingly on the American League or the NHL. What if this poor soul is 5'4" tall and weighs 120 lbs. Or perhaps someone loves music and wants to be a rock star. Chances are their garage band will never achieve the status of Freddy Mercury or Rod Stewart. While it's not totally impossible, the odds are highly unlikely. **Loving to do something does not necessarily mean you can earn a living at it.** But that doesn't mean we have to abandon our passion; just don't count on making a living at it. There are so many misleading examples of a singer, comedian, or artist becoming an "overnight success" when in reality they spent ten, twenty, or even more years honing their craft. The Justin Biebers and Mark Zuckerbergs of the world are an anomaly, not the norm.

I've just finished reading a book that I wish I'd been able to read forty years ago. *So Good They Can't Ignore You, Why Skills Trump Passion in the Quest For Work You Love,* written by Cal Newport. It really fired me up even though I'm retired and past caring about a career. A common sense, practical guide, it was all I could do to not bookmark every page I read. It confirmed what I've always believed, that young people today are being misled into thinking that following their passion is a guaranteed path to success. Those who accomplish both at the same time are in the minority.

If Steve Jobs had followed his passion, he'd have retreated to a Zen monastery contemplating *Financial independence is Step One in your journey to follow your passion.*

life instead of living life. He stumbled into the field of computers after picking apples and taking a course in calligraphy. He capitalized on the work of others and the rest is history. The same holds true for Mark Zuckerberg. Then, there's the flip side; doing what you love could kill you. Examples include Amy Winehouse and Robin Williams.

This certainly does not mean we have to slave at something we don't like for the rest of our lives and ignore our passion. Many years ago I read a book called *Your Money or Your Life* by Joe Dominguez and Vicki Robin. Reading that book more than twenty years ago prompted me to walk away from self-employment and return to a regular paycheque. It changed my life for the better. One of the most important messages I got from this book is that in order to have the time to do what you most enjoy (i.e. hobbies, your passion), you have to earn as much money as possible as early as possible in the short term and stash it away for that proverbial rainy day.

When you have financial independence you then have overall independence. Financial independence gives you *options* to do whatever you want with your time, to indulge your passions. But earning a living comes first. The sooner you have financial independence, the sooner you will have the freedom to follow your passion. That is not the message being passed along to young people today. No wonder they're disillusioned. There is some value in doing it the old boomer way. Get a job, any kind of job. Start living self-sufficiently to build independence, then you can do what you truly enjoy. It is an earned privilege.

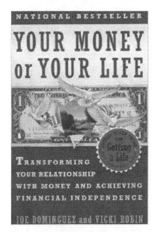 

I highly recommend both of these books. If they're not available at your local bookstore or library, you can order from Amazon.

Dear Santa: It's me again . . . Lynda

Dear Santa: All I want for Christmas this year is . . .

For the most part I have been a very good girl this year, more nice than naughty and I have generally tried to be a better person throughout the year. By Santa standards that should qualify me for plenty of loot under the Christmas tree but the truth is I do not want or need a single thing. I am incredibly lucky and the happiest I have ever been in my life. This was not always the case. In fact, it is the bumps in the road of life that make us truly appreciate the good times. Boomers are now reaching the age when we are losing friends, partners and family members at an increasing rate. Where we once spent a lot of time and money attending bridal showers, lavish weddings and baby showers, we now attend too many celebrations of life. Which is why I am celebrating the life I have now, every single day.

Over the years, holiday arrangements with family and friends gradually evolved toward less gift-giving and more sharing of good times. I have even heard about parents withholding some Christmas and birthday gifts from the grandchildren because they already have too much and do not appreciate it. We still remember the younger grandchildren in our family with gifts from Santa but that is only until they are launched. Everyone has more than enough in material goods and we no longer need to populate landfill with our accumulated and discarded frivolous consumption.

Not having to troll the crowded, over-heated stores and malls for questionable gifts that will only end up at a charity shop has been incredibly freeing. No more Secret Santa exercises and no more heart attacks and bouts of depression when we get our January Visa statement. And, how much does one really need when we have each other? That is more than enough by anyone's standards.

Dear Santa,

I already have everything I could possibly wish for this year. Got my family, good friends and LOVE. Please take care of those who need you. THANK YOU!! XX

So, to wrap up, dear Santa, here is my wish list for this year:

- Love, caring and an end to the violence for all victims of abuse.
- A warm, safe bed and home for the homeless.
- Free medical care for the sick and ailing.
- Plenty of healthy food for the hungry.
- Hope for the hopeless.
- Love and a safe environment for all the world's children.
- Peace on earth . . .

. . . and to all a good night.

Love, Lynda

Starting the new year with a clean sheet, metaphorically speaking

Ordinarily, I do not make New Year's Resolutions. That ensures I never have to deal with the added stress of achieving goals and the guilt that comes with not following through on fragile but usually ill-fated good intentions. This year is different and my awakening came when I was changing the sheets on our bed the other day.

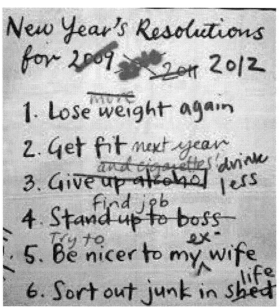

New Year's Resolutions
for 2009 ~~2011~~ 2012

1. Lose ~~more~~ weight again
2. Get fit ~~next year~~
3. ~~Give up alcohol~~ and ~~cigarettes~~ 'divine' less
4. ~~Stand up to boss~~ Find job
5. Try to Be nicer to my ex- wife
6. Sort out junk in ~~shed~~ life

I currently have three sets of sheets in rotation. My favourite sheets are like slipping into horizontal bliss, deliciously smooth and finely woven. They're 100 percent cotton and feel smooth and divine next to my skin. I can't remember where I bought them but if I could, I'd load up with more. My second set of sheets (by Martha Stewart) is lovely but they don't quite hit the mark like the first pair. And my third pair of sheets feel like canvas. They may have some astronomical thread count but those threads are coarse as tree bark and it's like sleeping under a tarp.

I probably spent more on that third set of sheets than I should have so I hate to part with them, but that's when my epiphany came. I've decided that at age 72 my life is now too short to spend it under sheets that are less than blissful. Those canvas jobs are going to the charity bin. Maybe someone with thicker, less sensitive skin will enjoy them, especially since they'll be free to whoever picks them up. They would be perfect drop-sheets for painting or to provide shelter should you need to pitch a sturdy tent in the Arctic.

Those sheets represent my new approach to life. **Whatever time I have left on this planet is going to be filled entirely with positive experiences and happy people.** It's a state of being that's largely within my control. I admit I cannot completely avoid loss, disappointment or sadness, but I can claim my full share of bliss in most areas of my life. As one of my former bosses used to say, "Shit happens". We all experience bumps in the road. That's life and we just keep motoring.

We alone are each responsible for own happiness. From now on I'm going to fill my life with joy. I already have so much to be thankful for and aging brings the knowledge that joy and contentment are not synonymous with expensive material possessions.

My library books give me unlimited joy and they're free. Snuggling with my little dog fills my heart with joy and she's happy to oblige at no cost. Walking in the sunshine on a clear day, enjoying the fragrance of fresh-cut grass or autumn leaves are all unbeatable pleasures. The company of people I love is the ultimate affirmation.

Baby boomers are reaching a point in life where the horizon is approaching and time is moving too quickly. We realize that every day is a gift and I've been examining my life in terms of how to maximize that gift of time I have left.

Happiness is free.

Part of that process means *eliminating sources of conflict or negativity from my everyday life.* Therefore, I rarely watch the news on television anymore. There's nothing to be gained by being subjected to daily updates of gun violence, car accidents, robberies, and political strife. If something important is happening in the world that I need to know, it'll reach me somehow. I don't need or want to be bombarded with negative news. It is truly soul-destroying.

My enlightenment has not been an overnight occurrence. Over the years I've gradually taken steps to eliminate toxic friends from my life. We've all encountered people along the way who suck the energy out of us; they're cynical, critical and generally unhappy. If that's the way they choose to live their lives, it does not have to be part of mine. It is not selfish; it's a matter of self-preservation.

There's a lot to be said for the old phrase, *"If you can't say anything nice, don't say anything at all."* I'm as guilty as the next person of being less than stellar in this regard, but I'm making a concerted effort to fix that. The fact that I'm retired and I'm now enjoying the best years of my life makes my pursuit of joy infinitely easier. Now that I'm no longer subject to the demands of disagreeable bosses, temperamental coworkers or the stresses of daily commuting, the majority of unpleasantness has been eliminated from my life. While work can be satisfying and enjoyable, I've found retirement is infinitely better.

If you're a regular reader of my blog, ***BoomerBroadcast.net***, you'll know I recently purged some of my personal belongings. I tossed stacks of uncomfortable bras, donated dozens of belts that I can no longer wear and eliminated everything from my wardrobe that didn't fit properly, didn't make me feel great or was simply a waste of space. The detritus of my everyday environment is being eliminated.

Now, I'm clearing psychic space, making room for only positive, joy-inducing experiences and activities. Frank Costanza's *"Serenity Now"* mantra on Seinfeld had a lot of merit. Unfortunately, screaming it at the top of your lungs in the midst of a crisis was obviously counter-productive. I have the option of easily tuning out or removing myself from confrontational conversations. I'm not interested in participating in or listening to complaining or bickering.

I've not yet reached absolute nirvana because I still can't purge those angry, hateful thoughts I have about the American and British political situations, nor can I disregard how our Canadian politicians have also been such a colossal disappointment. **Perhaps they too should consider casting aside negativity and start working in the spirit of kindness, goodwill and the betterment of humanity. Imagine how much different and better this conflicted old world would be.**

So, as I hang my favourite sheets outside to dry in the fresh breezes, I'm thankful that I have a safe, comfortable bed to climb into every night. I won't beat myself up when I enjoy a yummy cookie with my cup of tea and I'll continue to focus on positive experiences, joyfulness, and kindness. You're welcome to join me in saying *'No'* to negativity from now on. I have amazing friends and family and I'm clear about my priorities in life. They're simple, achievable, shareable and uplifting.

I wish every one of my very special readers a conflict-free, happy, healthy and fulfilling new year. **Be kind and be joyful mes très chères.**

About the Author

Lynda Davis is a baby boomer who retired as Corporate Marketing Manager for a major international construction company.

In search of a retirement project, Lynda planned to write a book of advice to young women on how to avoid the business mistakes and pitfalls she experienced during her working years. This idea was replaced by a blog www.boomerbroadcast.net targeted at baby boomers.

Lynda lives in Mississauga, Ontario, a suburb of Toronto, Canada and counts the present as the best years of our lives.

Manufactured by Amazon.ca
Bolton, ON

30332483R00157